Planning and Decentralization

One of the mos ‎al era is the decentralization ‎tral governments to localit ‎‎een actively promoted by p ‎Vorld Bank, the United Nat ‎‎ore recently, academics, prac ‎‎ critique of the widespread ‎

Yet, despit ‎‎ment, there is a limited unde ‎‎ing process, governance stru ‎ around the world. *Plannin* ‎‎original case study research d ‎h. The book examines the int ‎perspectives: the central state ‎‎nunity. It is aimed at acader ‎‎oolicymakers and developmer ‎

Victoria A. Bea ‎‎e University of California at ‎‎nal development planning, ‎‎ movements and poverty alle ‎

Faranak Miraftab is an Associate Professor of Urban and Regional Planning at the University of Illinois, Urbana-Champaign. Her research and teaching are concerned with transnational processes of community development, with special focus on grassroots strategies and mobilizations for access to housing and basic services.

Christopher Silver, FAICP, is Dean and Professor of the College of Design, Construction and Planning at the University of Florida. He has taught and consulted on urban development and planning in Indonesia over the past eighteen years. He is author of *Planning the Megacity: Jakarta in the Twentieth Century* (Routledge).

Planning and Decentralization

Contested spaces for public action
in the global south

Edited by
Victoria A. Beard, Faranak Miraftab
and Christopher Silver

Routledge
Taylor & Francis Group

LONDON AND NEW YORK

First published 2008
by Routledge
2 Park Square, Milton Park, Abingdon, Oxon OX14 4RN

Simultaneously published in the USA and Canada
by Routledge
270 Madison Avenue, New York, NY 10016, USA

Routledge is an imprint of the Taylor & Francis Group, an informa business

Typeset in Galliard and Helvetica by
Florence Production Ltd, Stoodleigh, Devon
Printed and bound in Great Britain by
TJ International, Padstow, Cornwall

British Library Cataloguing in Publication Data
A catalogue record for this book is available from the British Library

Library of Congress Cataloging in Publication Data
Planning and decentralization: contested spaces for public action in
   the global south/edited by Victoria A. Beard, Faranak Miraftab
   and Christopher Silver.
        p. cm.
      Includes bibliographical references and index.
   1. Decentralization in government—Developing countries.
   2. Political planning—Developing countries.   3. Public–private
   sector cooperation—Developing countries. 4. Local government—
   Developing countries.   I. Beard, Victoria A.   II. Miraftab, Faranak.
   III. Silver, Christopher, 1951–
   JS113.P53 2008
   320.809172'4—dc22   2007042981

ISBN10: 0–415–41497–0 (hbk)
ISBN10: 0–415–41498–9 (pbk)
ISBN10: 0–203–92826–1 (ebk)

ISBN13: 978–0–415–41497–5 (hbk)
ISBN13: 978–0–415–41498–2 (pbk)
ISBN13: 978–0–203–92826–4 (ebk)

Contents

Illustrations

Figures

Tables

Contributors

Victoria A. Beard is an Associate Professor of Urban Planning at the University of California at Irvine. Her research and teaching focus on international development planning, community-based planning, collective action and poverty alleviation. She has worked for the World Bank, the Asian Development Bank, RAND and the Research Triangle Institute.

Patrick Bond is a Political Economist and Director of the University of KwaZulu-Natal Centre for Civil Society, Durban, South Africa. He was educated in geography at Johns Hopkins University. Recent books include *Looting Africa: The Economics of Exploitation* (Zed Books and UKZN Press, 2006) and *Talk Left, Walk Right: South Africa's Frustrated Global Reforms* (UKZN Press, 2006).

Randi S. Cartmill is a Doctoral candidate in the Department of Sociology at the University of Wisconsin-Madison. Her research interests include gender, aging, work and social inequality.

Amrita Daniere is Chair of the Department of Geography at the University of Toronto at Mississauga and graduate chair of the Department of Geography and Planning at the University of Toronto. She published a book in 2002 (with Lois Takahashi from UCLA), entitled *Rethinking Environmental Management in the Pacific Rim*, about Bangkok's environmental problems. Her current research explores the notion of social capital and civic space in several Southeast Asian cities.

Linda Farthing is a writer, educator and editor who lived in Bolivia for eight years. She has extensive experience in grassroots community development, particularly with women, in both Bolivia and Nepal. She has taught university students, edited social science books, and authored over fifty articles and radio reports on Bolivia.

Benjamin Kohl is Associate Professor of Geography and Urban Studies at Temple University. He has worked on issues related to planning, development and politics in Bolivia for twenty years. Most recently, with Linda Farthing, he co-authored *Impasse in Bolivia: Neoliberal Hegemony and Popular Resistance* (Zed Press, 2006).

Neema Kudva is an Assistant Professor at Cornell University. Her research interests include the role of institutional structures and organizational practices in local level planning and development, focusing on the marginalized; and understanding the role of small cities and their regions in urban transformations in south-western India and East Africa.

Nora Libertun de Duren is an Adjunct Assistant Professor at Columbia University. She holds a PhD in Urban Planning from the MIT, a Master in Urban Design from Harvard University, and in Architecture from the University of Buenos Aires. Among other honors, she has been awarded the Fulbright Fellowship, the Harvard-Fortabat Fellowship, the MIT-Presidential Fellowship and the University of Buenos Aires Gold Medal.

Faranak Miraftab is an Associate Professor of Urban and Regional Planning at the University of Illinois, Urbana-Champaign. Her research and teaching concern transnational processes of community development, with special focus on grassroots strategies and mobilizations for access to housing and basic services. The empirical basis of her studies spans North America, Mexico and South Africa.

Kajri Misra is a Doctoral candidate at Cornell University. She has taught and worked as a planner in India, focusing on women's inclusion in local institutions, including *Panchayats* in Rajasthan, Gujarat, Orissa and Andhra Pradesh. Her dissertation examines the role of women in *Panchayat* planning processes in Kerala, Gujarat and Madhya Pradesh.

Menno Pradhan is a Senior Education Economist at the World Bank Indonesia office. Prior to joining the World Bank he worked as an Assistant Professor at the Free University in Amsterdam, and as a Visiting Fellow at Cornell University. He holds a PhD in Economics from Tilburg University.

Vijayendra Rao is a Lead Economist in the Development Research Group of the World Bank. His work, published widely in leading journals in economics and development studies, integrates economic and anthropological methods to inform poverty-reduction policies in poor countries.

Rivayani is a Researcher at LPEM FEUI and a Consultant for World Bank Jakarta and occasionally lectures in the Department of Economics at the University of Indonesia. She holds a Bachelor in Economics degree from the University of Indonesia and Master in Economics degree from Vrije Universiteit in Amsterdam.

Anny Rivera-Ottenberger, PhD Political Science, MIT, is an Adjunct Professor of Latin American Politics, Social Movements and Third World Development, University of Massachusetts, Boston. She was a post-doctoral Scholar in the Study of Democracy (2006) Wilson Center for International Scholars, a visiting researcher at ILPES-ECLAC, UN, and headed a program on communications, government of Chile (1994–8).

Gavin Shatkin is Assistant Professor of Urban Planning at the A. Alfred Taubman College of Architecture and Urban Planning, and Faculty Associate in the Center for Southeast Asian Studies at the University of Michigan at Ann Arbor. His research focuses primarily on globalization and urban poverty in Southeast Asian cities.

Christopher Silver, FAICP, is Dean (and Professor) of the College of Design, Construction and Planning at the University of Florida. He has taught and consulted on urban development and planning in Indonesia over the past eighteen years. He is author of *Planning the Megacity: Jakarta in the Twentieth Century* (Routledge).

Paul Smoke is Professor of Public Finance and Planning and Director of International Programs, Robert F. Wagner Graduate School of Public Service, New York University. His research and policy interests include public-sector decentralization and urban and regional development, with a particular focus on East and Southern Africa and Southeast Asia.

Tubagus Furqon Sofhani, PhD, is a Lecturer at the Department of Regional and City Planning, Institute of Technology Bandung (ITB), Indonesia. Through collaboration with non-government organizations, local governments, universities and community institutions, he has been involved in action research and advocacy to encourage participatory planning, community empowerment and fiscal decentralization in several regions in Indonesia.

James H. Spencer is Associate Professor of Urban and Regional Planning and of Political Science, as well as the Co-Director of the Globalization Research Center at the University of Hawaii. His prior work on public policy in the US has been published in *Economic Development Quarterly*, *Urban Affairs Review* and the *Journal of Planning Education and Research*. His current work focuses on water infrastructure planning in Southeast Asia, with a particular focus on Vietnam.

Lois M. Takahashi is Associate Professor in the Department of Urban Planning at UCLA. She has over fifty publications on her research interests, which include access to social services and overcoming the (NIMBY) "not in my back yard" syndrome in the US, and community participation and environmental governance in Bangkok, Thailand and Ho Chi Minh City, Vietnam.

Abbreviations

ASP	*Asemblea de Soberania de Pueblos*
BBGC	Barangay-Bayan Governance Consortium
BID	Business Improvement District
BKM	*Badan Keswadayan Masyarakat*
BMA	Bangkok Metropolitan Area
CBD	Central business district
CBO	Community-based organization
CDD	Community-driven development
CESCO	Economic and Social Council
CID	City Improvement District
CMP	Community Mortgage Program
COB	*Central Obrera Boliviana*
CoJ	City of Johannesburg
CSUCTB	*Confederacion Sindical Unica de Trabajores Campesinos de Bolivia*
CTCWSS	Can Tho Center for Water Supply and Sanitation
CTP	Cape Town Partnership
DC	District Commissioner
DDC	District Development Committee
DDP	District Development Plan
DDPR	District Development Program
DFRD	District Focus for Redevelopment Strategy
DIDECO	Directorate of Community Development
DPC	District Planning Committee
DPRD	*Dewan Perwakilan Rakyat Daerah*
GEAR	Growth, employment and redistribution
GPT	Graduated personal tax
GTO	Grassroots territorial organization
IDP	Integrated development plan
IFMS	Integrated Financial Management System
IMF	International Monetary Fund
ITB	Institute of Technology Banding

KLGRP	Kenya Local Government Reform Program
KSM	*Kelompok Swadaya Masyarakat*
LAD	Law of Administrative Decentralization
LADP	Local Authority Development Plan
LASC	Local authority service charge
LASDP	Local Authority Service Delivery Action Plan
LATF	Local Authority Transfer Fund
LDF	Local development fund
LG	Local government
LGC	Local Government Code
LGDP	Local Government Development Program
LGFC	Local Government Finance Commission
LLP	Law of Popular Participation
MAS	*Movimiento al Socialismo* (Movement towards Socialism)
MBL	*Movimiento de Bolivia Libre*
MFPED	Ministry of Finance, Planning and Economic Development
MIDEPLAN	Ministry of Planning and Cooperation
MIIU	Municipal infrastructure investment unit
MLG	Ministry of Local Government
MNDP	Ministry of Planning and National Development
MOF	Ministry of Finance
NCPC	Naga City People's Council
NCUPF	Naga City Urban Poor Federation
NIMBY	Not in my back yard
NPM	New public management
PAO	Provincial Administrative Organization
P5D	*Pedoman Penyusunan Perencanaan dan Pengendalian Pembangunan Daerah*
PDP	Provincial Development Plan
PLADECO	Municipal development plan
PO	People's organization
PPP	Public-private partnership
PR	Panchaytai Raj
PT	Brazilian Workers' Party
RAMS	Rates Administration Management System
SECPLAC	Planning Secretariat
TAO	*Tambon* Administrative Organization
TFESSD	Trust Fund for Environmentally and Socially Sustainable Development
UDHA	Urban Development and Housing Act
UF	Urban Foundation

UNDP	United Nations Development Program
UPP	Urban Poverty Program
VND	Viet Nam Dong
WO	Women's Office
YO	Youth Office

Chapter 1
Situating contested notions of decentralized planning in the global south

Faranak Miraftab, Christopher Silver and Victoria A. Beard

Introduction

One of the most pervasive trends of the current global era in developing nations is the devolution of governmental responsibilities from strong central governments to localities, a process generally referred to as decentralization. In the past two decades, decentralization has been actively promoted by powerful international organizations such as the World Bank, the United Nations and many bilateral development agencies. At global gatherings such as the 1992 United Nations' Conference on Environment and Development, in Rio de Janeiro, and the 1996 United Nations' Urban Summit, in Istanbul, international organizations identified local authorities (distinguished from central government agencies) as the lead agents for achieving sustainable development. Given the financial clout of the international agencies advancing this position, many national governments followed suit. Within the past decade, no fewer than sixty-five of the seventy-five developing nations with populations of over 5 million have had active decentralization policies or initiatives (Dillinger 1994).

Despite the global dimensions of the decentralization movement, little is understood about the rather dramatic transformation of the responsibilities of local planning and governance structures, or about the consequences of these transformations for other actors in planning. Decentralization policies in much of the global south, for example, have transferred the responsibility for providing basic services to local governments, yet often the transfer has occurred in the absence of demonstrated leadership capacity to meet service needs and also without the transfer of necessary decision-making power and financial resources. To handle their newly assumed responsibilities, some local governments have even had to divest themselves of the very powers conferred by decentralization. To achieve entrepreneurial governance for fulfilling their expanded yet under-funded mandate, they have turned to the private sector as well as to civil society organizations, and have adopted market principles. This shift has grave, but little understood, implications for local planners and urban managers, who have to redefine their roles and relationships vis-à-vis local governments, the private sector and non-state actors.

Practitioners as well as scholars often assume that several positive outcomes follow from decentralization. For example, decentralization is often associated with democratic reform and the strengthening of civil society (Diamond 1999; Manor 1999; Wunsch 1998). In terms of democratic reform, decentralization advocates assume that bringing the state closer to people allows more public participation in decision-making and ensures transparency and accountability (Diamond 1999). Advocates believe that curtailing centralized state power and national policies through the devolution of power yields a more responsive and inclusive governance (Bennett 1998; Blair 2000; Fiszbein and Lowden 1999). Other supporters promote decentralization in the belief that it increases the efficiency with which public goods and services are delivered (Bateley 1996; Burki *et al.* 1999; Savas 2000). One aspect of the efficiency argument contends that decentralized planning and service delivery can more accurately identify and satisfy local needs and expectations, especially those of marginalized populations (Burki *et al.* 1999; Cheema and Rondinelli 1983; The World Bank 2001). Another point put forward is that the private sector will deliver resources more effectively because a willingness to pay for services is brought into being by their being organized locally rather than provided by a distant regional or central government (Ostrom *et al.* 1961; Roth 1987).

Critics of decentralization, and especially of policies promoted in developing countries by large, global development institutions, draw upon a historicized understanding of the process. Critics emphasize the importance of the history of colonial domination and the role played by external institutions in developing societies. In the global south, colonialism worked against a tradition of local responsibility; over a long history it buttressed despotism to accommodate colonial rule. Decentralization critics underscore the dangers of an a historical understanding of decentralization, as when technocrats ignore the role of the global political–economic relations of dominance and how they shape the structure of governance in developing countries (Mamdani 1996). From this critique, what appears a straight forward process of devolving power may in actuality multiply the sins of the centralized state, creating a decentralized despotism (Agrawal and Ribot 1999). George and Sabelli (1994), for example, interpret the decentralization arguments based on prospects for "good governance" in developing countries as camouflage for a continuation of the colonial past. They see the celebration of decentralization for making government more accountable and transparent as yet another marketing strategy of international development agencies, such as the World Bank—a rubric under which to sell more debt and, hence, dependence. They argue that decentralized and participatory governance can actually work to sustain the status quo, by repackaging it in a new form aligned with the rhetoric of participation (Cooke and Kothari 2001).

To begin our exploration into the complex and often contradictory expectations and interpretations of decentralized planning, the chapter first sketches the genealogy of a global trend in decentralization policies and how such policies articulate with a widespread move from centralized to decentralized planning in the global south. Next, the chapter identifies and discusses significant sources of confusion and misinterpretation of decentralization that underlie the false expectations of it. Pointing out the contradictory potentials of decentralized planning, the introduction urges examination of those causal factors, conditions and contexts that can enable decentralization to produce more democratic, inclusive and equitable planning outcomes. The chapter concludes with a summary of the organization of the book and the contributions of each chapter.

The genealogy of decentralized planning

The call for governmental decentralization goes back to the 1970s' crisis of legitimacy for central government, with its lack of transparency and its exclusive decision-making processes (De Angelis 2005; Santos 2004). Movements included disenfranchised youth, ethnic minorities, women and the poor who all questioned the legitimacy of a state that monopolized the decision-making power over all local affairs. These movements sought greater inclusiveness in the state and demanded the participation of non-state actors in decision-making, some even calling for "governance without government" (Rosenau and Czempiel 1992). In the 1980s, a political opposition called for devolution of the state's decision-making power to lower levels of government, and for the state's permeability to disadvantaged groups. The objective was to achieve a more inclusive and transparent state and, consequently, processes of democratization.

Concurrently, proponents of post-cold-war economic liberalization pointed to the inefficiencies of government bureaucracies in the developing world as the root problem of state legitimacy. Economic neoliberals advocated decentralization to remedy the wastefulness of the state bureaucracy by opening the state and the government to presumably more efficient non-state actors (e.g. an increased use of the private sector in subcontracting, outsourcing and public–private partnerships). The intent was also to transfer management of local services from state responsibility to a business model in which individual residents would have to pay more of the real cost of basic services, and, as a result, state responsibility for providing basic service costs would shrink.

In the 1990s, this logic of state decentralization, by which restructuring of the state would facilitate neoliberal economic policies, overshadowed the earlier core logic of decentralization that sought political devolution and democratization (De Angelis 2005; Santos 2004). Thus the popularization of neoliberal economic policies as the way to "good governance" and their mainstreaming by international organizations are accomplished largely by subordinating decentralization's earlier political agenda. Decentralized planning, too, has gone through that transformation. Whereas the 1970s' and 1980s' call for decentralized planning had a political logic of democratic, inclusive and redistributive planning as articulated by equity planning and radical planning practice, the more recent rationale for decentralized planning has been an economic logic of efficiency, cost recovery and entrepreneurship.

Traditionally, the planning profession was equated with state planning in concert with problem-solving by technical experts. Since the 1960s, under substantial pressure from its critics both within and outside the profession, planning has broadened beyond a state-centered, elite-driven professional practice to acknowledge the important role of non-state actors (e.g. Castells 1983; Davidoff 1965; Douglass and Friedmann 1998; Escobar 1992; Fainstein 1992; Forester 1989; Friedmann 1987, 1989; Holston 1989; Krumholz 1982; Piven 1975; Sandercock 1998; Scott 1998). By the late 1980s, the problems with, and limitations of, centralized planning had been well documented (e.g. Hall 1980; Holston 1989; Peattie 1987). Centralized planning was criticized not only for its political elitism, but also for its limited administrative effectiveness and efficiency. An assertion now common in planning is that "urban infrastructure is definitionally harder to plan and control from the center" (Kingsley 1996: 1). These political and administrative rationales promoted a move away from top-down planning to diverse forms of decentralized planning. Decentralized planning broadens the planner's role to encompass being not only technical expert, but facilitator as well as social activist, so as to ensure the articulation and incorporation of local as well as professional knowledge in the planning process.

Although participatory planning and local community-based planning gained increased recognition and epistemological legitimacy in the 1980s, it was not until the next decade that decentralized planning was mainstreamed by government agencies and global development organizations. Global institutions and key global summits, such as the UN's 1992 Conference on Environment and Development in Rio de Janeiro and the 1996 Urban Summit in Istanbul, pushed a leading role for local authorities in development planning (Local Agenda 21) to the head of national agendas in the global south. The 1990s shift from centralized to decentralized planning was popularized and mainstreamed to an unprecedented extent. Development constituents had been demanding more public participation, a greater role for civil society, and more power in general over the planning process and its outcomes through the strategies of collaborative and community-based planning.[1] For example, during the 1990s, the fastest growing strategy for development assistance by the World Bank, which is the major engine for development planning in the global south, has been "community-driven development"—that is, projects that claim to increase community power over development (Dongier *et al.* 2002; Mansuri and Rao 2004).

The concurrence of the trends sketched above, in decentralization, economic liberalization, and participatory planning and civil society participation, should not be attributed to coincidence. Decentralization policies and the shift in planning articulate with the global trend of neoliberal state restructuring. It is unproductive, however, to embrace the position that decentralization is nothing more than a neoliberal strategy for advancing the project of capital accumulation by defusing authoritarian rule. On the other hand, it is overly simplistic to assume that decentralization will promote meaningful participation by communities and civil society organizations and therefore a more transparent and accountable local government. Hutchcroft (2001: 33) critiques a common oversimplification in much of the work from this perspective: "If the goal is to build analysis rather than propagate faith, it is essential to move beyond the association of authoritarianism with centralization and democracy with decentralization." From that perspective, we contend that it is essential to examine both empirically and critically the complex processes of decentralization and its potential for achieving democratic, inclusive and equitable planning.

This volume aims to take a first step in that examination. The research included here examines the articulation of decentralization policies and planning in diverse socio-political and institutional contexts. Some key questions are whether and under what conditions can decentralization lead to, and has it led to a more democratic, participatory and inclusive planning process? And if decentralization can have such disparate outcomes as the opening up of progressive spaces for political action and also the facilitation of market domination or capture by local elites, how should planners intervene to ensure that decentralized planning does promote more democratic, inclusive and equitable outcomes? Given the widespread implementation of decentralization policies, it is urgent to pursue these questions carefully. We hope that the case studies in this volume will contribute to a more empirically grounded understanding of decentralized planning and leave it less vulnerable to misinterpretation.

Conceptualization, contradictions and contested spaces for public action

Conflation of the terms used for the complex set of phenomena comprising decentralization is a significant source of confusion. Decentralization is commonly used as a general term that can refer to any of several distinct processes, which can occur in isolation, but which usually occur (to some degree) simultaneously—and which have distinct outcomes. For example, subtle yet important differences distinguish two forms of decentralization: administrative decentralization and political decentralization (Hutchcroft 2001).

Administrative decentralization concerns the "hierarchy and functional distribution of powers and functions between central and non-central governmental units" (Cohen and Peterson 1999: 23). It can entail either deconcentration, which moves the central government offices and administrative units to more localized government bodies (e.g. regional, provincial and/or municipal bodies) (Cohen and Peterson 1996),[2] or devolution, which is a more extensive transfer of authority and responsibility to local government bodies. Deconcentration can actually further centralize state power when, for example, it simply moves the guns of the capital city to the village (Slater 1989: 514); but it is hoped that devolution can result in more democratic decision-making if it is supported by a transparent and accountable political structure and by adequate financial resources. To voice that hope is not to imply a guaranteed democratic outcome for devolution of state decision-making power to local governments. Evidence from the global south, including some research in this volume, reveals how perverse outcomes of devolution can occur where democratic political institutions are weak and lack transparency and accountability. In such contexts, it is possible for decentralization to result in decentralized authoritarianism or elite control (see Beard *et al.* in this volume). Decentralization can also simply facilitate privatization, by which the local state sheds unfunded mandates and responsibilities (see, for example, chapters by Miraftab, Bond and Libertun de Duren in this volume).

Political decentralization attempts to build a democratic culture within a given polity—it is the transfer of political power to local government bodies and civil society organizations, and the inclusion of popular participation in governance and planning.[3] With respect to the interacting realms of administration and politics, it is often, though tenuously, assumed that changes in administrative structure will promote democratic reform. Some have pointed out, however, the danger in assuming that local democracy can be achieved while ignoring the national or macro-political structures (Mohan and Stokke 2000; Purcell 2006). Furthermore, the evidence from the global south, where decentralization policies have been aggressively promoted, challenges the assumed relationship between decentralization and democratization (see Crook and Manor 1998). A number of chapters in this volume examine that relationship. Silver and Sofhani, in Chapter 10, explore the relationship between political decentralization and democratization in Indonesia. That case exemplifies the rise of civil society and grassroots movements in the wake of decentralization in the global south. In Chapter 13, Shatkin explores these phenomena from a different perspective. Using a case study of Naga City in the Philippines, he analyzes the opportunities and limitations faced by progressive municipal leaders in post-authoritarian political contexts.

Other authors have emphasized the potential decentralization offers for community-based social transformation. In this volume, for example, Kohl and Farthing's study of decentralized planning points out precisely this dynamic in the Bolivian context. Bolivian decentralization began as part of a hegemonic project, but in the long term it was appropriated by grassroots activism: disenchanted communities long ignored by Bolivia's formal political structures used the decentralization channels for their own ends. Similarly, as documented by Misra and Kudva in this volume, the legal and administrative disjuncture in the decentralization mandates of the Indian government opened an opportunity for disadvantaged women to participate in *Panjayats* as a first step to move beyond gender-based exclusion.

Globally, decentralization policies have had mixed results for poor women. It is well documented that economic liberalization and privatization, by moving the burden of capital accumulation onto communities, families and the realm of social reproduction, shift the responsibility for securing livelihoods to households and women in particular (Aslanbeigui and Summerfield 2001; Bakker 2003; Beneria and Feldman 1992; Miraftab 2006b, 2001; Samson forthcoming). This shift, while it has increased the burden of poor women, has simultaneously increased their role as protagonists of community-based groups and neighborhood development (Beard and Cartmill 2007). The point to be noted here is that neo-liberalism creates new opportunities for local participation in decision-making. The mechanism may be motivated largely by interest in reducing the state's responsibilities. Nevertheless, local people use these political shifts to carve out innovative spaces of participation beyond those officially designated with the aim of stabilizing the conditions of capital accumulation. Citizens marginalized by the material forces of capitalism move their collective action beyond the limited coping strategy accommodated by local governments and community-based planning (Beard 2002, 2003). Using a combination of "invented" and "invited" spaces of participation (Miraftab 2006a), they transform their role to something more significant than simply providing cheap labor to predetermined projects that pretend to be participatory.

The potential of the current global decentralization era for inclusive or democratic planning is embedded in these contradictory processes. State decentralization may selectively decentralize and centralize various aspects of decision-making at global and local levels. It may also promote simultaneous processes of inclusion and exclusion through structures of participation and privatization (Miraftab 2005). Critical analysis of the outcomes that decentralization policies are producing on the ground is urgently needed, because such policies have the potential to create and reinforce both democratic and undemocratic practices. Thus the implications that decentralization in the global south has for citizenship and planning should not be taken as given. Decentralization comprises a set of contingent processes that vary across time and space and according to the social and historical specificities of the regions where they occur. The result is the emergence of highly contested spaces for public action.

Drawing upon original scholarship, this volume uses case studies to grapple with the nexus between decentralization and planning. It examines in detail the experiences of decentralizing states in the global south and the implications for planning. The contributions brought together in this volume constitute an effort to understand, not only how the two concurrent trends mesh, but also how such experiences vary across regional socio-political formations. It is our hope that the volume will open a dialogue on the divergent interpretations of the limitations as well as the potential of decentralized planning.

Organization of the book

The book is organized around three interrelated themes. The first section highlights the contentious notion of decentralization and how, in different political, administrative and fiscal contexts, the process can lead to different outcomes. The second section considers the challenges of fiscal and administrative decentralization, two pillars of state decentralization. The third and last section of the book highlights the role of local non-state actors, particularly citizens, community-based organizations and NGOs. This chapter concludes with a brief overview of the three sections of the book, followed by a summary of contributions from the chapters.

Section one

As discussed earlier, the notion of decentralization and the achievements of decentralized planning are highly contentious. Examining the decentralization experiences in South Africa, Argentina and Bolivia, contributors to this section highlight the complexities and contradictory outcomes of decentralization policies and processes. The case studies in Section One explore the range of social, political and economic conditions that can undermine the potential of decentralized planning for furthering social and spatial justice (as in the South African and Argentinian cases) and for empowerment of historically marginalized populations (as in the Bolivian case). Many scholars, including Bond, Libertun De Duren and Miraftab in this section, have shown how financially and politically constrained local governments, rather than promote social and spatial inclusion, actually facilitate greater inequality and privatization. Kohl and Farthing, in their examination of the Bolivian experience, on the other hand, show how vibrant social movements can take advantage of the spaces for public action created by decentralization to achieve positive social change. These authors underscore the tensions and dynamic power struggles generated by decentralization. As a contested space for public action, decentralized planning can constrain citizens' demands to local concerns, instead of allowing a focus on the impacts of larger structural, national and global policies; or, instead, in some cases, it can be used by disadvantaged groups to assert their interests.

In the opening chapter, Miraftab focuses on how the post-apartheid processes of decentralization built the rationale for the rise of entrepreneurial planning in Cape Town, South Africa. This chapter brings to light the paradox of decentralization: for decentralization to achieve inclusive development, strong regional and central governments are needed to support the capacity of local authorities and to intervene when local planning decisions permit uneven development across and within local government districts. Such interpretation is particularly important given how market participation in urban management and service provisioning is now promoted; that trend involves the risk that the private sector will cherry-pick the services to provide, and that cities will compete against each other. In Cape Town's city improvement districts (CIDs), a decentralized municipality lacking the financial and administrative muscle to fund its responsibilities, through innovative entrepreneurial strategies, enters imbalanced partnerships with a stronger and better organized private sector. In such contexts, decentralized local states undermine their integrationist agenda in order to attract more investment. As demonstrated in the CIDs case, the entrepreneurial strategy succeeds in achieving local development for an exclusive locality (downtown Cape Town), but it furthers social and spatial inequalities in the city at large. The chapter, however, like others in this section, stresses that the partnership is a dynamic terrain of power struggle and contestation, whose outcomes are not predetermined.

In Chapter 3, Patrick Bond further examines South Africa's decentralization as illuminated by the relationship between state restructuring, water privatization and its commercially based pricing system. Bond highlights the capital's drive to commodify public goods and identifies the underlying pressures that moved the post-apartheid state to outsource and privatize basic services including water. Bond argues that formal establishment of "water as an economic good" rather than a public good has been key to multilateral programs and to the multinational, corporate expansion of service provision and pricing. "In the course of outsourcing to private (or even NGO) suppliers," he argues, "the benefits of water as a public good . . . are generally lost. The lack of 'effective demand' by poor consumers," among other reasons, has produced a situation in which "the premier consumers are served and the masses are left behind" (46). Bond also highlights the countervailing pressures that have emerged, both implicitly in the form of poverty, and more explicitly from trade unions, community and consumer groups, environmentalists and other citizens' movements. The study of South African water provision during the first decade of post-apartheid democracy is illuminating, not only of the way that decentralization of financing limited access by the poor, but of the revealing ways by which, in this case, resistance shifted state policy to a "free basic water" tariff in 2001—although that left consumers still disempowered because it retained the crucial micro-neoliberal pricing.

Chapter 4 by Nora Libertun De Duren discusses the experience of decentralized planning in Buenos Aires, Argentina. This chapter focuses on the growth of gated communities in the poorest municipalities of Buenos Aires. It reveals how local governments in charge of infrastructure development, but lacking adequate resources, felt they had to use their control over land use and development permits to accommodate developers' interests. These municipal governments lured developers and allowed gated communities because the developers offered to fund needed infrastructure. The 1990s witnessed a phenomenal growth rate of requests (95 percent by 1999) for rezoning and land use changes to foster the development of gated communities in the poorest municipalities of Buenos Aires. In 1997, for example, 70 percent of the city's gated communities were located in

three of the poorest municipalities. Libertun De Duren's study links this phenomenon with the main administrative reforms in Buenos Aires provincial law. She
demonstrates that decentralized planning does not necessarily imply a more
inclusive local development, and that decentralized municipal governments may
foster higher levels of social inequality within their own boundaries.

Chapter 5, by Ben Kohl and Linda Farthing, demonstrates an outcome of
decentralization that stands in stark contrast to the other case studies in this section.
Their Bolivian case study demonstrates that, from a long-term perspective, the
decentralization legislation opened the formal political space to grassroots activism
and indigenous communities. The authors are cautious not to strike a celebratory
note when pointing out that Bolivian decentralization—the 1994 Law of Popular
Participation (LLP) and the Law of Administrative Decentralization, which were
part of an ongoing neoliberal restructuring—have had "the unintended result
of opening new political spaces to contest neoliberalism" (69). In Bolivia, the
decentralization strategy created a large number of new rural municipalities that
required thousands of municipal council representatives from indigenous and poor
rural populations. The new councilors, having gradually learned the skills for using
Western-style governing channels, then "fundamentally altered the discourse on
the rights of citizens in areas long abandoned by the state" (70). Viewing Bolivia's
decentralization over the last decade, the authors argue that the legislation intended
to extend the reach of the state instead extended the spaces of public action, so
that marginalized, disadvantaged populations' contestation in municipal formal
politics became possible. Despite the intended objectives, decentralized planning
and administrative decentralization, together with a law of public participation,
"changed the rules of the game and policy. . . . [It] served as a catalyst to mobilize
a marginalized population to adopt a new repertoire of political actions . . .
creating new expectations of the state" (80). To explain this positive outcome,
Kohl and Farthing note the existence of a strong social movement whose leadership
was capable of recognizing and exploiting the political opportunities created by
national elites and international financial institutions.

Section two

Chapters in the second section examine the basis of the decentralization movement: a changing economic development paradigm and fiscal decentralization. In
developing countries, replacing centralized economic planning with fiscal decentralization has been an important component of broader administrative and political
change. Seeking to make expenditure more efficient, international donor agencies
pressed to have authority for planning and implementing local services shifted
from central government agencies to local governments. Such fiscal restructuring was strengthened by related changes in the governance structure that gave
local governments the means to plan and deliver services. G. Shabir Cheema

and Dennis A. Rondinelli co-authored one of the pioneering studies of fiscal decentralization in the early 1980s, *Decentralization and Development: Policy Implementation in Developing Countries* (1983). This volume assessed the dynamics of decentralization versus centralization that was sweeping through the developing nations. One of the boldest experiments in fiscal and administrative decentralization was adopted by Indonesia in 1999, several decades after the international donor community's advocacy of the basic model of decentralization (Silver *et al.* 2001; Silver 2003). The push came from within, however, first to implement the model starting in 2001, and then to sustain the bold experiment during the trying political and economic times in subsequent years. The stimulus was the regional financial crisis that began in 1997 (the so-called Asian crisis) and the resulting demise of the discredited centralized system of governance under Suharto's New Order regime. Although much has been written on Indonesia's era of democratic decentralization, contributions to this volume offer fresh perspectives on the community outcomes of those reforms (see also USAID 2006).

Paul Smoke examines the decentralization through fiscal and administrative reforms that have occurred in Kenya and Uganda since the early 1990s, under pressure from the global donor community. These two African nations were emerging from the initial post-colonial experience of strong centralized regimes that marginalized local governments. Smoke argues that decentralization initiatives enjoyed widespread political support as part of a broad democratization, but also attempted to introduce more discipline to governmental management. His assessment finds that fiscal and administrative decentralization proceeded at different rates in the two countries, and with varying degrees of success. In Kenya, local governments had to compete with deconcentrated central government offices that had more financing to conduct similar functions, and they received only a limited direct funding from central government to support their expanded local responsibilities. In Uganda, the central government's financial transfers were more generous, accounting for nearly 80 percent of local government revenues in localities outside the capital city. The transfers, however, came with strings attached that limited how local planners could allocate the funds. In both Kenya and Uganda, the decentralization initiatives lacked meaningful citizen participation. Thus Smoke concludes that, despite an obvious commitment to expanded decentralization since the 1990s, "Kenya and Uganda still suffer from significant weaknesses in their subnational planning systems." (102)

In the case of Vietnam, fiscal and administrative decentralizations became possible in the wake of the government's decision, in 1986, to reduce state management of the economy to allow for limited privatization. As Spencer's study of the Can Tho City water delivery system shows, decentralization was carried out within the context of a socialist state and produced a unique brand of local community engagement in infrastructure management. The Can Tho water provision study also demonstrates that privatization comes in many forms: in this case local individuals worked directly with the water authority, and there was no corporate takeover of local functions. Spencer suggests that having community entrepreneurs manage the water distribution and fee collections for the water company offers a transitional model between the highly centralized state mechanism so prominent in Vietnam (as well as in other non-socialist developing nations) and the entirely locally controlled systems seen in more advanced decentralization. The unique role of local citizen managers as stakeholders in the Can Tho water delivery system underscores the importance of the participatory component that was lacking in Kenya and Uganda.

The Chilean case of decentralized planning and increased local governance examines how the participatory component played out differently in two otherwise comparable locales. As Anny Rivera-Ottenberger notes in her contribution, "Decentralization and local democracy in Chile: two active communities and two models of local governance," the local leadership style is a crucial component of decentralization. Chile's tradition of strong local governance was enhanced nationwide in the 1990s by the restoration of popular elections for local authorities. This central government-sponsored, "low-intensity democracy," as she phrases it, gave marginalized groups throughout Chile more voice in local policies. Yet, as the varying experiences of two local communities, El Bosque and Penalolen, indicate, the peculiarities of local political cultures shaped how their voices would be heard. In El Bosque, the mayor's strong support for empowering key community groups demonstrated that managerial success through decentralization need not impede implementation of progressive social policy. In Penalolen, in contrast, citizen organizations had no such "team" relationship with the local managers as existed in El Bosque, but rather depended as clients on local government support. As a result, some of their key needs were ignored. Although El Bosque is not without some lingering problems with empowerment, Rivera-Ottenberger concludes that, largely through a responsive local administrator "the participatory model of El Bosque captures the need for a place where rights are not only principles, but tangible distribution of benefits; a place to recover a sense of continuity, of community and of worth." (131)

Section three

The third section of the book examines the importance of civil society organizations, community-based organizations and residents in achieving the goals of decentralization. As stated earlier, two anticipated outcomes of decentralization are:

1   the efficient delivery of public goods and services; and
2   the empowerment of poor and marginalized segments of society.

That non-state actors can help achieve these goals rests on a series of assumptions often made by planning and development practitioners. First, it is believed that involving non-state actors, including private-sector and non-profit organizations, is more cost-effective because centralized state bureaucracies are corrupt as well as inefficient. Second, decentralization is thought to be a superior vehicle for incorporating the needs of, and targeting resources to, disadvantaged groups (i.e. women, the poor, squatters) because of its close geographic proximity and understanding of the local context. Third, the process of decentralization is expected politically to empower the poor and other marginalized segments of society, and in turn this empowerment is expected to safeguard decentralization from elite capture. Each of the chapters in this section critically examines one or more of these assumptions across a diverse set of geographic and socio-political contexts. In each chapter, decentralization partially achieves its objectives. However, the chapters illustrate how the complex dynamics of decentralization unfold on the ground, underscoring the oversimplifications of these assumptions and ultimately the contested relationship between state and non-state actors.

Beard *et al.*, in Chapter 9, examine decentralization and the role of non-state actors through the lens of the World Bank's Urban Poverty Program (UPP). The chapter tests two assumptions underlying both decentralization and community-driven development. The first is that, when governance and planning are decentralized and community actors are given more control, project resources are more likely to be targeted to appropriate beneficiaries. The second assumption is that decentralization and community-driven development empower local, non-state actors because they give them more voice and power over planning and development outcomes. The chapter begins with background information on decentralization, community-driven development and elite capture in the context of Indonesia's dramatic political transformation. Next it reviews the evolution of UPP. Then it analyzes individual characteristics that predict membership in microcredit groups as well as community boards. Microcredit group membership comprises project beneficiaries, whereas community board members are the project leaders. Surprisingly, the analyses find that, even though social and economic elites played a strong role in UPP project planning and implementation, project resources continued to be delivered to the poor. The findings point to a pattern of *elite control*, but not the corruption and misuse of power and resources usually associated with elite capture.

In Chapter 10, Silver and Sofhani examine a new paradigm in Indonesian local planning that emerged in the wake of decentralization and democratic reform. They do so by analyzing the case of a university–community partnership, the Jatinangor Project, in Indonesia. The objectives of the project were to establish a participatory forum of stakeholders to develop a planning agenda. The project engaged the local community, universities, government, the local legislative assemblies and non-governmental institutions down to the smallest spatial scale. The project built local capacity for community research, advocacy planning, new institutions and project monitoring. What was unique about the Jatinangor Project was that it went beyond simply achieving citizen participation in predetermined projects: through an intense, deliberative planning process, it strengthened the community's ability to place pressure on the local government. The chapter demonstrates how, in the context of a national political reform movement and decentralization legislation, progressive local actors were able to use new democratic ideals and expectations to transform local planning. As external support for the project now ends, a major question is whether the project will be able to maintain its open and inclusive planning process and avoid capture by local elites.

Misra and Kudva, in Chapter 11, examine the relationship between gender equity and decentralization through the lens of a constitutional amendment (1992–3) that reinstated *Panchayati Raj* (PR) in India. The amendment established gender quotas in the three tiers of local government. The authors critically examine how this decade-old experiment shapes our understanding of decentralized governance and the role of women. Their analysis combines work done by other scholars as well as observations in six states gathered over the past decade. The authors analyze women's involvement in three areas: presence, action and decision-making. Previous studies illustrate how caste norms, patriarchal practices, low educational attainment and the lack of political experience create obstacles to meaningful participation, but this study identifies a series of "gaps and disjunctures in the quota experiment that could impede change." (182) Identifying the differences in institutional arrangements across states, the authors recognize that greater decentralization may reinforce local practices that foster gender inequality. Considering such variations within states and even districts, they urge increased attention to the formal rules, regulations and procedures, mediated by a deeper understanding of place or local *Panchayats* context. In conclusion, the authors cautiously support the use of legal and institutional reforms to mandate the participation of women in planning and governance.

In Chapter 12, Daniere and Takahashi examine the possible linkages among decentralization, social capital and environmental planning and governance in Thailand. The authors use Evans' (1996) concepts of "complementarity" and "embeddedness" to explore those linkages. According to Daniere and Takahashi, both relationships may positively affect decentralization: complementarity helps to clarify the responsibilities of local governments and communities, and embeddedness helps to generate state and society networks. Their analysis is based on a series of surveys conducted in low-income communities in the Bangkok Metropolitan Area between 1995 and 2000, a period when citizen participation increased markedly. The authors tell a complex story, as their respondents reveal seemingly contradictory degrees of satisfaction as well as distrust of both NGOs and the state.

The authors conclude that, given the large number of residents who are unsure of whether they can trust government and NGO officials, there is "a significant window of opportunity to create and enhance embeddedness." (200)

Shatkin, in Chapter 13, addresses head-on one of the most fundamental problems of decentralization: the opportunities it creates for powerful political elites to pursue their own interests at the expense of the civil society organizations that represent community interests. He examines the problem in a case study of Naga City in the Philippines, where a mayor who gained office as a result of his membership of an elite family then shifted his power base by connecting directly with low-income communities. The case study documents the opportunities for progressive political leaders in post-authoritarian settings, a situation still rare in Asia compared with Latin America during the 1980s and 1990s. The case is of particular interest because the mayor was able to avoid the trap of patronage politics. Shatkin identifies two explanatory factors: first, the emergence of a competent, creative and reform-minded political leader who is committed to a redistributive and participatory agenda; and, second, the existence of civil society organizations that have strong community support and are willing to push the municipal government. The chapter concludes that, although decentralization does not guarantee empowerment of, and redistribution to, poor and marginalized groups, decentralization makes city politics increasingly important for pursuing those two goals.

The scope and variety of the decentralization policies that have changed planning, governance and management in the global south over the last two decades substantiate the need for critical, empirically based analysis of these policies and their outcomes. The cases presented here point to the roles played by local political culture, state and society relations, and the form and operation of certain standard features of decentralization schemes. Other key factors include the strength of social movements, the presence of local institutions that empower citizens to engage in planning and decision-making, and the role of the central state. The value of the cases offered in this volume is not only the range of examples of decentralization with varying degrees of success, but also the significant questions raised about the process itself—questions likely to prompt further research and analysis, certainly warranted by such a globally significant phenomenon.

Notes

1   This is not, however, to suggest a neat dichotomization between top-down and bottom-up planning. Indeed, a considerable body of recent research has indicated the importance of, first, effective central government and, second, a "state–society synergy" in order to achieve effective decentralization (Douglass *et al.* 2002; Evans 1996; Fox and Aranda 1996; Putnam 1993; Tendler 1997).

2   Although not discussed here, financial decentralization is encompassed in administrative decentralization.

3   Political decentralization is also sometimes referred to as devolution or democratic decentralization, thus resulting in confusion between administrative and political decentralization (Hutchcroft 2001; Manor 1999).

References

Agrawal, A. and Ribot, J. (1999) "Accountability in decentralization: A framework with south Asian and west African cases," *Journal of Developing Areas* 33: 473–502.

Aslanbeigui, N. and Summerfield, G. (2001) "Risk, gender, and development in the 21st century," *International Journal of Politics, Culture, and Society* 15 (1): 7–26.

Bakker, I. (2003) "Neoliberal governance and the reprivatization of social reproduction: Social provisioning and shifting gender orders," in I. Bakker and S. Gill, (eds) *Power, Production and Social Reproduction*, New York: Palgrave Macmillan, pp. 66–82.

Bateley, R. (1996) "Public–private relationships and performance in service provision," *Urban Studies* 33 (4/5): 723–50.

Beard, V.A. (2002) "Covert planning for social transformation in Indonesia," *Journal of Planning Education and Research* 22 (1): 15–25.

Beard, V.A. (2003) "Learning radical planning: The power of collective action," *Planning Theory* 2 (1): 13–35.

Beard, V.A. and Cartmill, R.S. (2007) "Gender, collective action and participatory development in Indonesia," *International Development Planning Review* 29 (2): 185–214.

Beneria, L. and Feldman, S. (eds) (1992) *Unequal Burden*, Boulder, CO: Westview Press.

Bennett, A. (1998) "Sustainable public/private partnerships for public service delivery," *Natural Resources Forum* 22 (3): 193–9.

Blair, H. (2000) "Participation and accountability at the periphery: Democratic local governance in six countries," *World Development* 28 (1): 21–39.

Burki, S.J., Perry, G.E. and Dillinger, W.R. (1999) *Beyond the Center: Decentralizing the State*, Washington, DC: World Bank. Available online at www.1.worldbank.org/public sector/decentralization/cd/Beyondthecenter.pdf.

Castells, M. (1983) *The City and the Grassroots*, Berkeley, CA: University of California Press.

Cheema, S.G. and Rondinelli, D.A. (eds) (1983) *Decentralization and Development: Policy Implementation in Developing Countries*, Beverly Hills, CA: Sage.

Cohen, J.M. and Peterson, S.B. (1996) "Methodological issues in the analysis of decentralization," Development Discussion Paper No. 555. Cambridge, MA: Harvard Institute for International Development.

Cohen, J.M. and Peterson, S.B. (1999) *Administrative Decentralization: Strategies for Developing Countries*, West Hartford, CT: Kumarian Press.

Cooke, B. and Kothari, U. (2001) *Participation: The New Tyranny?*, London: Zed Books.

Crook, R.C. and Manor, J. (1998) *Democracy and Decentralisation in South Asian and West Africa: Participation, Accountability and Performance*, Cambridge: Cambridge University Press.

Davidoff, P. (1965) "Advocacy and pluralism in planning," *Journal of the American Institute of Planners* 31 (4): 331–8.

De Angelis, M. (2005) "The political economy of neoliberal governance," *Review* XXIII (3): 229–57.

Diamond, L. (1999) *Developing Democracy: Towards Consolidation*, Baltimore, MD: Johns Hopkins University Press.

Dillinger, W. (1994) "Decentralization and its implications for urban service delivery," Urban Management Discussion Paper No. 16, Washington, DC: World Bank.

Dongier, P., Van Domelen, J., Ostrom, E., Rizvi, A., Wakeman, W., Bebbington, A., Alkire, S., Esmail, T. and Polski, M. (2002) "Community driven development," in J. Klugman (ed.) *A Sourcebook for Poverty Reduction Strategies*, Vol. 1, Washington, DC: World Bank, pp. 301–31.

Douglass, M. and Friedmann, J. (eds) (1998) *Cities for Citizens: Planning and the Rise of Civil Society in a Global Age*, Chichester: John Wiley & Sons.

Douglass, M., Ard-Am, O. and Kim, I.K. (2002) "Urban poverty and the environment: Social capital and state–community synergy in Seoul and Bangkok," in P. Evans (ed.) *Livable Cities? Urban Struggles for Livelihood and Sustainability*, Berkeley, CA: University of California Press, pp. 95–131.

Escobar, A. (1992) "Planning," in W. Sachs (ed.) *The Development Dictionary: A Guide to Knowledge as Power*, London: Zed Books, pp. 132–45.

Evans, P. (1996) "Government action, social capital and development: Reviewing the evidence on synergy," *World Development* 24 (6): 178–209.

Fainstein, S. (1992) "Planning in a different voice," *Planning Theory* 7/8: 27–31.

Fiszbein, A. and Lowden, P. (1999) *Working Together for a Change: Government, Civic, and Business Partnerships for Poverty Reduction in Latin America and the Caribbean*, Washington, DC: World Bank.

Forester, J. (1989) *Planning in the Face of Power*, Berkeley, CA: University of California Press.

Friedmann, J. (1987) *Planning in the Public Domain: From Knowledge to Action*, Princeton, NJ: Princeton University Press.

Friedmann, J. (1989) "The Latin American barrio movement as a social movement: Contribution to a debate," *International Journal of Urban and Regional Research* 13 (3): 501–10.

Fox, J. and Aranda, J. (1996) *Decentralization and Rural Development in Mexico: Community Participation in Oaxaca's Municipal Funds Program*, La Jolla, CA: Center for US–Mexico Studies, University of California at San Diego.

George, S. and Sabelli, F. (1994) "Governance: the last refuge?" in S. George and F. Sabelli (eds) *Faith and Credit: The World Bank's Secular Empire*, Boulder, CO: Westview Press, pp. 142–61.

Hall, P. (1980) *Great Planning Disasters*, Berkeley, CA: University of California Press.

Holston, J. (1989) *The Modernist City: An Anthropological Critique of Brasília*, Chicago, IL: University of Chicago Press.

Hutchcroft, P. (2001) "Centralization and decentralization in administration and politics: Assessing territorial dimensions of authority and power," *Governance: An International Journal of Policy and Administration* 14 (1): 23–53.

Kingsley, T.G. (1996) "Perspectives on devolution," *Journal of the American Planning Association* 62 (4): 419–26.

Krumholz, N. (1982) "A retrospective view of equity planning: Cleveland 1969–1979," *Journal of the American Institute of Planners* 48 (4): 163–78.

Mamdani, M. (1996) *Citizens and Subjects: Contemporary Africa and the Legacy of Late Colonialism*, Princeton, NJ: Princeton University Press.

Manor, J. (1999) *The Political Economy of Democratic Decentralization*, Washington, DC: World Bank.

Mansuri, G. and Rao, V. (2004) "Community-based and -driven development: A critical review," *The World Bank Research Observer* 19 (1): 1–39.

Miraftab, F. (2001) "Risks and opportunities in gender gaps to access shelter: A platform for intervention," *International Journal of Politics, Culture, and Society* 15 (1): 143–60.

Miraftab, F. (2005) "Making neoliberal governance: The disempowering work of empowerment," *International Planning Studies* 9 (4): 239–59.

Miraftab, F. (2006a) "Feminist praxis, citizenship and informal politics," *International Journal of Feminist Politics* 8 (2): 194–218.

Miraftab, F. (2006b) "Informalizing the means of reproduction: The case of waste collection services in Cape Town, South Africa," in L. Beneria and N. Kudva (eds) *Rethinking Informalization: Precarious Jobs, Poverty and Social Protection*, Ithaca, NY: Cornell University e-Publishing Program, 1438–162. Available online at http://hdl.handle.net/1813/3716.

Mohan, G. and Stokke, K. (2000) "Participatory development and empowerment: The dangers of localism," *Third World Quarterly* 21 (2): 247–68.

Ostrom, V., Tiebout, C.M. and Warren, R. (1961) "The organization of government in metropolitan areas: A theoretical inquiry," *American Political Science Review* 55 (4): 831–42.

Peattie, L. (1987) *Planning: Rethinking Ciudad Guayana*, Ann Arbor, MI: University of Michigan Press.

Piven, F.F. (1975) "Planning and class interests," *Journal of the American Institute of Planners* 41 (5): 308–10.

Purcell, M. (2006) "Urban democracy and the local trap," *Urban Studies* 43 (11): 1921–41.

Putnam, R.D. (1993) *Making Democracy Work: Civil Traditions in Modern Italy*, Princeton, NJ: Princeton University Press.

Rosenau, J. and Czempiel, E.-O. (eds) (1992) *Governance without Government: Order and Change in World Politics*, Cambridge: Cambridge University Press.

Roth, G. (1987) *The Private Provision of Public Services in Developing Countries*, New York: Oxford University Press.

Samson, M. (forthcoming) "Rescaling the state, restructuring social relations—A feminist analysis of local government transformation in post-apartheid Johannesburg and its implications for waste management workers," *International Feminist Journal of Politics*.

Sandercock, L. (1998) *Towards Cosmopolis: Planning for Multicultural Cities*, Hoboken, NJ: Wiley & Sons.

Santos, B. de Sousa (2004) "Governance: Between myth and reality," paper presented at the 2004 Law & Society Association Annual Meeting, Chicago, IL, May 27–30.

Savas, E.S. (2000) *Privatization and Public–Private Partnerships*, New York: Chatham House.

Scott, J.C. (1998) *Seeing Like a State: How Certain Schemes to Improve the Human Condition Have Failed*, New Haven, CT: Yale University Press.

Silver, C. (2003) "Do the donors have it right? Decentralization and changing local governance in Indonesia," *Annals of Regional Science* 37 (3): 421–34.

Silver, C., Azis, I.J. and Schroeder, L. (2001) "Intergovernmental transfers and decentralization in Indonesia," *Bulletin of Indonesian Economic Studies* 37 (3): 345–62.

Slater, D. (1989) "Territorial power and the peripheral state: The issue of decentralization," *Development and Change* 20 (3): 501–31.

Tendler, J. (1997) *Good Government in the Tropics*, Baltimore, MD: Johns Hopkins University Press.

US Agency for International Development (2006) *Decentralization 2006: Stock Taking on Indonesia's Recent Decentralization Reforms, Main Report*, Washington, DC: USAID.

World Bank (2001) "Making markets work better for poor people," in *World Development Report 2000/2001: Attacking Poverty*, Washington, DC: World Bank, pp. 61–76.

Wunsch, J.S. (1998) "Decentralization, local governance and the democratic transition in southern Africa: A comparative analysis," *African Studies Quarterly: The Online Journal for African Studies* 2 (1). Available online at http://web.africa.ufl.edu/asq/v2/v2i1a2.htm.

Section One

Decentralization: contexts and outcomes

Chapter 2

Decentralization and entrepreneurial planning

Faranak Miraftab

In the last two decades, the concept of state decentralization has been used to justify contradictory processes and decisions. Whereas advocates stress decentralization of state responsibilities and decision-making, so that inclusive decision-making and participatory planning can advance democratization, critics view state decentralization as a Trojan horse that brings the power of private-sector interests into public decision-making. The critique points to the outright privatization of public utilities as well as the invasion of the public-sector partnerships with private corporations.

Clearly, state decentralization is a complex and dynamic process. It may entail opposing outcomes. To use it in the interest of public good, planning professionals need critically to examine the links between state decentralization processes and planning practice, and then rethink the planners' role and responsibilities in that new context. They should be alert to the conditions under which the decentralization processes meant to empower localities to work more closely with constituents in inclusive planning may in fact, through an emphasis on entrepreneurial planning, introduce exclusive terms for urban citizenship.

Entrepreneurial planning refers to strategies that draw on—and also facilitate—the neoliberal policy framework known as entrepreneurial governance. Increasingly adopted by local governments around the world, entrepreneurial governance follows the new public management (NPM) guidelines, which embrace the principles of the for-profits private sector. To address public-sector inefficiencies, advocates of NPM counsel public administrators to adopt the management techniques and competitiveness of private businesses, market-based organizational structures and mechanisms, and performance measures and management by results (see Osborne and Gaebler 1992).

A frequent dilemma created by state restructuring processes occurs when more responsibilities are passed to local governments, but without adequate financial resources to carry them out. Local governments then turn for relief to the NPM prescription for operating as a private-sector entity, i.e. as a business. Short of outright privatization and sale of public assets, decentralizing local states often enter partnerships with private business to reap entrepreneurial profits. Their assumption is that doing so promotes a win–win situation, benefiting the citizens and the municipality's coffers as well as the local businesses.

In what follows, I interrogate a specific case of such a partnership in Cape Town, South Africa, which joined the decentralizing municipal government with private-sector business and commerce. The partnership created improvement districts, a strategy for local economic development through urban revitalization. Inspired by NPM's vision of entrepreneurial governance, the Cape Town municipality entered this partnership to benefit from the private sector's entrepreneurialism and thus improve its own financial ability to perform its responsibilities. Considering that the overarching agenda of the post-apartheid state restructuring process in South Africa has been to achieve urban integration and inclusive citizenship, I ask: Does the entrepreneurial urban strategy adopted by the decentralizing local state deliver the inclusive urban citizenship promised by the post-apartheid state restructuring?

I examine the Cape Town Partnership and the spread of City Improvement Districts (CIDs) across affluent areas of the city from inception in 2000 to 2006. First, background information is provided on Cape Town municipal government and the state restructuring context. Then, more details are given on CIDs' operation as an entrepreneurial strategy for urban economic development.

I analyze in this case study how the decentralizing local government's emphasis on urban entrepreneurship subordinates its political agenda for redistribution. Under contradictory pressures, the decentralizing local state in Cape Town moved from its initial post-apartheid objective of inclusive city and urban integration to creation of privileged urban zones such as CIDs, intended to attract new and foreign investments. In contrast to the political aspiration of decentralization—for inclusive citizenship—an entrepreneurial partnership risks continual social and spatial urban fragmentation.

For understanding the relationship between planning and decentralization, the South African experience is significant but not unique. Its importance lies in the fact that state restructuring had held out explicit promises for the post-apartheid social objectives of integration and equality; and also is seen in the planning profession's key role in both the making and the unmaking of apartheid's social and spatial inequalities. The South African experience, moreover, has global relevance. The decentralizing local government of Cape Town, caught between its mandate for economic growth on the one hand and its mandate to achieve inclusive urban citizenship on the other, faced a conundrum shared by many municipalities around the world. The planning implications of these contradictory pressures on Cape Town, as in many other cities, have brought officials to adopt entrepreneurial planning.

The municipal government and state restructuring

The paradox of South Africa's post-apartheid state is its simultaneous political liberation and economic neoliberalization, a condition that is the key to understanding the challenging relationship there between decentralization and planning. The paradox of neoliberal economics and political liberation illuminates many aspects of the contradictory pressures shaping South Africa's decentralization as it pursues the ambitious goal of inclusive citizenship and urban integration through entrepreneurial governance and planning.

In 1996, two years after the negotiated political settlement that brought the ANC to power, the ANC's redistributive platform, RDP, was replaced by a homegrown neoliberal policy package, growth, employment and redistribution (GEAR). Whereas RDP had called for economic growth through redistribution, GEAR asserts that distribution will happen through the economic growth to be achieved through liberalization of trade and market-led development. In 1996, when the shift to GEAR took place, South Africa also adopted a new constitution. This progressive document establishes a series of substantive citizenship rights, including housing and basic services, as universal rights for all citizens.[1]

Two aspects of the new constitution are important for our discussion:

(a)   the constitutional call for deracialized citizenship, which expanded the responsibilities of the South African state and mandated for social and spatial integration; and

(b)   the constitutional mandate for state decentralization comprising national, provincial and local governments, and the transfer of responsibility for delivering public services to the local governments.

The goal of inclusive citizenship was to be achieved through state decentralization, facilitated by processes of integrated development planning within municipalities and district councils. In actuality, however, the integrated development plans (IDPs) received little political or financial backing for their implementation (see Harrison 2006; Parnell and Pieterse 2002). South Africa's state restructuring transferred functions to local governments, but not financial power.[2] (For more detailed documentation of this disjuncture see contributions to Pillay *et al.* (2006) entitled *Democracy and Delivery.*)

In the absence of adequate transferred funding for their expanded responsibilities, and within a growth-oriented policy framework favoring entrepreneurial governance, local governments hasten to shed responsibilities and their costs and improve their revenues by participating in private-sector and market-based strategies. Indeed, specific institutions such as the Municipal Infrastructure Investment Unit (MIIU) were created to help municipalities to adopt the private business sector's principles of operation with the aim of cost efficiency, and to establish partnerships with private businesses (see Pillay and Tomilson 2006).

To cut their costs, local governments have turned to privatizing or contracting out basic public services to private companies, or have created public–private partnerships (PPPs) for developing infrastructure and providing public services.

However, the strategy's relief for costs depends on full cost recovery by the private or partnership businesses—from the citizens' user fees.[3] The new system then is "no fee, no basic service." The chapter by Patrick Bond in this volume explains this system well. I refer readers to his chapter for a detailed discussion of the pricing system for water services and its implications for exclusive citizenship in the context of South Africa's state decentralization. In a further move to increase their revenue and income bases, municipal governments have prioritized, making the city or selected zones of it more marketable for investment and attractive to lucrative consumption. The adoption of CIDs has been one such urban strategy, promising to improve revenues by bringing in foreign investment and lucrative tourism.

The CIDs, by giving private stakeholders a bigger hand in shaping and managing urban space, facilitate a shift from political to market-based steering mechanisms. In South Africa, this shift and the emergence of entrepreneurial enthusiasm in local government can be traced to some of the same ideologies, pundits and institutions of knowledge production that have influenced state restructuring in the US and the global north (Bond 2000; Harrison 2006; Pieterse 2005). For example, the guide to "reinventing government" published in the US by Osborne and Gaebler (1992) influenced South Africa's New Public Management approach, which assumes bureaucracy to be the root of problems in local government (see Harrison 2006). In my interviews with city officials about efforts to bring in the private sector, they often referred to expecting the state to steer rather than row—an analogy popularized by Osborne and Gaebler.

CIDs embody the rise of "urban entrepreneurialism" or "entrepreneurial governance" (Hall and Hubbard 1996), in which, to survive, financially strapped cities decide that their only option is to think and act like private-sector entities, turning themselves into some sort of "Municipality Incorporated." Municipality Incs. aim not only to be fiscally disciplined and market savvy, but also to participate in efforts to dissolve the public realm (Brown 2003; Clark 2004; Harvey 2005).

Clearly the story of CIDs in Cape Town is closely related to the many stories from other parts of the world about market-led, local economic projects; contradictory pressures are experienced globally between political citizenship, or formal rights, and substantive citizenship, or economic rights. (I have elaborated on those pressures at length elsewhere: see Miraftab and Wills (2005) and Miraftab (2006).)

The Cape Town Partnership

In 1997, the city government of Cape Town, facing expanded responsibilities but with no increase in material resources, considered the proposal made by an agglomeration of commercial property and business owners in the city center. The proposal was to establish a PPP to fund and manage an example of the urban revitalization strategy known as CIDs. Popularized by Mayor Giuliani for New

York City in the 1980s and widely adopted in the US and Europe, these are known elsewhere as Business Improvement Districts (BIDs).

In 2000, the City of Cape Town approved the establishing of a partnership with the city's private sector to support CIDs, with the expectation that they would create employment and relieve the City's financial distress, both by bringing in new investment and by preventing the flight of businesses located in the improvement districts. The Cape Town Partnership (CTP) was created to manage the first CIDs established in the city, located in the central business district (CBD) and in three adjacent areas (Green Point; Sea Point and Oranjekloof). CTP, a non-profit, private entity, comprises partnerships of the local government with business and commerce organizations to oversee services within the CIDs, both from the municipality and private subcontractors.[4] The CTP Board of Directors comprises members from both the public and private sectors.[5] CTP is active in the reformulation and enforcement of city by-laws about the use of the public spaces in its territory, with particular attention to informal traders, parking attendants, street children, the homeless and panhandlers. As the managing body of the most powerful CIDs in Cape Town, CTP is subsidized by the Cape Metropolitan Council.[6]

Any area can declare itself an improvement district, as long as 51 percent or more of the area's property owners vote to create one and, hence, have additional fees (close to 13 percent of the property rate) added to their municipal bills, which are collected by the City.[7] Neither residential nor commercial tenants have any say about establishment of CIDs; voting is tied to property ownership. Since their inception in Cape Town, the number of CIDs has risen to fourteen, in affluent areas of the city.

Downtown extreme makeover

CTP, using public and private funds, undertook a sort of "extreme makeover" of downtown Cape Town that intended making it "a world class city, . . . with globally competitive product offerings" (Partnership's CEO, interview in 2001). The Partnership's strategy towards that goal was to create exclusive and disciplined zones that are clean, not only of trash, but also of unwanted citizens. The strategies to regulate not only the use but even the users of public space in the improvement districts included policing the public space and also hiring many private security agencies to police it, trying to regulate the use of public space by informal traders and eliminating from the streets, not only trash, but also poverty, as embodied in street children and the homeless.

Elsewhere I have discussed in detail the strategies applied in such disciplined urban zones and their social sanitation (see Miraftab 2007). Briefly, CIDs' disciplinary work can be summarized in three areas:

(a)   Regulating public space by restricting of informal trade: CTP has tried to limit the presence of informal traders in improvement districts by restricting them to specific areas and converting markets in the downtown CID to be only upscale, tourist-oriented markets. Those moves have met with fierce resistance from the informal traders, who accuse the City of partnering with formal big business to sacrifice the informal traders. They point out that, although not big in the amounts of their capital, they are large in number and thus in aggregate economic impact. The CID controversy has brought into opposition the city's informal and formal business sectors—both powerful, but constituted of, and catering to, very different socio-economic constituencies. Whereas CIDs, representing formal business, try to attend to the interests of the fee-paying property owners in their zone, informal traders cater to the majority poor of the city and offer as well a major source of livelihood for the city's many unemployed. The struggle between CTP's big business interests and the interests of informal traders and majority citizens is ongoing.

(b)   Conferring legibility on the informal parking attendants by incorporating them into privatized parking management: parking attendants are historically an informal network of unemployed people who steer people and cars in the congested downtown, point drivers to available curbside parking and protect their parked vehicles.[8] This is a major source of livelihood for unemployed youth in the downtown. In 2001, supported by CTP, the City passed a by-law that required parking attendants in the CBD to be employed by a subcontracted, private parking management company; to wear uniforms and name tags, and to issue company receipts for the parking fees collected. The private company was to pay its contracted fee to the City and a fixed wage to formalized parking attendants, called wardens, who would be hired according to specific criteria. That aspect of the plan was upset, however, by the existing informal network of parking attendants, who are strongly territorial and were not easily pushed aside by the new, uniformed wardens. Nor was there a long line of educated applicants with reference letters, seeking these jobs with the lowest pay. Thus the scheme's recruitment criteria fizzled out. For the most part, the same parking attendants, uniformed and name-tagged, have returned to work, carrying the companies' receipt booklets.

(c)   Surveillance of public space, not only against crime but also against the presence of street children and homeless, who might be perceived as a threat to security: the public space and its users in central city CIDs are policed by a horde of surveillance: private security officers on foot, bicycle and horses; City and national police forces; and 24-hour, closed-circuit TV cameras. This policing of public space is funded not only by the CIDs' privately raised funds, but by their drawing down a lion's share of Unicity's security enforcement.[9]

That distribution of forces is notably unrelated to need, as the City's areas with the highest crime rates receive no remotely comparable share of its security enforcement. The rationale is strictly economic: to displace crime from affluent areas with lucrative consumption into less lucrative—and so less privileged—areas, whose property owners cannot afford to purchase more safety.[10]

The CTP surveillance strategy vis-à-vis the street children and the homeless has undergone some changes. Since 2003, CTP no longer rounds up street children and the homeless into the backs of private security trucks, which happened routinely during the first three years of the partnership. Since late 2003, CTP has relied instead on an NGO-run assessment center's six outreach workers to keep street children and homeless people off CID territory. The multi-service assessment center enters street children into a database when they are brought in by the outreach workers. Those with no criminal charges pending are taken back either to their families or to one of the NGO-run shelters located outside the CIDs.[11]

The efforts to contain informal traders within designated, privatized market places and to make parking attendants legible goes hand in hand with the surveillance and registration of homeless children and adults. In combination, these strategies socially sanitize and discipline urban public spaces. Their aim is to improve the perception of safety held by visitors, tourists and affluent consumers who frequent CIDs. In a city that, as a whole, was fragmented and polarized, downtown Cape Town thus posed as a commodity for sale. Indeed, it has become a hot spot for international real estate developers and tourism development companies, who have bought downtown blocks and turned them into luxury apartments and lofts, predominantly for foreign tourism.

Between 2000 and 2003, the real estate redevelopments in downtown had an accumulated value of R8.2 bn, equivalent to US$1.6 bn[12] (*The Saturday Argus* July 5, 2003). In 2003 alone, this investment was worth R3.4 bn (US$0.68 bn) (www.capetownpartnership.co.za, accessed July 2005). These developments, which brought major economic currency to the city's business district, also made the private-sector-dominated CTP an extremely powerful actor in the city's management —so much so that its entrepreneurial CEO, Michael Farr, was referred to by many Cape Townians as the city's unofficial mayor.

In 2003, however, an important turning point occurred in the development of CTP and of the CIDs in Cape Town's city center. Several conditions, discussed below, exacerbated tensions both within CTP and between CTP and the City, and brought CTP to crisis. Under the city government's threat to pull out of the partnership, the political posturing within the CTP swiftly changed. The shrewdly entrepreneurial CEO, Farr, stepped down. A charismatic, anti-apartheid activist and former city manager, Andrew Boraine, stepped in to lead the CT partnership.

To distance CTP from the positions of the previous CEO, he announced, "We can't create an island of prosperity in a sea of poverty"; his public speeches stated that "poverty is not a crime."

Partnership as a terrain of power struggle

In 2004, the political composition of CTP and its discourse, practices and methodology were transformed. The private sector to a certain degree lost its dominance of the partnership, as the former city manager was brought in to lead it. Some may say the CIDs became victims of their own success; their large and rapid encroachments on the urban landscape brought law suits against them in which rental residents and even property owners sought redress for the CIDs pushing them out; the CIDs' elitist practices with respect to the homeless, the street children and the informal traders sharpened the conflicts within the municipality between the more socially minded and the more growth-minded factions, and between the municipality and the business-dominated Partnership.

Other factors dampened the enthusiasm for CIDs, as well. The ANC gained the city council and Cape Town's mayorship in 2003. Social movements arose that opposed the evictions, privatization and service cut-offs sweeping across the townships and poor neighborhoods. These movements, claiming citizenship rights and the right to a just city, gained strength and legitimacy. It should be remembered that the cities have been the core of the citizenship struggle in the apartheid and the post-apartheid eras.

A unique factor in the change in the Partnership's balance of power was the tragic murder of two street children in downtown CIDs by white business owners. One murder was recorded on the city's CCTV. A public outcry arose, as most South Africans were reminded of apartheid's brutality against blacks, unwanted in the Cape Town's white downtown spaces (*Cape Argus* May 17, 2004). Soon after the murders, the ANC mayor of Cape Town, Nomaindia Mfeketo, launched the Smile-A-Child Campaign, which pledged "there will be no more street children within a year" (*Cape Towner* June 10, 2004). The mayor announced funding for NGOs to eradicate this problem (though one would hope not the children).[13] CTP launched a social development program, helping to finance an NGO-run center and a staff of social workers to work with street children. Through these NGOs, CTP keeps street children out of its zones: outreach workers register and create records for street children brought into the center. If they are not wanted by the judicial system, they are sent to the appropriate service agencies and to their families if they can be located, or to shelters the NGO runs in townships outside the CBD. This system differs markedly from the previous CTP practice of regularly rounding up homeless and street children into the backs of private security trucks.

We must not, however, exaggerate the nature and extent of the 2004 changes. Despite the CTP's changed composition and new rhetoric, it cannot be said to have resolved the tension between the goal of social integration and that of entrepreneurial governance. Unless a way is found to address the structural basis of inequalities and poverty, Boraine's limited social service interventions in Cape Town may displace, but are unlikely to resolve, the problems of crime, homelessness and drug abuse harming children as well as adults. For the CBD's business sector, the children on its streets mean simply an economic liability to its image of the city for tourism, for global investment and for the 2010 World Cup in Cape Town, as an NGO staff pointed out in an interview (2006). That perspective makes the financial tie between NGOs and the business sector dubious and casts a cold light on the CTP's narrow territorial concern.

Boraine's pro-poor statements certainly help to humanize the CIDs—and also, it should be noted, help to justify resistance to the practices of law enforcement officers by traders, homeless, street children and others in a refusal of the exclusionary project of urban revitalization. But it is not clear how far he can move CIDs from exclusionary outcomes and practices. Boraine himself recognizes the limitations he faces: he argues the necessity of a nationally coordinated policy so that "investors cannot leave one city [whose policies protect the poor] for another with more favorable conditions" (interview 2004).

In the context of South Africa's deep socio-spatial inequalities, CIDs' territorial focus does risk displacing crime to areas that cannot afford to purchase better safety, and displacing street children to areas where no NGOs are paid to do outreach. The territorial focus also increases the urban fragmentation of an apartheid city. It defeats social and spatial integration, the stated goal of both urban and regional development policies. Improvement districts, by tying extra services, whether waste collection, safety or social outreach work, to property owners' ability to pay more in fees, perpetuate the infamous urban spatial inequalities of apartheid. Urban scholars have documented such fragmentation and polarization of the post-apartheid cities (Watson 2002; Harrison *et al.* 2003), whereby the privileged areas continue as before to receive better services (McDonald and Smith 2004) and to enjoy a disproportionate share not only of private business investments but also of public resources (Turok 2001). The basis of exclusion may have shifted from race to class, but the citizen's relationship to the state is still tied to urban location—a prominent feature of apartheid spatiality.

Articulation of decentralization and planning

The creation of improvement districts and their management through a PPP highlight the entrepreneurial planning that has arisen with the global trend towards neoliberal governance. Entrepreneurial planning subordinates decentralization's political agenda to an economic one. The post-apartheid objectives of state restructuring were defined initially as inclusive citizenship and participatory planning to ensure more voice and control for disadvantaged groups. Subsequently, however, the turn toward decentralization guided by neoliberal economics has validated entrepreneurial planning that yields control to privileged corporations and private-sector developers. That process is often disguised by the language of "partner-ship" and "power sharing," which celebrates with undifferentiated terminology the state's sharing of power with a spectrum of actors—all wrapped in the guise of "non-state actors." Collapsing actors with sharply conflicting interests into one all-encompassing category is one of the factors leading to the contradictory outcomes that have been seen for decentralization.[14]

Studying the dynamics of the CTP during the first six years of its operation reveals important insights into the articulation of decentralization and planning and into their expected outcomes.

First: PPPs, though often celebrated as an achievement of decentralization and power sharing or cooperative governance, do not deliver guaranteed outcomes. The political context and environment of a partnership matter greatly as to whether it does or does not achieve a public good—in this case, social and spatial integration. When the political logic of state restructuring is conflated with its economic logic, decentralization, in actuality, has exclusionary outcomes. This case study reveals, however, the contentious nature of partnerships as a terrain of power; their out-comes are thus inherently not predetermined, but rather responsive to the power dynamics among the differing actors/partners. In the changing dynamics of the CTP, the approach, methodology and rhetoric of the partnership were observed to be subject to change from a combination of local resistance within and outside the partnership structure. It is deceptive, therefore, to consider partnerships as fixed or static arrangements and, therefore, to assume decentralization leads to a predictable outcome such as democratization or inclusive planning.

Second: decentralization may pose a critical danger of setting up "local traps" —i.e. limiting the realm of action and change to spatially bounded, politically and economically isolated territories (Purcell 2006). Assuming that the problems of inequality and injustice can be fixed at the local level without taking into account the dynamics of the larger structures and specific contexts—what Mohan and Stokke (2000) call localism—is a danger in uncritically advocating decentralization. As seen in this case of CIDs' implementation, spatially bounded strategies for local economic development face unavoidable tensions within both the public and private structures, among citizens, city officials and planners. Tensions arise between market-driven, local economic development, aimed at growth and global competitiveness, and socially aspired agendas for social equity through regional and metropolitan integration. The work of Iris Young (1990) has effectively exposed the danger that local participation can indeed generate greater injustice from the inequality among local communities. She therefore calls for regional planning and the coordination of local or community-based initiatives at the regional level. Young warns against celebrating local decision-making without being alert to the inequalities embodied by and across communities. Similarly, Janet

Abu-Lughod (1998) cautions against uncritically romanticizing local communities and decentralized decision-making, and reminds us of such reactionary agglomerations as KKKs and elitist homeowner associations.

Third: transnational models of urban economic development, such as CIDs, do not simply roll out over a smoothed global space. Their implementation involves a contentious process of responding to local conditions. Conceptualizing CIDs as part of a global mode of neoliberal governance is useful and illuminating, but may assign too much power to the global agenda for capital accumulation and overlook how local specifics change the process and outcomes of such partnerships. I argue here that the practices the CTP has foregone in response to pressures it faced on the ground must analytically be taken into account. A combination of residents' resistance and the scheme's irresponsiveness to the historical particularities of the local context brought CTP face to face with local specifics of global neoliberalization. The disjunction had an important impact on how the Partnership managed CIDs. Just as the parking attendants' recruitment criteria were abandoned, so too the earlier, heavy-handed treatment of the homeless was defeated by the recognition that police and their pickup trucks could not simply "clean up" poverty from the streets of downtown, nor would NGO social workers consent to do so.

While concluding that decentralization is not a static model that necessarily achieves democratization and inclusive planning, I now call attention to certain conditions that can improve their democratic potential: all administrative levels of the state and coordinated, regional decision-making bodies, if they have appropriate tools and implementation powers, can help to eliminate the "local trap" lurking in decentralization. Strong social movements and civil society groups rooted in the struggle of the disadvantaged citizens can launch incursions into decentralization's terrain of power and prevent its domination by private-sector interests through entrepreneurial planning. In that paradoxical way, decentralized planning might indeed produce more inclusive and egalitarian decision-making and outcomes. It need not inevitably be taken over by interests of the stronger localities and narrowly focused local decision-making bodies (e.g., such area-based partnerships as CIDs). Clearly, a strong governing body to oversee the at-large interests of cities and regions would be useful. Even though social and spatial fragmentation is a corollary of contemporary neoliberal capitalism, a centralized state power responsive to vigilant social movements of disadvantaged groups could counter the splintering affects of decentralization.

Notes

1   Article 26 of the 1996 constitution states: "everyone has the right to access to adequate housing . . . No one may be evicted from their homes, or have their homes demolished, without an order of court made after considering all the relevant circumstances. No

legislation may permit arbitrary evictions." Article 27 states: "every one has the right to have access to . . . sufficient food and water and social security, including, if they are unable to support themselves and their dependants, appropriate social assistance."

2   For example, in the case of Cape Town, 90 percent of the Cape Town Unicity's budget comes from local revenues. Those revenues include the sale of bulk services, such as water, sanitation and electricity (85 percent), and to a limited extent property rates and levies (Watson 2002: 77, citing Ministry of Provincial Affairs and Constitutional Development 1998). Even the devolution of political power has been limited. That may be explained by the nature of the negotiated political settlement in South Africa, which required local government structures to inherit officials of the former white local authorities, often reluctant and sometimes hostile to changed policies.

3   This strategy is also referred to as "cost reflective pricing" or full recovery of service costs, "wherein the entire cost of service delivery, including infrastructure maintenance and replacement, is structured into rates" (see Bond in this volume). In this system, black areas with inferior infrastructure incur higher service delivery costs, whereas white suburbs, historically subsidized by the apartheid state for their infrastructure development, enjoy lower service delivery costs. Such "cost reflective pricing" of services does not allow for cross-subsidy between the areas; hence, residents in black townships pay more than do those in affluent white areas for identical services. High unemployment, intense poverty and greater service delivery costs burden the black townships; nevertheless, impoverished residents who cannot afford their service payments have increasingly had service disconnected.

4   Of the currently active improvement districts in Cape Town, the CBD and three areas adjacent to CBD are managed by CTP. The other districts fall outside the CBD, and each is managed by a single agency. For example, Wynberg, Claremont, Fish Hoek and Muizenberg each have their own managing company.

5   The composition of the board has changed since its inception. The earlier CTP board comprised three members of the public sector and nine members of the organized business sector, including Chambers of Commerce; the South Africa Property Owners Association; Corporate Cape Town (twenty-six companies, such as banks and finance companies); Cape Town Heritage Trust; Cape Town Tourism; the Convention Center Company; Business Against Crime; and the City-Community Patrol Board. The most recent composition of the CTP board, however, is more diverse, including some members of the non-profit, NGOs. The current board comprises members of the following organizations: Mandela Rhodes Foundation; Hermans & Roman Property Solutions; Mayoral Committee for Housing, City of Cape Town; Table Mountain National Park; University of Cape Town; I & J company; Haven Night Shelter; SA Black Technical & Allied Careers' Organisation (SABTACO); City Manager, City of Cape Town; Former Arts & Culture Manager, District 6 Museum Foundation; Special Advisor to the Premier, Western Cape Provincial Government; Business Against Crime; RMB Properties; Cape Town Heritage Trust; Member of the Mayoral Committee for Planning and Environment, City of Cape Town; and Cape Regional Chamber of Commerce (www.capetownpartnership.co.za).

6   The City pays one-twelfth of CTP's budget plus 3 percent of the bad debt provision.

7   This is a unique feature of South African CIDs. Elsewhere, the public sector does not bear the burden of fee collection and property confiscation should rate-payers fail to pay the additional levies for CID privatized services and management.

8   Laurie Scott (2003: 31) cites a survey conducted by the Catholic Welfare Development that was conducted in 1996 among the homeless population of downtown Cape Town.

Over 70 percent of the respondents cited parking and/or washing cars as their source of income.

9   Of the CCTVs purchased by Cape Town Unicity in 1999, seventy-two are installed in the CBD alone; twelve in the adjacent, up-market, ocean-front Seapoint; and forty-three along a main artery road, Vanguard Drive—to monitor criminals' likely escape route. Of the 900 city police officers operating in all of metropolitan Cape Town, about 150 are assigned to the CBD and Seapoint (interview 2006).

10 There is, of course, an additional economic rationale for the discourse of safety and security: one that extends beyond individuals' bodily safety to the collective economic security of the city. Rationalizing the policing of public space, CTP's founding CEO argues that "expenditure on policemen is not consumptive. It is investment expenditure. Because if crime is addressed, more investment is brought in" (interview 2001).

11 The Mayor's Campaign made some funds available to the local NGOs in the CBD that had for decades worked with the center city street children, but it did not consult with them (interview with a local NGO 2006). The bulk of the Mayor's funds went to the one NGO (City Mission) jointly contracted with CTP to run the Assessment Center, targeting CBD's street children specifically.

12 Based on the exchange rate in July 2004, US$1 = R5. Cumulative investment in the Central City since 2000, measured in terms of the capital value of current leases, new developments, investment purchases, upgrades and renewals, is R11 bn (CTP website, accessed June 2007).

13 There is no precise estimate of the number of street children in Cape Town. In the CBD alone, NGOs estimate about 300 street children. In the city as a whole, a 2000 survey estimated there were 800 street children.

14 The PPP literature indeed collapses efficiency, effectiveness and equity and indeed does not engage with the question of equity and social justice (e.g., USAID 1997; Fiszbein and Lowden 1999; DFID 1999; Bennett 1998). Dominated by mechanistic accounts of the PPPs (i.e. the logistics and typology, the forms of contracts and the terms of concessions—it has little to say about the power relations and the importance of the environment within which partnerships are implemented. Topics such as the political, economic, social and cultural environments of the PPPs and how they influence the ability of partnerships to serve the goal of public good are thinly treated (Osbourne 2000; Payne 1999). This literature often falls short in examining whether and how these partnerships could replace the public sector's responsibility to serve the public good. (For a fuller discussion of that issue, see Miraftab 2004.)

References

Abu-Lughod, J. (1998) "Civil/uncivil society: Confusing form with content," in M. Douglas and J. Friedmann (eds) *Cities and Citizen*, New York: John Wiley & Sons, pp. 227–38.

Bennett, A. (1998) "Sustainable public/private partnerships for public service delivery," *Natural Resources Forum* 22 (3): 193–9.

Bond, P. (2000) *Elite Transition: From Apartheid to Neoliberalism in South Africa*, London: Pluto Press.

Brown, W. (2003) "Neoliberalism and the end of liberal democracy," *Theory and Event* (7): 1.

Clark, J. (2004) "Dissolving the public realm? The logic and limits of neoliberalism," *International Social Policy* 33 (1): 27–48.

DFID (Department for International Development) (1999) *Public–Private Partnerships in Infrastructure. Department for International Development*, London: DFID.

Fiszbein, A. and Lowden, P. (1999) *Working Together for a Change: Government, Civic, and Business Partnerships for Poverty Reduction in Latin America and the Caribbean*, Washington, DC: World Bank.

Hall, T. and Hubbard, P. (1996) "The entrepreneurial city: New politics, new geographies," *Progress in Human Geography* 20: 153–74.

Harrison, P. (2006) "Integrated development plans and third way politics," in U. Pillay, R. Tomilson and J. DuToit (eds) *Democracy and Delivery: Urban Policy in South Africa*, Cape Town: HSRC Press, pp. 186–207.

Harrison, P., Huchzermeyer, M. and Mayekiso, M. (eds) (2003) *Confronting Fragmentation: Housing and Urban Development in a Democratising Society*, Cape Town: Cape Town University Press.

Harvey, D. (2005) *A Brief History of Neoliberalism*, Oxford, New York: Oxford University Press.

McDonald, D. and Smith, L. (2004) "Privatizing Cape Town: From apartheid to neoliberalism in the mother city," *Urban Studies* 41 (8): 1461–84.

Miraftab, F. (2004) "Public-private partnerships: The Trojan horse of neoliberal development?," *Journal of Planning Education and Research* 24 (1): 89–101.

Miraftab, F. (2006) "Feminist praxis, citizenship and informal politics: Reflections on South Africa's anti-eviction campaign," *International Feminist Journal of Politics* 8 (2): 194–218.

Miraftab, F. (2007) "Governing post-apartheid spatiality: Implementing city improvement districts in Cape Town," *Antipode: Radical Journal of Geography* 39 (4): 602–26.

Miraftab F. and Wills, S. (2005) "Insurgency and spaces of active citizenship: The story of Western Cape anti-eviction campaign in South Africa," *Journal of Planning Education and Research* 25 (2): 200–17.

Mohan, G. and Stokke, K. (2000) "Participatory development and empowerment: The dangers of localism," *Third World Quarterly* 21 (2): 247–68.

Osbourne, S. (2000) *Public–Private Partnerships for Public Services: An International Perspective*, London: Routledge.

Osborne, D. and Gaebler, T. (1992) *Reinventing Government: How the Entrepreneurial Spirit is Transforming the Public Sector*, Reading, MA: Addison-Wesley.

Parnell, S. and Pieterse, E. (2002) "Developmental local government," in S. Parnell, E. Pieterse, M. Swelling and D. Wooldrigde (eds) *Democratising Local Government: The South African Experiment*, Cape Town: Cape Town University Press.

Payne, G.K. (1999) *Making Common Ground: Public–Private Partnerships in Land for Housing*, London: Intermediate Technology Publications.

Pieterse, E. (2005) "Political inventions and interventions: A critical review of the proposed city development strategy partnership in Cape Town," in S. Robins (ed.) *Limits to Liberation After Apartheid: Citizenship, Governance and Culture*, Oxford: James Curry, pp. 113–33.

Pillay, U. and Tomilson R. (2006) "Conclusion," in U. Pillay, R. Tomilson and J. DuToit (eds) *Democracy and Delivery: Urban Policy in South Africa*, Cape Town: HSRC Press, pp. 302–19.

Pillay, U., Tomilson, R. and DuToit, J. (eds) (2006) *Democracy and Delivery: Urban Policy in South Africa*, Cape Town: HSRC Press.

Purcell, M. (2006) "Urban democracy and the local trap," *Urban Studies* 43 (11): 1921–41.

Scott, L. (2003) "The mechanics and implications of city improvement districts in Cape Town," unpublished Master's thesis, Dept. of Urban and Regional Planning, University of Illinois, Urbana-Champaign, December.

Turok, I. (2001) "Persistent polarization post-apartheid? Progress towards urban integration in Cape Town," *Urban Studies* 38 (13): 2349–77.

USAID (1997) *New Partnership Initiative: A Strategic Approach in Development Partnering*, Washington, DC: USAID.

Watson, V. (2002) *Change and Continuity in Spatial Planning: Metropolitan Planning in Cape Town Under Political Transition*, London, New York: Routledge.

Young, I.M. (1990) *Justice and Politics of Difference*, Princeton, NJ: Princeton University Press.

Chapter 3

Decentralization, privatization and countervailing popular pressure

South African water commodification and decommodification

Patrick Bond

This chapter considers the underlying pressures to decentralize and privatize state water services, rooted in capital's drive to commodify. The 1990s and early 2000s witnessed the formal establishment of "water as an economic good" in multilateral programs and multinational corporate expansion of service provision. But, in addition to various forms of economic logic that have driven water commodification, countervailing pressure emerged, both implicitly in the form of poverty, and more explicitly from trade unions, community and consumer groups, environmentalists and other citizens' movements. The case of South African water during the first decade of post-apartheid democracy is illustrative, not only for the way decentralization of financing initially limited access, but also for the revealing ways resistance shifted state policy to a "free basic water" tariff in 2001, which still left consumers disempowered because it retained crucial micro-neoliberal pricing principles.

Introduction

The decentralization of state services generally entails the shifting of delivery mandates from higher to lower scales but with fewer resources, a problem known as "unfunded mandates." It is sometimes argued that the core *economic* objective behind decentralization is increased efficiency, but what this means in practice, as we will see in our case study, can better be termed "commodification." Simultaneously, urban areas are under much more severe competitive pressures, as decentralized planning compels a shift to entrepreneurial management. The most extreme case may be the full transfer of state responsibilities to households, under the guise of "community-based management" and "participation." In many rural areas suffering lack of state capacity, decentralization reflects a rollback of state service delivery commitments altogether. These features of decentralization have had a devastating impact upon water/sanitation access for poor people, and throw into question the over-reliance upon decapacitated municipalities for essential state services such as water.

In these respects, decentralization is a symptom of a deeper set of adverse state–society relationships that have emerged in the past three decades or so, which follow the globalization of capital and widespread adoption of neoliberal policy frameworks and which, in turn, reflect changes in class power, especially as applied to urban municipal management. Consistent with the critique of "accumulation by dispossession" by David Harvey (2003), a "double movement" emerges, consistent with Karl Polanyi's (1956) analysis. As we will observe, commodification has been joined and rebuffed by decommodification pressures from grassroots communities. Harvey cites the South African water sector as an exemplar of accumulation by dispossession, among other examples of the ways profits are being sought, not only at the point of production and through the expanded reproduction of capital, but also through systems such as privatization, which transfer common resources and values from society or nature, into capital assets. For Third World municipalities in particular, decentralization led to "a mismatch between financial authority and functional responsibility," as Patricia McCarney (1996: 19) observed.

During the late twentieth century, these processes unfolded via central–local shifts in governmental responsibilities and were codified through entrepreneurial competition between cities, which put added pressure on services for low-income people. For roughly two decades after the 1986 launch of the World Bank's New Urban Management Program, a neoliberal *interurban* Washington Consensus unfolded, especially in relation to urban water and sanitation delivery. The Bank's 1991 policy paper on urban management, the 1996 United Nations Conference on Human Settlements in Istanbul, the UN Development Program's Municipal Services Program and Habitat housing division adopted similar strategies, alongside the US Agency for International Development, British Department for International Development, Canadian CIDA and other official donor agencies. The overall orientation paralleled austerity and structural adjustment policies at the macro-economic scale, with US AID consultants from the Urban Institute (1991) spelling out the:

> important change in policy thinking in the developing world closely linked to the acceptance of market-oriented economies: the growing acceptance of rapid urbanization. . . . An emphasis on national economic growth and export-led development will usually mean that new investment resources must be directed to already successful regions and cities. . . . Governments have considerable control over the entire cost structure of urban areas. Public policy should be directed to lowering these costs.

"Lowering these costs"—especially by lowering the social wage (including subsidies for water)—is crucial for the more direct insertion of "competitive" cities into the world economy. The focus here is not merely on limiting public financing of social services to those deemed to add value (though this is one of the more obvious effects of structural adjustment and the catalyst for many an IMF riot). Just as importantly, the New Urban Management Program also highlights the *productivity* of urban capital as it flows through urban land markets (now enhanced by titles and registration), housing finance systems (featuring solely private sector delivery and an end to state subsidies), the much-celebrated (but extremely exploitative) informal economy, (often newly privatized) urban services such as transport, sewage, water and even primary health care and educational services (via intensified cost-recovery on "human capital" investments), and the like.

The problem also became severe in Third World rural areas where, as Ugandan scholar Mahmood Mamdani (1996: 111, 287) has shown for Africa, local-level state administration often amounted to "decentralized despotism," even prior to the 1980s–90s rise of neoliberalism. Even in the best case, Museveni's Uganda, where local-level power relations inherited from centralized despotic rule had to be thoroughly broken, there remained a "bifurcated" duality of power: between a centrally located modern state (sometimes directly responsible for urban order in primate capital cities) and a "tribal authority which dispensed customary law to those living within the territory of the tribe." With this observation, Mamdani sets the stage for the problem of global–national–local processes:

> In the absence of democratization, development became a top-down agenda enforced on the peasantry. Without thorough-going democratization, there could be no development of a home market. The latter failure opened wide what was a crevice at Independence. With every downturn in the international economy, the crevice turned into an opportunity for an externally defined structural adjustment that combined a narrowly defined program of privatization with a broadly defined programme of globalization.

As state service delivery withered under pressure of this sort during the 1980s–1990s, World Bank (1994) decentralization and community participation programs were introduced to "improve quality, effectiveness and sustainability . . . [and] strengthen ownership and commitment." The Bank's (2000: Annex 2) *Sourcebook on Community Driven Development in the Africa Region: Community Action Programs* captured the contradictions associated with an instrumental approach to decentralization and participation:

> Fifteen years ago, community based management and user friendly handpumps were introduced [across Africa], together with VIP latrines. Communities had to manage and pay for the maintenance of their handpumps. The approach was received with great skepticism by sector ministries: "Villagers can't possibly maintain a pump." Today community based management is accepted by all sector professionals across Africa as the only sustainable approach to village water supply and sanitation (with construction of low cost latrines) and increasingly to town water supply. Demand responsiveness where communities choose the facilities they want, decide how to manage and finance them, and pay part of the capital cost is also widely accepted as fundamental to sustainability.

Before considering how widely these ideas are indeed accepted—and can be sustained financially—in the water sector, we might first examine how urban South Africa came under immediate pressure to decentralize state services during its critical 1990s transition period.

Decentralization hits democratic South Africa

The African National Congress government of Nelson Mandela (1994–9) articulated the pro-globalization, entrepreneurial sensibility of decentralized urban neoliberalism in its 1995 *Urban Development Strategy (UDS)*: "Seen through the prism of the global economy, our urban areas are single economic units that either rise, or stagnate and fall together. . . . South Africa's cities are more than ever strategic sites in a transnationalized production system" (Ministry of Reconstruction and Development 1995: 17, 41). As intrametropolitan struggles over resources intensified, the competition in laxity that South Africa began experiencing at the regional level via 1970s and 1980s apartheid-era decentralization initiatives (Bond 2000) jumped scale to the international level.

With apartheid running out of steam and Mandela released from jail in 1990, the main corporate advocates for urban neoliberalism, a think tank developed by Anglo American Corporation and other business leaders, the Urban Foundation (UF) (1990: 59), called for a "'bottom-up' regional development policy, in which functionally-defined regions compete with one another for development funds on the basis of their local and regional comparative advantages." The "winner region" would be Johannesburg, whereas the demise of decentralization incentives—to the benefit of large metropolitan corporations—also meant the demise of household living standards in peripheral areas. Based upon Mike Morris and Dave Kaplan's (1987) analysis of a potential South African post-fordism, the UF (1990: 12) cele-brated decentralized industrial systems on the grounds that "just-in-time production technology requires spatial compactness and spatial integration of metropolitan areas in order to ensure rapid interactions between complementary firms."

The result would be intensified uneven development in the country's system of cities and towns, combined with political decentralization of a rather circum-scribed sort. In 2006, the South African Presidency (2006: 20, 22) of Thabo Mbeki announced its National Spatial Development Perspective's three objectives: "Focus investment and development interventions to ensure maximum and sus-tainable impact; spatial arrangements to facilitate nation building and social and economic inclusion; ensure government implements its programmes taking into account economic, social and demographic realities." Notwithstanding talk of inclusion, in reality the second of these three—decentralization of resources to rural areas (especially ex-Bantustans) suffering underdevelopment—is systematically undermined by the strategy's second "normative principle," drawn from the economic "realities" of apartheid-era capitalism: "focus economic infrastructure development on *localities of economic growth and/or economic potential* in order to gear up private sector investment, stimulate sustainable economic activities and create long-term employment opportunities" (emphasis added). This is the key linkage, then, between the amplification of inherited local spatial patterns and the needs of the world economy, a phenomenon known as glocalization.

As a result, political decentralization—including the rationalization of 843 apartheid-era local governments in 1994 into 284 "wall to wall" municipalities by 2001—occurred during an economic rescaling that rewarded already-rich regions. One result was an acute case of unfunded mandates for lower-income municipalities, as central government shrunk central-local operating subsidies by 85 percent in real terms during the 1990s. This left municipalities incapable of drawing upon external resources for infrastructural operating/maintenance (Bond 2000). At the same time, the local authorities' capacity to generate cross-subsidies from differential prices to high-income residents and corporations was also declining owing to interurban competition and services commercialization. There is no better case to illustrate the problems associated with these trends towards uneven development than the urban water sector, where access by poor people has been threatened by intensified commodification and diminished state subsidies. Indeed, paying for water systems has proven an exceptionally difficult task, one that soon generated riots and a partial state concession: "free basic water."

Financing water infrastructure

From the very outset of organized water provision, the institutional delivery mechanism was decentralized in most countries, at the municipal scale. However, the New Public Management paradigm focused much more attention on gaining efficiencies through restructured water supplies that more closely related retail *prices to costs* (Bond 2004, Wilson 2006). Indeed, the main dilemma, posed by neoliberals aiming to roll back state support for water services, is how such systems should be financed, not only for initial capital investment to expand the water reticulation grid, but especially with respect to the operating and maintenance costs that bedevil so many delivery systems.

Since the early 1990s, privatization and commercialization of water supplies have expanded in many parts of the world. The intense conflict over the economics of water resources' allocation was prefigured by the 1992 International Conference on Water and the Environment in Dublin, where water was formally declared an "economic good" by key multilateral officials and firms active in the sector. Four years later, the Global Water Partnership and World Water Council advanced the position that commodification of water would lead to both private-sector investments and more efficient utilization. In the same spirit, 1997 witnessed the first World Water Forum in Marrakesh, the founding of the World Commission for Water in the 21st Century.

At the same time, the International Monetary Fund (IMF) and World Bank became much more explicit in promoting water commodification through what were once mainly macro-oriented structural adjustment programs, whether called the Enhanced Structural Adjustment Facility, Poverty Reduction and Growth Facility or Poverty Reduction Strategy Programme (Hennig 2001). According to one NGO critique by the Globalization Challenge Initiative (2001):

> A review of IMF loan policies in 40 random countries reveals that, during 2000, IMF loan agreements in 12 countries included conditions imposing water privatization or full cost recovery. In general, it is African countries, and the smallest, poorest and most debt-ridden countries that are being subjected to IMF conditions on water privatization and full cost recovery.

In early 2006, the European Union's attempt to have water included within the World Trade Organization's General Agreement on Trade in Services as a tradeable service—in the process subjecting water to further competition/privatization pressures—appeared to falter, based largely on strong alliances between Third World movements and Scandinavian activists. However, in 109 bilateral requests made by European governments of trade partners in 2000, water was included in seventy-two requests, indicating the underlying water commercialization pressure.

With the 2006 Nobel Prize award to Muhammad Yunus, founder of Bangladesh-based Grameen Bank, the idea that even decentralized microfinance could fund water systems became more credible. The most extreme form of this position came from Yunus himself (1998: 214): "I believe that 'government', as we know it today, should pull out of most things except for law enforcement and justice, national defense and foreign policy, and let the private sector, a 'Grameenized private sector,' a social-consciousness-driven private sector, take over their other functions." Yet the private provision of water—whether a major commercialized municipal operation or microsupply of water through small-scale retail outlets—is often so prohibitively expensive (compared with state-supplied water), that even the United Nations Development Program (UNDP) (2003: 106) is forced into a contradiction, by first demonstrating that cost-recovery on water is prohibitively expensive, but then, second, insisting that microcredit is the solution:

> How difficult is it for poor people to cover the costs of water and sanitation infrastructure? Consider an example from Bolivia and some cost estimates for water and sanitation from a project in El Alto:
>
> - Average monthly income: $122 ($0.80 a day per capita).
> - Connection costs: $229 for traditional water, $276 for sanitation (excluding trunk infrastructure).

- Connection costs for condominial technology with community participation: $139 for water, $172 for sanitation.

An important additional cost for poor households is the construction of a bathroom or similar in-house facility, including a toilet. In El Alto these costs averaged $400, plus 16 days of labour. These costs are typically not factored into costing exercises for water and sanitation. Even with microfinance available the costs were too high for most poor people. But with hygiene education, the demand for toilets more than doubled. Where poor people struggle to cover charges, they should be helped through credit schemes. Bangladesh's Grameen Bank has been extending credit for water and sanitation, on a group basis, for years.

(United Nations Development Program 2003)

The UNDP's (2006: 120) *Human Development Report* on water also assumes that sometimes the state should allow the market to take over (in a site where the "flying toilet" of excrement in small plastic bags hurled from private to public spaces is common):

In Kibera, Nairobi, constructing a pit latrine costs about $45, or two months of income for someone earning the minimum wage. To help poor households meet the financing requirements of improved sanitation, arrangements are needed that provide subsidies or allow payments to be spread over time through microcredit.

The same report claims progress in rural sanitation in Lesotho, where state involvement has shrunk:

The full cost-recovery and zero-subsidy policy has created incentives for innovation. But even basic latrines are still beyond the means of the very poor. Only recently have measures been put in place to reduce the costs of latrines through microcredit programmes offering extended loan repayment periods.

(UNDP 2006: 125)

Setting aside the problem of the state shirking its historic responsibility to fund water (as Yunus apparently celebrates), there are numerous dangers associated with microcredit, especially where the link between financing and productive sector activity is tenuous, and in so many situations where women discover that the expensive (high interest rate), overly indebting and residual-patriarchal features of microcredit are opposite to that advertised (Bond 2007).

The gap for such initiatives comes from system state failure—not surprising given the various ways African states have been financially and politically disempowered in recent years (Mkandawire and Soludo 1999). In large African cities, the commercialization of water is typically introduced so as to address classic problems associated with state control: inefficiencies, excessive administrative centralization, lack of competition, unaccounted-for consumption, weak billing and political interference. The desired forms will vary, but the options include private outsourcing, management or partial/full ownership of the service. In the field of water, there are at least seven institutional steps that can be taken towards privatization: short-term service contracts, short/medium-term management contracts, medium/long-term leases (*affermages*), long-term concessions, long-term Build (Own) Operate Transfer contracts, full permanent divestiture, and an additional category of community provision, which also exists in some settings. Aside from French and British water corporations, the most aggressive promoters of these strategies are a few giant aid agencies (especially US AID and British DFID) and the World Bank.

For example, "The World Bank has worked with the City [of Johannesburg (CoJ)] in recent years to support its efforts in local economic development and improving service delivery," according to World Bank (2002) staff and consultants. Early interventions included a 1993 study of services backlogs and the new government's 1994 Municipal Infrastructure Investment Framework. More recently, according to the Bank (2002), Johannesburg's vision strategy document for 2030:

> draws largely on the empirical findings of a series of World Bank reports on local economic development produced in partnership with the CoJ during 1999–2002, and places greater emphasis on economic development. It calls for Johannesburg to become *a world-class business location* . . . The World Bank's local economic development methodology developed for the CoJ in 1999 sought to conceptualize an optimal role for *a fiscally decentralized CoJ* in the form of a regulator that would seek to alleviate poverty . . . through job creation by creating *an enabling business environment for private sector investment* and economic growth in Johannesburg. (emphasis added)

This short-termist commitment to urban entrepreneurialism negates the needs of poor people for higher levels of municipal services paid for through cross-subsidies from business, for Johannesburg would become less competitive as a base within global capitalism if higher levels of tariffs were imposed. Throughout the 1990s, precisely this sort of pressure intensified in South African cities, especially Johannesburg, to outsource a variety of functions. Among key pilot projects were late-apartheid water supply projects established by the Suez-controlled company Water and Sanitation South Africa in three Eastern Cape towns: Queenstown (1992), Stutterheim (1994) and Fort Beaufort (later named Nkonkobe) (1995). Similar supply deals with foreign firms in Nelspruit and the Dolphin Coast were temporarily stalled in 1998 by trade union-led resistance, but were resuscitated in 1999. Johannesburg followed in 2001.

The primary advocates of privatization were the World Bank and its private sector investment arm, the International Finance Corporation, as well as local and international firms. For example, Banque Paribas, Rand Merchant Bank, Colechurch International, the Development Bank of Southern Africa, Générale des Eaux, Metsi a Sechaba Holdings, Sauer International and Suez had all met with officials of South Africa's fifth largest municipality by 1997, in the wake of a week-long 1996 World Bank study of the council's waterworks that suggested just one policy option: full privatization (Port Elizabeth Municipality 1997). Many municipalities had closed down their public housing and, in some cases, civil engineering departments during the 1980s as part of the first wave of municipal state shrinkage. The adoption of municipal neoliberalism intensified thanks to dramatic shortfalls in central–local operating subsidies, late 1990s legislation favoring PPPs, and a large US Aid grant for the development of PPP business plans in various towns.

In this context, the World Bank felt able to continue promoting privatization (including in its *World Development Report 2004* (2003), which offered Johannesburg as a success story box). In addition to its ideological commitment to the market, the Bank also would have considered self-interest in safeguarding its vast sunk investments in water systems. The International Consortium of Investigative Journalists found that, during the 1990s, the Bank lent $20 bn to water-supply projects and imposed privatization as a loan condition in one third of the transactions (Logan 2003). To protect these loans and investments, the Bank and other financiers participated in the 2002–03 World Panel on Financing Infrastructure that reported to the World Water Forum in Kyoto. Chaired by former IMF Managing Director Michel Camdessus, it brought together the Global Water Partnership, presidents of major multilateral development banks (IADB, ADB, EBRD, WB), representatives of the International Finance Corporation, Citibank, Lazard Frères, the US Ex–Im Bank, private water companies (Suez, Thames Water), state elites (from Egypt, France, Ivory Coast, Mexico and Pakistan) and two NGOs (Transparency International and WaterAid).

Among Camdessus' recommendations were that international financial institutions should increase guarantees and other public subsidies for private water investors. Camdessus called for $180 bn in capital expenditure, even though just one-sixth of that would be earmarked for investments aimed at meeting drinking water, sanitation and other hygiene needs. A primary reason for the Commission's existence was that, after the East Asian, Russian, Brazilian and South African crises of the late 1990s, the dramatic increase in private water investments in the Third World suddenly reversed. With Suez in trouble in Argentina and many other settings, Camdessus was required as a means of generating greater risk and currency insurance for the large French and British water firms. Assisted even by an NGO (WaterAid), Camdessus designed a "devaluation liquidity backstopping facility" to those ends, as well as a "revolving fund" to cover the "large fixed cost of preparing Private Sector Participation contracts and tenders." Public Services International (2003), whose union affiliates boast 20 million members, declared:

> The bankers' panel pursues the goal of having private corporations manage and profit from delivering the world's water. They want these companies to serve the world's cities, and to build more dams and reservoirs . . . [yet] there is no attempt to address the issue of how the international community can effectively cross-subsidize the provision of clean water for the poor.

Pricing water

Cross-subsidization of water in South Africa often occurred from national to local scales, a practice that the Department of Water Affairs and Forestry began phasing out in the late 1990s. For consumers in some rural areas of KwaZulu-Natal Province, the decision fully to decentralize water provision in search of full cost-recovery suddenly became clear when their previously free water was switched off in early August 2000, when they failed to pay a $7 connection fee. The country's worst-ever recorded cholera crisis broke out within one week. Six months later, the government's failure to decentralize sanitation services to community and household scale became evident, as a journalist reported:

> Communities in cholera-ravaged northern KwaZulu-Natal were on Monday told they had to build their own toilets if they wanted to win the war against the disease, which has claimed 66 lives and infected nearly 20,000 people in the province since August last year. Provincial health MEC Zweli Mkhize told communities in the worst hit areas of Empangeni/Eshowe that 87,000 households in northern KwaZulu-Natal—between the Tugela and Umfolozi rivers—still did not have proper sanitation facilities . . . The department [of Water Affairs and Forestry] came under fire earlier this year for failing to spend less than half of its sanitation budget of $1.7 million earmarked for the [KwaZulu-Natal] province for the current financial year. The department claimed there had been a "lack of interest" from rural communities. Community leaders at Ntambanana on Monday told government officials that their numerous calls for toilets over the past few years had fallen on deaf ears. "We have asked for toilets, but we got nothing . . . we have taps, but no water. We would not have had an outbreak if we had water and toilets," one elderly man said.
>
> (South African Press Association January15, 2001)

As both Public Services International and *The Economist* agree, hence, the crucial controversy is the way water services are priced under conditions of commercialization. In the course of outsourcing to private (or even NGO) suppliers, the benefits of water as a public good (or "merit good")—namely, environmental, public health, gender equity and economic multiplier features (Bond 2000:

Chapter 4)—are generally lost. The lack of "effective demand" by poor consumers, and the difficulty in identifying accurate "shadow prices" for subsidies, together make it very difficult to internalize these externalities via the market. Regulation is normally insufficient in even middle-income countries such as South Africa, as the cholera case shows. Indeed, the aspect of water commodification that is both most dangerous from the standpoint of low-income people, and most tempting from the side of management, is the reduction of cross-subsidization within the pricing system, sometimes termed "cherry-picking" so as to signify that, within a local retail market, the premier customers are served and the masses are left behind.

When the World Bank (2000: Annex 2) instructed its field staff on how to handle water pricing in both urban and even impoverished rural Africa, the mandate was explicit, for, if it is accepted that communities should benefit from a "sustainable" and "demand-responsive" strategy based on their own "choices," then state support to water schemes, via subsidies, should—as a matter of policy, regardless of affordability—be terminated, in favour of full cost-recovery:

> Work is still needed with political leaders in some national governments to move away from the concept of free water for all . . . Promote increased capital cost recovery from users. An upfront cash contribution based on their willingness-to-pay is required from users to demonstrate demand and develop community capacity to administer funds and tariffs. Ensure 100% recovery of operation and maintenance costs.

In most urban systems, the cost of supplying an additional drop of water—the "short-run marginal cost curve" (line A in Figure 3.1)—tends to fall as users increase their consumption, because it is cheaper to provide the next unit to a large consumer than a small consumer. Reasons for this include the large-volume consumers' economies of scale (i.e. bulk sales), their smaller per unit costs of maintenance, the lower administrative costs of billing one large-volume consumer instead of many small ones, and the ability of the larger consumers to buy water at a time when it is not in demand—e.g., during the middle of the night—and store it for use during peak demand periods. The premise here is that the pricing of water should correspond directly to the cost of the service all the way along the supply curve. Such a system might then include a profit mark-up across the board (line B), which ensures the proper functioning of the market and an incentive for contracting-out or even full privatization by private suppliers.

The progressive principle of cross-subsidization, in contrast, violates the logic of the market. By imposing a block tariff that rises for larger consumers (line C), the state would consciously distort the relationship of cost to price and, hence, send economically "inefficient" pricing signals to consumers. In turn, argue neoliberal critics of progressive block tariffs, such distortions of the market logic introduce a disincentive to supply low-volume users. For example, in advocating against South Africa's subsequent move towards a free lifeline and rising block tariff, the World Bank advised that water privatization contracts "would be much harder to establish" if poor consumers had the expectation of getting something for nothing. If consumers didn't pay, the Bank suggested, South African authorities required a "credible threat of cutting service" (Roome 1995: 49–53).

The progressive rebuttal is that the difference between lines A and C allows not only for free universal lifeline services and a cross-subsidy from hedonistic users to low-volume users: there are also two additional benefits of providing free water services to some and extremely expensive services to those with hedonistic consumption habits: higher prices for high-volume consumption should encourage conservation, which would keep the longer-run costs of supply down (i.e. by delaying the construction of new dams or supply-side enhancements); and benefits accrue to society from the "merit goods" and "public goods" associated with free provision of services, such as improved public health, gender equity, environmental protection, economic spin-offs and the possibility of desegregating residential areas by class.

Another progressive critique of private suppliers who require tariffs reflective of marginal cost plus profit is that water infrastructure is a classical natural monopoly, so that competition in building multiple piping systems is irrational. The large investments in pipes, treatment centers and sewage plants are "lumpy" insofar as they often require extensive financing and a long-term commitment, to which the state is more suited. Furthermore, replying to the argument that a private-sector supplier might still meet social objectives through a strong state regulator, progressives mistrust "captive regulators," given the long history of corruption in the water sector. Rebutting those who argue that African states are intrinsically incapable of providing water services, progressives cite more proximate reasons for the recent degeneration of state water sectors: 1980s–90s structural

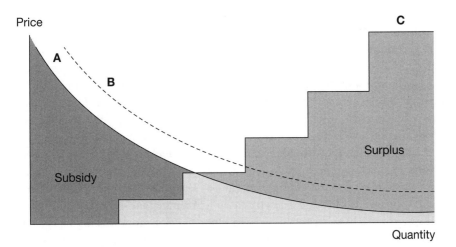

3.1 Pricing water: marginal cost (A), for-profit (B) and cross-subsidized lifeline plus block tariff (C).

adjustment programs, which decapacitated most states; corrupt state bureaucrats; weak trade unions; and disempowered consumers/communities. All can be reversed with sufficient political will.

Finally, the progressive argument for making a water subsidy universal—not means-tested for only "indigent" people—is both practical and deeply political. If the service is means-tested, it invariably leads to state coercion and stigmatization of low-income people by bureaucrats. Further, it is an administrative nightmare to sort out who qualifies, as so many people depend upon informal and erratic sources of income. More philosophically though, it is a premise of most human rights discourse that socio-economic rights such as water access are *universally* granted, not judged on the basis of a subjective income cut-off line, especially given the differences in household size for which different low-income people are responsible. This is partly because international experience shows that defense of a social welfare policy requires universality, so that the alliance of poor, working-class and middle-class people who usually win such concessions from the state can be kept intact (Esping-Andersen 1990).

As *The Economist* observed in mid 2003, one of the most important sites to consider the economics of water resources allocation is South Africa. One reason is that, because of the international drive to commercialize water, even post-apartheid South African citizens were subject to neoliberal cost-recovery and disconnection regimes. This affected many who simply could not pay their bills. From the late 1990s through 2002, as a result, approximately 10 million people suffered water disconnections (McDonald and Pape 2002). Africa's worst-ever recorded cholera outbreak—affecting more than 150,000 people—can be traced to an August 2000 decision to cut water to people who were not paying a South African regional water board. After the ruling African National Congress promised free basic water supplies in December 2000 during a municipal election campaign, the same bureaucrats responsible for water disconnections began redesigning the water tariffs.

In July 2001, revised price schedules provided a very small free lifeline: 6,000 liters per household per month, followed by a very steep, convex curve (see Figure 3.2). However, the next consumption block was unaffordable, leading to even higher rates of water disconnections in poor areas. The 6,000 liters represent just two toilet flushes a day per person for a household of eight, for those lucky enough to have flush toilets. It left no additional water to drink, wash with, clean clothes or for any other household purposes. In contrast, from the progressive point of view, an optimal strategy would provide a larger free lifeline tariff, ideally on a per-person, not per-household basis, and then rise in a *concave* manner to penalize luxury consumption. Johannesburg's tariff was set by the council, with help from Suez Lyonnaise des Eaux, a Paris-based conglomerate, and began in July 2001 with a high price increase for the second block of consumption. Two years later, the price of that second block was raised 32 percent, with a 10 percent overall increase, putting an enormous burden on poor households that used more

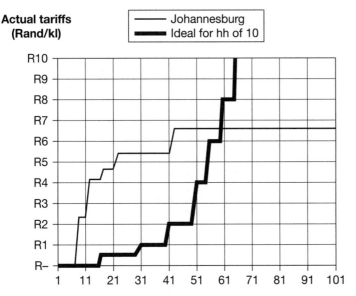

3.2 Divergent water pricing strategies: Johannesburg (2001) versus ideal tariff for large household.
Source: Johannesburg Water and own projection.

than 6,000 liters each month. The rich got off with relatively small increases and a flat tariff after 40 kiloliters per household per month, which did nothing to encourage water conservation and, hence, did not mitigate the need for further construction of large dams, which in turn would drive up the long-run marginal cost curve and further penalize low-income Johannesburg townships residents.

In Durban, the 1997 consumption of water by the one-third of the city's metered (and regular bill-paying) residents who have the lowest income was 22 kiloliters per household per month (see Figure 3.3). Shortly afterwards, a "Free Basic Water" strategy was adopted (for just the first 6 kiloliters per household per month), but steep increases in price for the next blocks of water were imposed. By 2003, the price of the average liter of water consumed by the lowest-income third of billed residents had doubled from R2 in 1997 (about US$0.30) to R4. According to Reg Bailey, that price increase resulted in average consumption by some low-income consumers diminishing to 15 kiloliters per household per month during the same period. The price elasticity for water was, hence, a disturbing −0.55—an extremely large impact for what should be a basic need and, hence, relatively impervious to price change. In contrast, for middle- and high-income consumers, the price rise was higher, but the corresponding decline in average consumption far less (Bailey and Buckley 2005). Indeed, the UNDP's 2006 *Human Development Report* indicates that Durban has a convex-shaped tariff curve, compared with several other Third World cities. Durban charges by far the highest

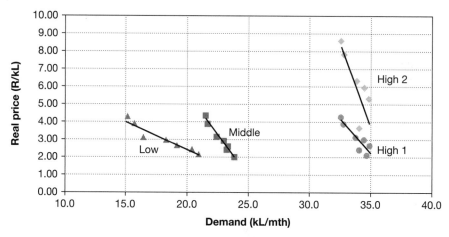

3.3 The impact of price on consumption for different income groups in Durban: from 1997 (lower price, higher volumes) to 2003 (higher price, lower volumes).

Source: Buckley and Bailey 2005.

Step increases in block water tariffs, 2001–05 (US$)

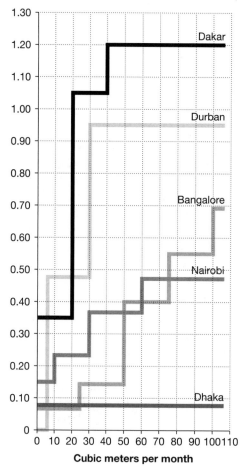

3.4 Durban's tariff compared with four other cities.

prices in the 6–20 kiloliters per month range, the block in which many of the lowest-income people consume (see Figure 3.4).

Conclusion: advocacy for decommodification

What kinds of countervailing strategy are being experimented with to counter the negative trends? First, it is important not to overstress the merits of centralization, as if geographical scale is the central criterion. As Wittvogel famously argued, centralized–despotic regimes of ancient India, Egypt and China were underpinned by vast irrigation infrastructures whose maintenance needed legions of workers, artisans and bureaucrats. These "hydraulic civilizations" oversaw a vast system of agricultural production and environmental and social management.

In contrast, strategic debates among progressive water activists combine centralized–democratic financing systems with decentralized–participatory state service delivery. Mamdani (1996: 287) argues that rural and urban alliances are vital here:

> Decentralized democratization confined to the local state is both partial and unstable. It harbours contradictory possibilities: the point of reform of rural power can just as easily be to link up with representative demands from urban civil society as it can be to check these. If the objective is an overall democratization, it requires a balance between decentralization and centralization, participation and representation, autonomy and alliance. But if it is to checkmate civil society, a one-sided glorification of decentralization, autonomy and participation will suffice because, in the final analysis, it is bound to exacerbate the breach between the urban and the rural . . . This tendency needs to be seen as a negative development.

Perhaps most importantly, water resources-allocation debates under conditions of decentralization demonstrate, simply, that pricing is highly political. Indeed, commodification in the water sector has generated some of the most intense local social-justice struggles in the world today, calling into question the very tenets of neoliberalism in state services provision, even when—as in South Africa—a small concession is made in the form of circumscribed "free basic water."

Needless to say, outside South Africa (where redistributive water pricing is feasible at the municipal scale for more than half the population in major urban centres), a prerequisite for improving state supply of water is a greater central–local subsidization, which in turn requires dramatically intensified advocacy for debt repudiation and the implementation of exchange controls, so as to halt the outflow of finances that would make expanded systems financially feasible. Given the depth of the legitimacy crisis associated with globalization and commodification, new social forces have emerged to contest these processes. Many of these groups have coalesced around opposition to privatization.

The strategy adopted by so-called "water warriors"—a component of the global justice movements—in anti-privatization campaigns is typically to defend elected municipal government as the key institution for delivering water. They argue that, in most societies, the state remains the main agent that can redistribute resources and organize purified, high-pressure water in sufficient quantities to serve public health, gender equity and other broader eco-social goals (Barlow and Clarke 2002; Friends of the Earth International 2003; Grusky and Fiil-Flynn 2004; McDonald and Ruiters 2005; People's World Water Forum 2004; Polaris Institute 2003; Public Citizen 2003a; 2003b; Shiva 2002; Transnational Institute 2005).

Networked transnational civil society forces opposed to the commercialized model of water delivery, and generally in favour of reasserted state provision of water, include citizens' organizations (Council of Canadians in Ottawa, Public Citizen in Washington and the World Development Movement and War on Want in London); trade unions (Public Services International and their affiliates); indigenous people's movements; environmental groups (especially the International Rivers Network and Friends of the Earth); think tanks (e.g., the PSI Research Unit at Greenwich University, Polaris in Ottawa, the TransNational Institute in Amsterdam, the Agriculture and Trade Policy Center in Minneapolis, the Municipal Services Project involving three universities in South Africa and Canada, Parivartan and the Centre for Science and the Environment in New Delhi, Food and Water Watch in Washington, and the International Forum on Globalization in San Francisco); and high-profile community leaders, intellectuals and politicians.

Many of these water warriors emerged from urban community revolts against privatization, in sites ranging from Detroit, Atlanta and several French cities, to Accra, Dar es Salaam and Soweto in Africa, to Cochabamba and El Alto in Bolivia, Buenos Aires, and Asian cities including Manila and Jakarta, as well as Auckland, New Zealand. In Vancouver, a 2001 "Blue Planet" conference gathered activists; in Delhi, the 2004 People's World Water Forum brought the movements into alignment on analysis and common targets; and in 2006 these forces—numbering at least 10,000 activists—marched on the World Water Forum in Mexico City. The World Social Forum (in Porto Alegre, Mumbai and Nairobi), as well as regional Social Fora, provides space for water activist assemblies. Email listserves such as "water warriors," "reclaiming public water" and "right to water" permit information exchange and coordination.

The campaigns for decommodification of water have been successful, in many settings, in driving out the water privatizers who have sought profits under conditions of decentralized financing in which desperate municipalities search for new sources of capital. What they have not yet done, however, is take control of sufficient national state power to establish redistributive national–local subsidization systems. Even in Bolivia, where the Cochabamba and El Alto water wars were one reason state power shifted to the Movement Towards Socialism in late 2005, more than a year of hard work in establishing a water ministry and national water agency did not result in lower retail prices. These struggles continue and are a crucial signifier of whether neoliberal, decentralized forces driving towards commodification can be repelled by citizens' movements demanding decommodification.

References

Bailey, R. and Buckley, C. (2005) "Modelling domestic water tariffs," presentation to the University of KwaZulu–Natal Centre for Civil Society, Durban, November 7.

Barlow M. and Clarke, T. (2002) *Blue Gold*, New York: New Press.

Bond, P. (2000) *Cities of Gold, Townships of Coal*, Trenton, NJ: Africa World Press.

Bond, P. (2004) "New municipal public management in South Africa: The rise and fall of water commercialization," in P. Dibben, G. Wood and I. Roper *Contesting Public Sector Reforms*, Basingstoke: Palgrave Macmillan.

Bond, P. (2007) "Microcredit evangelism, health and social policy," *International Journal of Health Services*, 37 (2): 229–49.

Esping-Andersen, G. (1990) *The Three Worlds of Welfare Capitalism*, Princeton, NJ: Princeton University Press.

Friends of the Earth International (2003) *Water Justice for All*, Amsterdam: Friends of the Earth International.

Globalization Challenge Initiative (2001) "The World Bank, the IMF and the right to water." Available online at www.isodec.org.gh/Papers/saragruskyMay2001.pdf.

Grusky, S. and Fiil-Flynn, M. (2004) *Will the World Bank Back Down?* Washington, DC: Public Citizen.

Harvey, D. (2003) *The New Imperialism*, New York: Oxford University Press.

Hennig, R. (2001) "IMF forces African countries to privatize water," February 8. Available online at www.afrol.com.

Logan, M. (2003) "Multinationals ride wave of water privatization," *OneWorld US*, February 4.

Mamdani, M. (1996) *Citizen and Subject*, Princeton, NJ: Princeton University Press.

McCarney, P. (1996) "Introduction," in P. McCarney (ed.) *The Changing Nature of Local Government in Developing Countries*, Toronto, ON: University of Toronto Centre for Urban and Community Studies; Ottawa, ON: Federation of Canadian Municipalities.

McDonald, D. and Pape, J. (2002) *Cost Recovery and the Crisis of Service Delivery in South Africa*, Pretoria: Human Sciences Research Council Press.

McDonald, D. and Ruiters, G. (2005) *The Age of Commodity*, London: Earthscan.

Ministry of Reconstruction and Development (1995) *Draft Urban Development Strategy*, Pretoria: Ministry of Reconstruction and Development.

Mkandawire, T. and Soludo, C. (1999) *Our Continent, Our Future*, Ottawa, ON: IDRC.

Morris, M. and Kaplan, D. (1987) "The implications of the new technology for industrial location," unpublished paper, Johannesburg: Urban Foundation.

People's World Water Forum (2004) "Declaration of the People's World Water Movement." Available online at www.citizen.org/cmep/Water/conferences/articles.cfm?ID=11053.

Polanyi, K. (1956) *The Great Transformation*, New York: Beacon Press.

Polaris Institute (2003) *Global Water Grab*, Ottawa, ON: Polaris Institute.

Port Elizabeth Municipality (1997) "Public private partnerships for municipal services," report by Director: Administration to the Executive Committee, February 4.

Public Citizen (2003a) *The Evian Challenge*, Washington, DC: Public Citizen.

Public Citizen (2003b) *Water Privatization Fiascos*, Washington, DC: Public Citizen.

Public Services International (2003) "The report of the World Panel on financing water infrastructure," Geneva, March 12.

Roome, J. (1995) "Water pricing and management: World Bank presentation to the SA Water Conservation Conference," unpublished paper, Washington, DC: World Bank, October 2.

Shiva, V. (2002) *Water Wars*, Boston, MA: South End Press.

South African Presidency (2006) *National Spatial Development Framework*, Pretoria: South African Presidency.

South African Press Association (2001) "Government running low on funds: People must build their own toilets," January 15.

Transnational Institute (2005) *Reclaiming Public Water*, Amsterdam: Transnational Institute.

United Nations Development Programme (2003) *Human Development Report 2003*, New York: UNDP.

United Nations Development Programme (2006) *Human Development Report 2006*, New York: UNDP.

Urban Foundation (1990) *Regional Development Reconsidered*, Policies for a New Urban Future Series, 3, Johannesburg: Urban Foundation.

Urban Institute (1991) *Urban Economies and National Development*, Washington, DC: US Agency for International Development.

Wilson, Z. (2006) "Water: a global contestation," in F. Holland and W. Dicke (eds) *Global Civil Society 2006/07*, London: Sage.

World Bank (1991) *Urban Policy and Economic Development: An Agenda for the 1990s*, Washington, DC: World Bank.

World Bank (1994) *The World Bank and Participation*, Washington, DC: World Bank.

World Bank (2000) *Sourcebook on Community Driven Development in the Africa Region: Community Action Programs*, Africa Region, Washington, DC: World Bank.

World Bank (2002) "South Africa: Monitoring service delivery in Johannesburg," Washington, DC, Southern Africa Department: Africa PREML, April.

World Bank (2003) *World Development Report 2004*, Washington, DC: World Bank.

Yunus, M. (1998) *Banker to the Poor*, Dhaka: University of Bangladesh Press.

Chapter 4

Decentralized planning and metropolitan growth

Poverty and wealth in Buenos Aires suburbs

Nora Libertun de Duren

Decentralization, the devolution of power from central to local government agencies, was promoted as one way to increase local say in government and, hence, advance a more equal distribution of goods in society (Stiglitz 1999; UNDP 2004). However, some studies of urban planning practices suggested that decentralized governments may further the opposite outcome, an even less equal distribution of resources (Prud'Homme 1995; Wood 1958). Indeed, after more than a decade of changes towards decentralization, the correlation between a decentralized government and a more equal society is not evident. Moreover, many empirical studies on decentralization have shown that, after decentralization, the socio-economic differences among decentralized localities have risen (e.g. Bird and Smart 2002). We know little, however, about how decentralization affects social equality *within* localities. Given the evidence that high income levels are correlated with active political participation (Alford and Friedland 1975; Mollenkopf 1989), decentralization in societies marked by inequalities may allow for policies to be disproportionately influenced by the goals of affluent groups, and thus may further local inequality. How do the pre-existing economic and political conditions in localities influence the social outcome of decentralization? Under which conditions might decentralized democratic governments foster greater levels of social inequality within their own boundaries?

This chapter examines those questions in the case of the growth in Buenos Aires since the late 1970s. Although Argentina's economy has been unstable, oscillating between development and decay, public and private ownership, its social polarization has steadily increased (Turn and Carballo 2005). That polarization has been encrypted in its urban landscape: industrial neighborhoods have declined, while new gated communities and select urban locations have received the bulk of both local and international investments (Svampa 2001). In addition to the development shifts, urban planning power has undergone continual decentralization that has increased the authority of municipalities over land-use decisions. By looking in detail at the growth of Buenos Aires' urban peripheries, where the changes in real-estate development have been most notable, I explore the conditions that led democratic, decentralized municipalities to foster uneven urban development within their boundaries. The following pages present a brief introduction to the case of the Buenos Aires metropolis. Then, the main features of urban planning decentralization in the Province of Buenos Aires are outlined. The chapter then explains how impoverished municipalities used their newly acquired land-use management rights to facilitate the development of gated communities.[1] In the conclusion, some principles are extracted that may be useful for thinking about decentralization and inequality in underdeveloped countries.

National development and suburban Buenos Aires in the 1970s

With more than a third of the country's 36 million residents, though less than 2 percent of its land (307,571 square kilometers), Buenos Aires is by far the largest metropolis in Argentina. The country's geographical development has been uneven since Hispanic times (Suarez 1999), and Buenos Aires became the economic node it is today only after the industrialization of the twentieth century, sponsored by Peron's mid twentieth century presidency (Dorfman 1983; Scobie 1964). By providing subsidies and protecting Argentinian industries from international competitors, the Peronist state fostered the clustering of most industrial establishments and labor in Buenos Aires and its surroundings. In the long run, such concentration of national development in the Buenos Aires metropolis was prejudicial to sustainable development for its citizens. The impoverishment of the rest of the country brought a continuous flow of migrants to the city. Then, when the state stopped sponsoring industrialization, hundreds of Buenos Aires residents had to settle for unstable and underpaid jobs, and many urban structures became obsolete. As early as the 1960s, the Peronist model was showing signs of exhaustion, and more than 460,000 city dwellers—about 5 percent of the metropolitan population—were living in shantytowns (Pirez 1994). In 1976, after a long succession of national political crises, a military coup seized the national government. The dictatorship imposed its discriminatory principles on the city through police power, reserving the city life of the urban core to be only "for those who deserved" (Oszlak 1994) and launching a massive slum removal program.

During the seven years of the dictatorship, more than 200,000 slum dwellers were forced to relocate outside the city (Oszlak 1984). Poor foreigners living in the slums, most of whom were from Paraguay, Chile, Uruguay and Bolivia, were repatriated. The nationals were either moved to their native provinces or, in most cases, dispersed to towns in the less urbanized suburbs (Bermudez 1985).

The dictatorship also replaced the state-led industrialization that had created and sustained many of the economic activities of the suburbs with a market-led economy (Diaz Alejandro 1970; Dornbusch 1986; Kosacoff and Ramos 2001). The military regime had an economic and ideological prejudice against urban industries, viewing them as not only inefficient but potentially dangerous given the regime's fear of labor mobilization (Schvarzer 1987). Therefore, the government limited credits to large industrial compounds (Azpiazu 1985; Kulfas and

Schorr 2000) and gave tax incentives only to industries located at least 60 kilometers from the city center (Ferruci 1986). As a consequence, most of the small industrial establishments around the city closed their doors, and industrial employment declined.

Most of the densely industrialized suburbs to the west and south of the city owe much of their growth to the intense, state-promoted industrialization of the mid twentieth century, when many industrial establishments and also most of the industrial labor forces located there (Mora y Araujo and Smith 1983). That was when these suburbs acquired a well-developed infrastructure: piped water, sewerage, electricity, paving and a fairly dense urban grid. The infrastructure fostered relatively even development throughout nearly all the western and southern industrial suburbs. In contrast, the suburbs bordering the metropolitan conglomeration to the north presented only a few small towns, and the rest of their vast territory lacked almost all infrastructure and was used mostly for agriculture or recreation (Bariffi 1981; Union Industrial Argentina 2001). Hence, after the 1976 *coup d'état* ousting Ms Peron, the change in the national development policy did not affect all suburbs in the same way. Jurisdictions with the bulk of industrial establishments suffered the immediate consequences of the decline of local industry, but municipalities that still had vast areas of under-used land lost their chance to develop their infrastructure through industrialization.

It was in this social and economic context of industrial stagnation, slum clearance and population relocation that the first comprehensive law mandating the decentralization of land management began. In 1977, the Province of Buenos Aires transferred planning power from the provincial government to the municipal governments. However, the dictatorship's aim in mandating that decentralization of planning was to relieve the national budget; ironically, it was far from the democratic aims of the decentralization that took place after 1983, when democratic institutions returned to Argentina. Moreover, though successful, the transfer's long-term impact of this regulation was not what the dictatorship had intended for Buenos Aires. As we shall see, the dictatorship's decentralization of land-use regulation did make land available for the needs of the urban core. However, as these needs changed, urbanization patterns did not follow the urban model envisioned by the dictatorship, with the city free of slums and its suburbs containing the poorest segments of the population. Rather, making land available for housing consumption, at the same time that the industrial project of the suburbs was in decline, generated a constituency in the suburbs ready to allocate land for gated communities, which triggered the transformation of the suburban polity (see Table 4.1).

Decentralizing urban planning

It is no coincidence that, as the national government halted its support for urban labor and industries and was forcing poor residents from Buenos Aires city into

Table 4.1 Shifts in the geographical distribution of industrial establishments
(in percent)

Industrial establishments	1947	1954	1964	1974
Buenos Aires City	29	26	21	20
Buenos Aires suburbs	28	31	38	37
Rest of Argentina	43	43	41	43
Total	100	100	100	100

Source: Ferrucci 1986.

the suburbs in the Province of Buenos Aires, the provincial government launched a series of legislations that increased the difficulty of acquiring residential land (Clichevsky 2002). Furthermore, the legislation delegated the responsibility for providing infrastructure to the municipal jurisdictions, which were hardly capable of such a financial undertaking.[2] It was also at that time, 1977, that the first official land-use planning code of the Province of Buenos Aires was passed.[3] Amidst the absolute suspension of constitutional rights and repression of civic participation, this code (Urban Code 8912/77) called for the principles of municipal self-govern-ance and decentralization (Badia 2004). However, as might be expected in this context, the code contained no provision for increased participation by residents. Until the passage of this provincial law, there had been a vacuum in the body of law that regulated urban planning. In practice, most decisions affecting Buenos Aires were made at the provincial if not the national level, while municipal govern-ment functioned simply as the bureaucratic institution. However, the new law made municipal authorities responsible for designating land uses and approving new developments, and expressly recognized the municipality as the main planning entity. Without exception, the municipality could designate all land as either rural or urban, to reflect the character of its current usage. Undeveloped land was desig-nated according to its desired future use. Also, as the resources for affordable housing disappeared, gated communities were explicitly addressed for the first time in the urban code. Minimum and maximum population densities were established for three main categories: rural settlements, urban settlements and gated com-munities.

This foundational document of municipal planning gives a disproportionate priority to the development of weekend houses. Even though at the time of the regulation, gated communities were used by less than 1 percent of the province's population and affected less than 10 percent of the province's total area, the planning code devotes an entire chapter specifically to the regulations of these gated enclaves. This concern may be due to the conspicuous growth rate of gated com-munities, which contrasted with the overall decline of the suburbs. Until 1970, there were about twenty gated communities in the region; five years later, their number had doubled. In addition, their locations next to the main arteries connecting to the capital city made them highly visible (Libertun de Duren 2006).

Besides the kinds of land use the planning document promoted, the process of planning itself also was highly exclusionary. Neither the 1977 code, nor the additions in the 1980s, nor even those of the post-dictatorship in the 1990s, required public participation. Neither did they require that municipal authorities publicize their planning decisions in their communities. This exclusionary view of the role of planning reflected the institutional beliefs of the dictatorship that governed from 1977 until 1983. The absence of civic participation in that era is not surprising. However, none of the successive legal reforms under democratic governments made public participation a condition for approvals for investment or development. Eventually, private investors in the democratic era took advantage of the top-down approach embedded in the planning code inherited from dictatorship days.

Nonetheless, the rate of construction of gated communities was erratic. During the first half of the 1980s, almost no development occurred, and no laws changed. In 1985, however, the growth of gated communities peaked again, and, in late 1986, another planning decentralization decree was approved that affected gated communities. The new regulation gave municipal authorities discretion in applying some of the restrictions on gated communities that had been established by the 1977 code, namely, the location of gated communities in rural lands and the requirement for at least 7 kilometers between any two gated developments. Twelve years later, following a spectacular peak in the investment in gated communities, another provincial decree further increased the discretionary powers of municipal authorities. This time, all area requirements and location restrictions were dropped. Final approval and monitoring of the actual layout became a responsibility of the municipality. For the first time, the codes did mention local participation, requiring an informational public forum 10 days before the decision about the municipal permit. However, the decree clearly stated that neither the municipal government nor the developers were bound by any views expressed in these meetings.

It was noticeable as early as the 1970s that gated communities were clustering in poor municipalities. By 2000, almost twenty-five years after the first law mandating the decentralization of urban planning from the provincial to the municipal level, about two-thirds of the region's new gated communities were located in the northern, less industrialized municipalities, where, according to the national census data of 1980, one out of every three households was living in precarious conditions.[4] The presence of new gated communities in impoverished jurisdictions thus widened the gap between the affluent and the poor, at the same time that it increased the physical proximity of the two groups.

In actuality, it was not the decentralization that generated the initial impulse towards developing gated communities. Rather, it is likely that the demand for

Table 4.2 Contribution of industrial activities to Argentine economy (in percent)

Year	1950–9	1960–9	1970–9	1980–9
Variation on Argentina's GDP[a]	3.1	3.8	2.7	–2.1
Industrial share of Argentina's GDP[b]	25	28	27	24

Sources: (a) Dornbusch 1986. (b) Kosacoff and Ramos 2001.

Table 4.3 Northern municipalities' poverty levels and gated communities

Municipalities along northern highway, within 60 km of BA city

	1981[a]		1991[a]		2001[a]		2001[b]
	All households	% poor	All households	% poor	All households	% poor	Gated communities
Pilar	20,340	33	31,259	25	58,313	21	115
Escobar	19,681	33	30,893	22	45,347	19	45
Tigre	50,502	28	64,370	23	79,807	18	60
San Fernando	34,509	25	38,668	20	42,059	14	15
Campana	14,819	21	18,498	16	22,773	14	7
San Isidro	76,721	12	82,960	9	88,054	7	29
Average	36,095	25	44,441	19	56,059	16	45

Sources: (a) 1981, 1991, 2001 National Argentine Censuses (INDEC). (b) Real-estate brokers' data.

these developments resulted from the rising prices of urban housing together with the heightened perceptions of urban crime. The gated communities also depended on the existence of the highway network, managed by the private sector and supervised by the national government. Nevertheless, it was the decentralization laws that enabled local municipalities to rezone land, so the new gated communities could be developed within their jurisdictions. In fact, there is a noticeable correlation between planning decentralization and the variation in the number of gated communities funded each year. Consistently, a revision of the planning laws followed each sharp rise in the number of gated communities. In turn, the new legal framework augmented land availability, minimized requirements about area and location, and increased municipal autonomy (see Tables 4.2 and 4.3).

The suburban prospect

The combination of obsolete industrial suburbs with an influx of displaced poor from the city core who had to provide their own services left local governments with few resources at a time when they needed them most. To make matters worse, the changes in national development policies favored large industrial holdings, which located further from the urban periphery and rendered the existing industrial fabric of the western and southern suburbs obsolete (Colman 1987). Those policies also deprived the little-industrialized northern suburbs of the flow of industrial investments. By the early 1980s, the changes in the urban social structure following on from these spatial rearrangements became apparent: while poverty decreased in the city's core, the indigent population swelled in the periphery (Bermudez 1985). Moreover, these shifts, which were the consequence of both market rationale and government policies, had an enduring effect on the nature of the polity.

Throughout the 1980s and 1990s, municipalities within 60 kilometers of the city core were seriously impoverished. However, consistently with the divergence seen in the 1970s, each municipality had different conditions. The south and west suffered the effects of the stagnant local economy; the suburbs farther north, however, had never seen the benefits of an even industrialization, and, in their vast, unserviced territory, as many as a third of all households were living in poverty (INDEC 1980, 1991 and 2001).

It was under those conditions that the municipalities functioning under a decentralized regime in the recently democratized Argentina used their planning powers to foster exclusive enclaves such as gated communities in order to bring fresh investments and infrastructure to their localities. As expected given the contrast between the old and the new residents, the new enclaves were physically set apart from the rest of a municipality. That separation intensified the differences within the municipalities. The local governments and their middle- and low-income residents saw the allocation of land for gated communities as a means of upgrading their municipalities. In the eyes of the municipal governments, once the state support for local industries had halted, such investments were the only feasible way to bring infrastructure to unused lands.

By 1998, after the upgrading of the highway connecting the city of Buenos Aires and these northern municipalities, those along the corridor accounted for more than 70 percent of all the suburban gated communities (Pirez 2002). Even within this region though, the new gated communities were not evenly distributed, but clustered disproportionately in the three municipalities with above average percentages of poor households. This distribution pattern cannot be explained as a direct consequence of municipal size, as the other municipalities also had undeveloped land, and gated communities can be created from existing developments. Furthermore, though land prices in these three impoverished municipalities were slightly lower than in neighboring municipalities during the 1980s, their land values had record-high increases after the highway upgrade, jumping from $50 to between $70 and $100 per square meter in less than a year.

In short, the loss of state support for urban industries, the upgrade of the northern highway and the decentralization of urban planning led to the concentration of gated communities in the poorest northern jurisdictions. Although the industrial policy and the highway upgrade recentered national policies, decentralized planning capacities made local government active players as well, able to lure gated-community developers to their jurisdictions. Gated communities were perceived as a strategy for local development that could replace falling industrial investment and activate the local economy. In the words of one local mayor:

> Nowadays there are private neighborhoods flourishing all over. We almost have no room for the location of industries. We have made an effort to provide clear and precise norms—through judicial security- so that those who invest in the district will not find unpleasant surprises in the future. All this has made investing in Tigre [municipality] very easy, and contributed to large capitals coming to the area. This had been supported with the recovery of land not able to be urbanized without capital investment.[5]

Municipalities took advantage of the decentralization of the development permits process to control local land uses so as to accommodate developers' needs. Chronologically, there is a correlation between the rate of gated-community development and the number of changes in land-use regulations in favor of gated communities: the more new gated communities developed, the more municipal ordinances changed. Furthermore, in the poorest municipalities—which contain 70 percent of all gated communities, but account for only one-third of the ten municipalities' total area—the frequency of these zoning amendments increased dramatically after each decentralization measure.[6] Taking the main reforms in the Buenos Aires Provincial law (1977, 1986 and 1999) as keystones, we can compare three stages of decentralization. In the first stage, 20 percent of rezoning changes took place in the three poorest municipalities of the region; in the second stage, the proportion is 37 percent; and, from the last decree until 2000, 95 percent of rezoning changes were located in this area.

Decentralizing the suburbs and the polity

One of the mayors of the municipality with the highest number of gated communities, who was later forced out owing to corruption charges, said:

> While it is true that the building of the Bingo [a gambling centre] was a corruption scandal during the previous administration, today, under our government they are compacting fifty blocks of [the town of] Del Viso at their cost. [Why?]. Because they came to talk to me and I told them that any investment in Pilar has the moral obligation of giving something back to the community. Of course we did not ask them for a bribe, but we did ask them to collaborate with the people. They put 130,000 US $ without giving a single coin to the Municipal Government. We just supervised the works. In the same sense, Pilar del Este [a new gated community] is paving one and a half

kilometers in a street which used to be in terrible shape. That is the mother idea: If the Municipality cannot, let the private sector give us a hand.[7]

Besides detailing the particulars of one municipality, that statement reveals the public sector's relationship with investors to be an exchange of reciprocal favors that are not governed by formal regulations and in which residents have no say, as they are presented as the outcome of the goodwill of developers and local politicians. Arguably, this is one of the outcomes of a law whose basic principles were those of a de facto government. Yet, it seems that current residents living outside the gated communities—the majority of local population—have not resented their lack of involvement in the local planning process. Municipal political parties have enjoyed voters' loyalty more often than the provincial or national government have. In the municipalities with a high concentration of gated communities, the governing parties have won all municipal elections since 1987.

The stagnation of industrial establishments in the suburbs parallels to the worsening economic conditions of middle- and low-income households. In this context, many suburban residents see gated communities as a source of employment and, hence, lend their support to them. Mayors in these localities calculate that for each new house inside a gated community, there are at least five more jobs outside it.[8] In Pilar municipality, for example, local officials estimate that gated communities gave employment to about 30,000 people, making them one of the most significant job generators for local residents. The mayor of Tigre municipality explains:

> Creating jobs is the most important thing. Many new developments solved problems of the older neighborhoods. Today, there is a line of workers waiting at the door of these new gated communities. Construction jobs are really active here. And services are too, there are some of these developments which give employment to six to 1,000 people. And all this is very relevant for us, because these are new jobs.[9]

By the year 2000, gated communities, one of the most profitable real-estate investments in the suburbs (Coy and Pholer 2002), were overwhelmingly located in those municipalities that had had less industrial development in the 1970s and the highest percentages of poor households in the 1980s. As a consequence, however, these localities now have larger income gaps among their residents—larger than those of the 1970s, when they received the inflow of displaced slum residents, and larger than those of the impoverished old industrial suburbs, which did not receive a similar inflow of gated communities in the 1990s (see Figure 4.1). Not only did the strategy of luring gated communities into municipalities with high percentages of poor households raise social differences within them, as they became centers of unskilled employment, new shantytowns arose in their

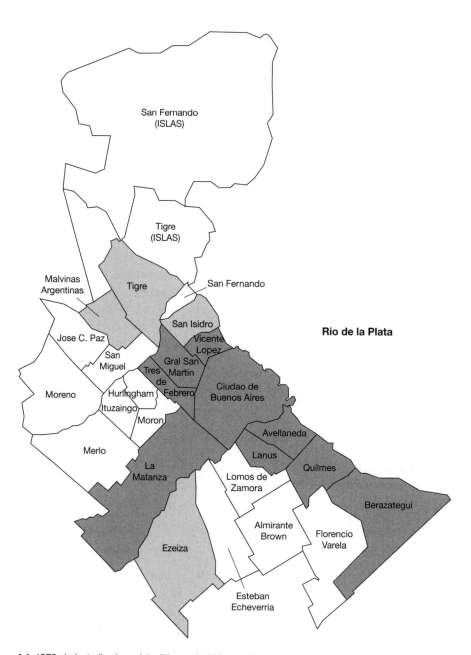

4.1 1970s industralized municipalities and 1990s gated communities.

Note: Dark grey shows jurisdictions which had the bulk of industrial development in the 1970s. Light grey shows jurisdictions with a high concentration of gated communities in the 1990s.

Source: Own elaboration based on *Argentine Industrial Census* (1978), *Real Estate Listings* (2002), *UIA* (1995–2000).

surroundings. Census numbers show that in Escobar and Pilar—two of the main centers for gated communities—the numbers of poor residents increased, suggesting that the inflow of wealth has had no parallel in a politics of redistribution.

Conclusions

This paper began by asking how pre-existing local economic and political conditions influence the social outcome of decentralization, and sought the conditions under which decentralized and democratic governments would foster higher levels of social inequality within their own boundaries. The case of gated communities in the outskirts of Buenos Aires since the 1970s has cast light on those enquiries. I have assumed that an urbanization model based on gated communities promotes evident discontinuities in the quality of the city and, hence, is a symptom of social fragmentation. Tracing the dynamics that create spatial differences in the urban form also hints at those that foster social inequality.

This study also provides evidence that the characteristics of the 'suburbanizing elites' (Blackely and Snyder 1995; Cicollela 1999; Torres 2001; Webster *et al.* 2002) offer relevant but not sufficient explanation of the urbanization patterns of the suburbs. The specific intramunicipality geography of inequality can be explicated only by considering the local conditions in which suburbanization took place. In the eyes of suburban mayors, the juxtaposition of declining industrialization and under-utilized land made gated communities a desirable land use. As those new land uses took place in previously undervalued lands, gated communities increasingly were located next to shantytowns, hence creating a new micro-pattern of social polarization in the suburbs.

The decentralization of planning capacities from the province to the municipalities allowed local governments of the poorest municipalities to change land uses according to their own criteria. By the year 2000, while the former industrial suburbs were struggling to revitalize their obsolete industrial infrastructure, those suburbs whose land had been mostly under-used until the 1980s received a boost from investments in gated communities. The 1970s dictatorship had crafted the original legal framework of decentralized planning with almost no provision for residents' participation. Yet, once a democratic regime was back in office, there was no widespread demand for more participation in local planning. Local residents perceive gated communities as potential sources of employment and as a way of protecting the market value of their own property, and therefore they have accepted the municipal government manipulation of land uses.

In this instance, the extreme social contrasts of the suburbs are the result of residents' choices within a scenario marked by the infrastructural and economic possibilities of their localities. Decentralization was a mechanism that allowed suburban municipalities to lure private developers to their lands, and, hence, the extreme contrast in the infrastructure of the region was a prerequisite for producing the current suburban geography. Thus, this case study shows that physical scenarios condition democratic performances. It also shows how inequality promotes a dynamic that depends on the perpetuation of social differences, not only for economic transactions, but also for physical planning. Finally, this case study reveals that decentralization does not necessarily lead to a more equal distribution of resources, even when there is local participation. Therefore, the quest for social justice cannot be satisfied simply by ensuring political rights, insofar as the material context for exercising these rights is already deeply imbalanced. It is likely that, in a market-led society the choices of citizens living in unequal conditions will tend to reproduce the same inequalities.

Notes

1   This term does not distinguish between different varieties such as "barrios cerrados," "clubes de campo" and "country-clubs."
2   Law 9347.
3   Urban Code 8912.
4   I use the NBI value as defined by the Argentine census (INDEC). To be classified as an NBI, a household has at least one of these characteristics:

   (a)   more than three people per room;
   (b)   unsound building structure;
   (c)   no water-closet;
   (d)   at least one child aged between 6 and 12 who does not attend school;
   (e)   four or more people depending on one single breadwinner who has no schooling beyond third grade.

5   Interview conducted by the author with Tigre planning officer, August, 2004.
6   The Northern area is composed of the following municipalities: Vicente Lopez, San Isidro, San Fernando, Tigre, Escobar, Pilar, Malvinas Argentinas and San Miguel.
7   "No quiero que Pilar sea una ciudad dormitorio," *La Nación* June 11, 2000.
8   Interview conducted by the author with Pilar and Tigre planning officers, August, 2004.
9   Interview conducted by the author with Pilar and Tigre planning officers, August, 2004.

References

Alford, R. and Friedland, R. (1975) "Political participation and public policy," *Annual Review of Sociology* 1: 429–79.

Azpiazu, D. (1985) *La Promoción Industrial en la Argentina: Efectos e Implicancias Estructurales, 1973–1983*, Buenos Aires: CEPAL.

Badia, G. (2004) "Cambiando el foco: La decentralizacion de Buenos Aires y la region metropolitana," in M. Escolar, G. Badia and S. Frederic (eds) *Federalismo y Decentralizacion en Grandes Ciudades*, Buenos Aires: Libros Prometeo.

Bariffi, A.C. (1981) "La gran industria," in H. Diffieri (ed.) *Atlas de Buenos Aires*, Buenos Aires: Municipalidad de la Ciudad de Buenos Aires.

Bermudez, E. (1985) *La Disputa por un territorio: los Partidos del Gran Buenos Aires*, Buenos Aires: CICSO.

Bird, R. and Smart, M. (2002) "Intergovernmental fiscal transfers: International lessons for developing countries," *World Development* 30 (6): 899–912.

Blackely, E.J. and Snyder, M.G. (1995) *Fortress America: Gated communities in the United States*, Washington, DC, and Cambridge: Brookings Institution Press and Lincoln Institute of Land Policy.

Cicollela, P. (1999) "Globalización y dualización en la region metropolitana de Buenos Aires. Grandes inversions y restructuración socioterritorial en los años 90," *Eure* 25 (76): 5–27.

Cicollela, P. and Mignaqui, I. (2002) "Buenos Aires socio spatial impacts of the development of global city functions," in S. Sassen (ed.) *Global Networks, Linked Cities*, New York: Routledge.

Clichevsky, N. (2002) "Tierra vacante en Buenos Aires. Entre los loteos 'populares' y las 'áreas exclusivas," in *Tierra vacante en países latinoamericanos*, Cambridge: Lincoln Institute of Land Policy.

Colman, O. (1987) *La Región Bonaerense. Desarrollo Productivo, Estrategias Laborales, Decentralizacion Estatal y Financiera*, Buenos Aires: Fundación Friederich Elbert.

Coy, M. and Pholer, M. (2002) "Gated communities in Latin American mega cities: Case studies in Brazil and Argentina," *Environmental and Planning B: Planning and Design* 39: 355–70.

Diaz Alejandro, C. (1970) "Stages in industrialization in Argentina," in *Essays in the Economic History of Argentina*, New Haven, CT: Yale University Press.

Dorfman, A. (1983) *Cincuenta Años de Industrializacion en la Argentina. 1930–1950*, Buenos Aires: Ediciones Solar.

Dornbusch, R. (1986) "Argentina after Martinez de Hoz," in G. Di Tella and R. Dornbusch (eds) *The Political Economy of Argentina*, London: Macmillan Press.

Ferrucci, R. (1986) *La Promocion Industrial en la Argentina*, Buenos Aires: Eudeba.

INDEC Instituto Nacional de Estadísticas y Censos (National Insitute of Statistics and Censuses) (1980/1991/2001) "Argentina: Series Provincia de Buenos Aires y Ciudad Autónoma de Buenos Aires, 1980–1991–2001."

Kosacoff, B. and Ramos, A. (2001) *Cambios Contemporaneos en la Estructura Industrial Argentina (1975–2000)*, Bernal, Provincia de Buenos Aires: Universidad Nacional de Quilmes.

Kulfas, M. and Schorr, M. (2000) "Concentracion en la industria manufacturera Argentina durante los anos noventa," *FLACSO, Publicaciones del Area de Economia y Tecnología*, July.

Libertun de Duren, N. (2006) "Planning à la carte: The location patterns of gated communities around Buenos Aires in a decentralized planning context," *International Journal of Urban and Regional Research* 30 (2) June: 308.

Mollenkopf, J. (1989) "Who (or what) runs cities, and how?," *Sociological Forum* 4 (1) March: 119–37.

Mora y Araujo, M. and Smith, P. (1983) "Peronism and economic development," in F. Turner and J.E. Miguens (eds) *Juan Peron and the Reshaping of Argentina*, Pittsburgh, PA: University of Pittsburgh Press.

Oszlak, O. (1984) *Proceso, crisis y transición democrática Bs. As.*, Buenos Aires: Centro Editor de America Latina.

Pirez P. (2002) "Fragmentation and privatization of the Buenos Aires metropolitan city," *Environment & Urbanization* 14 (1) April.

Pirez, P. (1994) *Buenos Aires Metropolitana. Politica y Gestion de Ciudad*, Buenos Aires: Centro Editor de America Latina.

Prud'Homme, R. (1995) "Dangers of decentralization," *World Bank Research Observer* 10 (2): 201–20.

Rabinovitz, F. and Trueblood, F. (1971) *Latin American Urban Research*, Beverly Hills, CA: Sage Publications.

Schvarzer, J. (1987) *Promocion Industrial en Argentina: Caracteristicas, Evolucion y Resultado*, Buenos Aires: CISEA.

Scobie, J.E. (1964) *Argentina*, Oxford: Oxford University Press.

Stiglitz, J.E. (1999) "Wither reform? Ten years of transition," paper prepared for World Bank Annual Conference on Development Economics, Washington, DC, April.

Suarez, O. (1999) *El Territorio Argentino*, Buenos Aires: FADU, Universidad de Buenos Aires.

Svampa, M. (2001) Los *que ganaron. La Vida en los Countries y en los Barrios Cerrados*, Buenos Aires: Biblos.

Torres, H. (2001) "Cambios socio territoriales en Buenos Aires durante la década de 1990," *EURE (Santiago)* May 27, 80: 33–56.

Turn, F. and Carballo, M. (2005) "Argentine, economic disaster and the rejection of the political class," *Comparative Sociology* 4: 1–2.

Union Industrial Argentina (2001) *Evolucion Territorial-Sectorial de las PYMIS. 1994–2000*, study directed by Dr Vicente Donato. Buenos Aires: Observatorio Permanente de las PyMIs Argentinas.

United Nations Development Programme (2004) "Decentralized governance for development: A combined practice note on decentralization, local governance and urban/rural development," *UNDP Publications*, April.

Webster, C., Glasze G. and Frantz, K. (2002) "The global spread of gated communities," *Environment and Planning B: Planning and Design* 29: 315–20.

Wood, R.C. (1958) *Suburbia: Its People and Their Politics*, Boston, MA: Houghton Mifflin.

Chapter 5

New spaces, new contests
Appropriating decentralization for political change in Bolivia

Benjamin Kohl and Linda Farthing

> The United States will use this moment of opportunity to extend the
> benefits of freedom across the globe. We will actively work to bring the
> hope of democracy, development, free markets, and free trade to every
> corner of the world.
>
> (Bush 2002)

For forty years, political and administrative decentralization has been integrated
as a core component of the global neoliberal ideology described above by US President George W. Bush (Kohl and Farthing 2006; Peck 2001; Peet 2003). As a
result, both high- and low-income countries have transferred planning and
administrative responsibilities from national to subnational governments (Oyugi
2000; Samoff 1979; Wunsch 2001). These policies are based on the assumption
that decentralized governments are not only more efficient and less corrupt than
centralized ones, but also more democratic (World Bank 1997, 2000). In fact,
expanding citizen participation in planning is only one of several potential outcomes
of decentralization, as experience has demonstrated around the world (Huerta
Malbrán *et al.* 2000; Hutchcroft 2001; Oxhorn, *et al.* 2004; Schönwälder 1997;
Wanyande 2004).

Some critical scholars argue that the focus on formal democracy aims to
ensure the political stability that global markets require to operate successfully
within national economies. They contend that the focus on formal democratic
processes channels citizens' demands to limited local concerns and a tepid and
tidy range of choices expressed at the ballot box (Gill 2002; Kohl 2002; Robinson
1996, 2003; Slater 1989). These scholars also concur, however, that under certain
conditions decentralization programs can have the unintended result of opening
new political spaces to broaden local control and contest neoliberalism. In Bolivia,
decentralization legislation written in 1994 took place in a context of long-
established trajectories of political resistance and contributed to the conditions that
culminated in the December 2005 election of coca grower Evo Morales, a self-
proclaimed socialist and the country's first indigenous president. These events did
not take place in isolation but within a context of a growing economic and political
crisis after 1999, which was triggered by:

(a) declining government revenues after the privatization of the hydrocarbons company;
(b) the forced eradication of coca; and
(c) declining remittances from the 17 percent of Bolivians working in crisis-torn Argentina (Kohl and Farthing 2006).

The power of social movements in Bolivia has been well reported since the 2000 Cochabamba water war (Albro 2005; Assies and Salman 2003; Olivera 2004; Shultz 2003). Hylton and Thomson (2005) point out that these movements are built on legacies of resistance in the Andes dating from the Spanish Conquest. The formal political side of the process that laid the groundwork for Morales' election in 2005, however, is not as well understood. In this chapter we address this gap, demonstrating how, in a context of long-standing popular mobilization, political decentralization increased local participation in planning and facilitated the transformation of a contentious social movement (Tarrow 1998) into a dominant political force.

To detail the success of these counter-hegemonic movements, we draw on the social mobilization tradition of planning theory. We contend that, with its emphasis on transformative and structural change in capitalism through direct collective action from below, it provides the most appropriate lens to comprehend what has occurred in Bolivia (Friedman 1987: 83). In a poorly integrated country, planning has never been the exclusive domain of the state; rather, as social mobilization theory proposes, planning manifests as a form of politics (Friedmann 1987). The primacy of social mobilization in determining the country's course is exemplified in Bolivia's 500 years of steadily recurring cycles of contention, mostly under authoritarian regimes, as an impoverished, indigenous majority has struggled against a small, wealthy elite of European origin. Its salience has only increased in the formally democratic neoliberal era since 1985, with the state retreat from an active role in planning, shifting the locus in local decision-making to civil society (Douglass and Friedmann 1998). Therefore, we squarely place Bolivia's story within the insurgent planning histories described by Holston (1998) and, following Friedmann (1987: 250), we define planning "as an activity in which knowledge is joined to action in the course of social transformation."

Two key interrelated legal processes facilitated the political rise of counter-hegemonic movements. First, the 1994 LPP, along with the related Law of Administrative Decentralization (LAD), created over 250 new, small and largely indigenous and rural municipalities with planning oversight delegated to local organizations. These newly formed municipalities required thousands of council representatives and, as the indigenous and urban poor increasingly assumed office, they acquired some of the formal skills associated with Western-style government. This change fundamentally altered the discourse on the rights and roles of citizens in areas long abandoned by the state (Kohl 2003b). Second, changes in electoral laws in 1996 and 2004 led to greater representation of mostly male indigenous and *campesino* leaders in the national congress, which allowed them to transform traditional peasant and neighborhood organizations into formal political parties.

To clarify the changes decentralization has wrought in Bolivia, we briefly consider the nexus between decentralization and broader political participation as reflecting an ideological process with uneven results in practice. We then turn to the Bolivian experience to reveal the unintended consequences of the efforts of multinational institutions in collusion with national elites to construct limited, technocratic and contained citizen participation in planning. We contend that Bolivia provides an excellent example of the social mobilization tradition of planning theory, demonstrating how well-organized social movements have proven capable of appropriating the spaces decentralization provides. The Bolivian case is considered in comparative perspective in order to draw conclusions that suggest which factors may be critical for social movement success.

Decentralization as a strategy for increasing political participation

During the 1990s, decentralization reemerged as part of the "new development paradigm," which emphasized "community development, deregulation, privatization, minimal government, popular participation and flexible forms of foreign aid" (Werlin 1992: 223). Oxhorn (2004) has discovered a strong tendency in the most recent wave of decentralization policies towards a normative assumption that directly links decentralization with improved electoral democracy. Others argue that this assumption reflects an ideological faith in market democracy rather than either rigorous analysis or well-articulated concepts.

Such ideological assumptions are evident in an eighty-country study conducted by Huther and Shah (1998) that measures the degree of citizen participation only by the extent of political freedom—defined as voting—and stability—defined as democratic transitions of power. Huerta Malbrán *et al.* (2000: 225) identified similar narrow and technocratic approaches to defining citizen participation in their study of fifteen municipalities in Chile, Colombia and Guatemala. Schönwälder (1997) describes this type of participation in planning as a means to an end, the end being to improve the efficiency of development projects. Huerta Malbrán *et al.* concur and argue that, within the framework of neoliberalism, increased citizen participation is "more directed to transforming the community and citizens into project managers, administrators and public works builders than into political actors with decision-making power" (2000: 225, our translation).

Oxhorn (2004) contends that contradictory theoretical tendencies have muddied analysis of decentralization's links to increased democracy and points out that, in fact, the empirical results tend to be ambiguous and contradictory. In studies from across the global south, scholars have found that decentralization is often a top-down process that can disempower marginalized peoples and reinforce the control by local elites, particularly where civil society is fragmented and weak (Bienen *et al.* 1990; Huerta Malbrán *et al.* 2000; Nickson 1995; Wunsch 2001).

Critics of neoliberal decentralization stemming from the social mobilization tradition also note that any authentic increase in citizen participation in planning processes must serve to strengthen the participation of the poor and address issues of power (Schönwälder 1997; Slater 1989). Wanyande (2004) argues that, for political decentralization to be effective, citizens must have the skills to participate in decentralized structures and be willing to commit time to these projects, a condition that depends on the combination of political consciousness with a strong civil society.

Schönwälder (1997) notes that political decentralization presents poor-peoples' movements with the old dilemma either of maintaining autonomy by continuing to apply pressure from outside the system or of taking advantage of new political opportunities but risking cooptation. This predicament is at the heart of the challenge faced by the social movements that form the base of Bolivia's current government under the MAS (*Movimiento al Socialismo*—Movement toward Socialism): they must help the government they put into office maintain domestic peace while simultaneously demanding responses to their collective agenda.

Bolivia's decentralization

Bolivia is about twice the area of France or Texas, is organized into nine departments and has a population of 9 million, the majority of whom are from Quechua and Aymara ethnic groups.[1] Since the mid sixteenth century when the colonial mines of Potosí produced more than half the world's gold and silver (Klein 1998), Bolivia's natural resource wealth has benefited global, rather than local, economic interests. As with many low-income countries, the successive resource booms driven by silver, quinine, rubber, tin and, most recently, coca (and its derivative cocaine) and hydrocarbons have done little to construct the foundations for continued economic growth (Sachs and Warner 1999). About half the population still lives as semi-subsistence farmers in rural areas, and these *campesinos*[2] provide much of the country's food.

Bolivia has the dubious reputation of having had the largest number of *coups d'état* in the world since winning independence from Spain in 1825 (Morales 1992). Although frequently controlled by military governments, since the return to civilian rule in 1982 the country has celebrated seven constitutional transfers in administration. (In 2003 and 2005, while presidents were forced to resign in the face of massive popular protests, the transitions followed constitutional procedures.) During the eighteen years of dictatorship prior to 1982, oppositional forces utilized what Beard (2003) calls covert planning to keep a sense of collective agency alive.

Between 1952 and 1985, the government served as the country's prime economic actor. The transition to a market-dominated economy followed the 1986 IMF structural adjustment package that introduced a neoliberal economic model (Sachs 1987). Structural adjustment led to a sell-off of government firms and, through 2003, a trend towards the privatization of basic services.

In a poorly integrated country where pressures for greater local autonomy have been constant, Bolivia's 1994 LPP reflected longstanding efforts by regional movements, on the one hand, to obtain more resources and decision-making power and, on the other, by NGOs, to shift resources to long-neglected rural communities (CIPCA 1991; Medina 1997; Molina Monasterios 1997). Grindle (2000) contends that, for the government in power, the goals were to: extend the reach of the state (a frequent outcome of decentralization programs); to develop a stronger sense of national identity; to control endemic corruption; and to confront regional (mostly urban) elites' demands for political autonomy by focusing resources in rural hinterlands, a strategy that Tulchin and Selee (2004) have discovered has been utilized by national elites elsewhere. It also reflects the notion of planning as a neutral technocratic process that serves as what Sandercock (1998: 24) calls an "ordering tool . . . a kind of spatial police."

Before the LPP, most of the country fell outside any municipal jurisdiction at all. Municipal elections, held every five years since 1987, were relatively unimportant before 1999 as they only took place in the nation's largest cities.[3] Municipal governments only encompassed towns and cities, whose formal boundaries were never registered nationally and often fluctuated in accordance with the interests of the mayor in office. The rural areas, from the perspective of the national government, were largely ignored and, in many areas, the local government was a community organization, whether a "traditional" *ayllu* or *capitania* or a "modern" *campesino* union that operated independent of local municipalities (Albó *et al.* 1990; Ejdesgaard Jeppesen 2002: 36).[4] The structure of the national budget also reflected the centralization of formal government: 10 percent was targeted for the nine departmental capitals, with other towns and rural areas competing for funds from an additional 10 percent channeled through regional development corporations.

In 1994, the LPP and related legislation changed that. The laws combined the funds directed to departmental capitals and regional development corporations and allocated them to municipal governments on a per capita basis. In the process, the laws created over 250 new municipal governments, almost three-quarters of them "rural" municipalities with populations of less than 15,000 people. However, undoubtedly the principal innovation was the mandating of participatory planning and fiscal oversight by neighborhood and indigenous organizations (Kohl 2003a).

Prior to decentralization, candidates in countrywide elections needed affiliations with a national party, which led to political elites, typically from the largest cities, exerting undue influence on local politics. Through the 1993 national elections, all members of both houses of congress were elected through a proportional-representation system that drew on party lists to field candidates. This style of electoral politics kept indigenous rural and (increasingly indigenous) urban political actors from meaningful political participation. As a result, historically disenfranchised rural communities expressed their voices through the contentious politics associated with social movements.

That began to change owing to a 1996 electoral law that called for one-half of representatives to be chosen from district-level competitions, in a hybrid proportional-representation system following the German model (Domingo 2001).[5] This required political parties, which traditionally lacked formal rural organizations, to field district-level candidates beginning in 1997.

The opening of political space

The LPP led to a major political accomplishment: for the first time, the government formally recognized traditional organizations, including urban neighborhood organizations, pre-Hispanic indigenous organizations (*ayllus* and *capitanías*) and modern *campesino* unions, and mandated a formal role for them in local planning.[6] The government registered almost 15,000 widely disparate grassroots territorial organizations (GTOs) between 1994 and 1997 and gave them responsibility for creating community development plans, ensuring local oversight of projects, and mobilizing community labor for the construction and maintenance of public works. In rural municipalities, GTOs can have as few as sixty members, whereas in the country's largest cities they number as many as 3,000 (Kohl 2003a).

Conspicuously absent from recognition were labor unions, reflecting the continued government determination to prevent any legitimate role for Bolivia's once powerful *Central Obrera Boliviana* (COB), which had co-governed during the 1950s and brought down dictatorships in the 1970s and early 1980s (Ejdesgaard Jeppesen 2002; Medeiros 2001).

The national Confederation of Unions of *Campesino* Workers of Bolivia (*Confederación Sindical Unica de Trabajadores Campesinos de Bolivia* (CSUTCB)) initially opposed the recognition of GTOs outside the union structure, as governments had historically sought to create parallel organizations to undermine *campesino* unions. In a reaction similar to that found in the Philippines by Angeles and Magno (2004), the CSUTCB greeted the sudden change in government discourse that transformed *campesinos* into "subjects of participation" with mistrust, as the state had traditionally operated in opposition to, rather than in support of, the unions (Ejdesgaard Jeppesen 2002). Formal union opposition to the LPP weakened steadily as its male leadership realized that the law did indeed offer new political and social opportunities for Bolivia's indigenous majority, and, in May

1995, the CSTUCB signed an agreement with the government allowing local unions to serve as GTOs (Grindle 2000). The CSUTCB announced in their 1996 Congress that they would "radicalize popular participation to the extreme," heralding how popular organizations planned to utilize the LPP to pursue their own counter-hegemonic agendas (Ejdesgaard Jeppesen 2002: 37).

Although the LPP formally commits itself "to promote equal access of women and men" (Ley 1551 Article 8 1994), it contains a structural bias against women. Grassroots Bolivian women's organizations, which began organizing in the 1960s with the formation of housewives' committees in the mines, have been organized along sectoral rather than territorial lines. Consequently, they do not qualify as GTOs. Even when women's organizations have a territorial basis, they are generally subordinate to the male-dominated unions. This has resulted in a systematic exclusion of women from equal participation in the LPP, even as other laws attempt, with limited success, to increase their participation in planning and politics.[7]

Issues concerning the composition, legitimacy and representation of GTOs reflect the difficulty of legislating democratic participation in planning among highly heterogeneous populations (Kymlicka 1995). Although none of these problems has been resolved, the LPP indicates a shift in the character of politics in Bolivia. Before the LPP, grassroots groups and unions saw few options but to engage in oppositional politics to exercise demands on the state; in the era of popular participation, groups began to make some of those demands through formal political channels. This shift in political culture is an ongoing process: grassroots groups still use the oppositional techniques that had been developed centuries before the LPP. It is no surprise to see, for example, fifty or 100 members of a neighborhood organization at the entrance to a municipal building demanding attention from their representatives. And even with Evo Morales as President of both the nation and the confederation of coca growers from the Chapare, coca growers' unions still mobilize to make public demands on their leader in this combined role.

The LPP sought to channel Bolivia's traditionally unruly political protest to a local level and contain it within prescribed limits. Medeiros argues that the LPP embodied a "highly regulated construction of a modern participatory citizenry" as part of a hegemonic project that sought to "predefine the limits to what can be achieved" (2001: 401), and, in the short run, the LPP achieved moderate success in this dimension.

The LPP, electoral politics and social movements

Between 1995 and 1999, the LPP allocated enough resources to municipalities to attract the attention of local populations while simultaneously redefining the spaces for opposition. Before the 1985 structural adjustment program broke the back of the miners' union, opposition to the government was national and class-based. Drawing from Friedmann's (1987: 273–97) typology of social mobilization strategies, the period of COB predominance was based on a formal organization, strongly influenced by vanguardism that focused on what it was against rather than for and worked outside the system in oppositional, but generally non-violent, forms to achieve what many of the Marxists who dominated the labor movement believed was the inevitable collapse of capitalism.

Owing to the structural adjustment's successful assault on the COB, by 1995 labor resistance primarily followed sectoral lines. Such fragmentation rendered the union movement largely ineffective. In its place, rural indigenous social movements, most notably coca growers in the Chapare region east of Cochabamba, rose to become the most important opposition force in the country. The constant repression associated with the US-financed drug war, which fell most heavily on *campesinos*, combined with unfulfilled economic development promises, forged them into a powerful political movement with strong grassroots and almost exclusively male leadership, directly accountable to their bases (Farthing and Kohl 2001; 2005).

As the national labor movement and its formal organizational structures disintegrated, much of the focus turned to more informal and local processes, and opposition centered on GTOs and municipal struggles. During the first five years of the LPP, indigenous groups and *ayllus*, which had been able to command attention through national protests, generally did not register the same gains through participation in planning within municipal borders where they confronted entrenched local elites. There were, however, some important exceptions: the coca producers, the highland Aymara and to a lesser degree the lowland Guaraní, Bolivia's third largest indigenous group. These groups, often under powerful and charismatic male leaders, managed to reach beyond municipal boundaries and extend political alliances along ethnic lines, or, in the case of the coca producers, along economic interests, to develop a base for broader formal and contentious political activity. Compared with the era under COB leadership, actions during this period reflected the opposite end of the spectrum delineated in Friedmann's 1987 typology: they were mostly informal and spontaneous, tended to greater violence and counted on less clear authority and leadership. Nonetheless, social resistance remained clearly outside the system and continued in a tradition of opposition rather than proposition.

The LPP became a site for local confrontation as the widespread tensions that exist in rural Bolivia between townspeople and rural indigenous people were brought to the surface (Farthing and Kohl 2005; Medeiros 2001). Because of the LPP, the ubiquitous second-class status of indigenous citizens was contested throughout Bolivia (Ejdesgaard Jeppesen 2002). Just as Ducci (2004) discovered in Chile, the process of decentralization fed political opposition as it generated expectations that governments could not fulfill, no matter how extensive citizen participation in planning, as annual per capita disbursements from the national government never exceeded US$30.

With the introduction of municipal elections, popular movements gained entry to formal political spaces and began to transform social movements into political parties. In the 1995 municipal elections, thirteen political parties fielded candidates, and *campesino* and indigenous representatives were elected to 29 percent (464 of the 1624) of the seats in 200 of the country's 311 municipalities (MDH-SNPP 1996). In this first election, however, most successful candidates represented the traditional parties, rather than more populist ones (Albó 1996: 14).

The large number of political parties made it attractive for the smaller parties that lacked a national organization to open their doors to indigenous and rural people as the best way to field candidates. The success of some of the smaller parties, especially the Assembly for [Indigenous] Peoples' Sovereignty (*Asamblea de Soberania de Pueblos* (ASP)) and the Free Bolivia Movement (Movimiento Bolivia Libre (MBL)), in winning seats in rural municipalities alerted the traditional parties to the need for a stronger rural presence.

Although only four indigenous candidates, all representing the coca growers' movement, reached Congress in the 1997 national elections, their success inspired other *campesino* and indigenous organizations and convinced small political parties to "loan" them their party slates during municipal elections in 1999.[8] Many of the candidates in the 1995 and 1999 municipal elections participated as national candidates for the MAS in 2002 (Healey 2005). Indigenous councilors won seventy-nine seats in seven of nine departments, although mostly through the traditional parties (Van Cott 2003: 763).

As Gray Molina (2003: 351) argues, the LPP fundamentally "restructured the rules of the game for political intermediation and policy making in rural areas." The 1995 municipal elections marked an important turning point and signaled the eventual demise of a peculiar form of Andean apartheid that had kept indigenous people from meaningful participation in electoral politics and local planning. Increasingly, *campesino* unions and other indigenous organizations worked with small, progressive political parties and in some cases began to form their own parties. The steady growth in local electoral participation, especially among rural voters, increasingly complemented union politics with party politics (Gray Molina 2003).

It was only in the 2002 combined presidential and congressional elections that the MAS broke beyond the boundaries of the Chapare to take second place nationally with 20 percent of the popular vote. Although Morales' showing exceeded expectations, the party was still perceived as a regional one. In the largely

Aymara department of La Paz, Felipe Quispe, "*El Mallku*," captured much of the indigenous vote, winning about 6 percent nationally and gaining six seats in the lower house.

Gonzalo Sanchez de Lozada assumed the presidency in August 2002 at the head of a weak coalition government, which represented the worst of what Eduardo Gamarra (1996) refers to as Bolivia's "pacted" democracy. Political pressure came from two fronts. On the one hand, social movements built on the symbolic success of the 2000 Cochabamba "water war" to continue pushing continually weaker and more incompetent administrations that failed to convince the people that they operated in the best interest of the majority of Bolivians (Kohl and Farthing 2006). On the other hand, the growing formal political participation of opposition movements led by Morales and the MAS pushed for reforms that further opened the political process. Although the MAS had little legislative power as a minority party, Morales took up the fight not only in the halls of Congress but also in the streets as Sanchez de Lozada's government thrashed about, reacting to social and political crises rather than governing proactively.

The opposition grew increasingly strident, and, after 14 months of almost continual chaos, on October 17, 2003, Sanchez de Lozada resigned as 500,000 people marched from El Alto to La Paz, demanding his departure for sanctioning lethal force against unarmed civilian demonstrators in a presidential decree. Following constitutional protocol, his vice-president, Carlos Mesa assumed office with a promise to address the issues of the "October Agenda": a constitutional assembly, decentralization and regional autonomy, nationalization of gas, and corruption. In the municipal elections of December 2004, the MAS, although failing to win in major cities or an overall majority of seats, had the strongest showing of any party, particularly in rural areas.

Mesa, who resigned from office in June 2005 in the face of massive protests for failing to enact the "October Agenda," brought two important changes during his tenure. Notably, given Bolivia's repressive history, he refused to order the military to shoot civilians. He also modified electoral rules to allow social groups to field candidates for municipal office without having to integrate into political parties, which allowed for more direct indigenous participation. This further extended the space for formal political contestation, and, in the 2004 municipal elections, in Bolivia's largest cities, 30 percent of elected councilors represented citizen groups rather than political parties.

Eduardo Rodriguez Veltzé, the president of the Supreme Court, replaced Mesa with the sole mandate of organizing elections within 180 days. Although constitutional procedure only called for presidential elections, broad-based social pressure forced Congress to pass a law that recalled the entire national legislature while it also required the direct election of departmental prefects. This election put Morales in office with an unexpected 54 percent of the vote, even as his party lost six of nine prefectural races to a mix of traditional party candidates and strong local leaders (*caudillos*), who took advantage of new electoral laws to form their own parties.

Bolivia's experience in comparative perspective

Social movements in other Latin American countries have had a mixed experience with political decentralization as a tool to advance their agenda. In Colombia, social movements have not appropriated the newly established participatory planning mechanisms but rather have continued to direct their demands at the central government, and for the most part Colombian labor unions have ignored municipalities (Ahumada Beltrán and Velasco 2000). In Chile, where municipal elections were held for the first time after the Pinochet dictatorship in 1992, Pressacco and Huerta (2000) found that the weaknesses of social organizations limited active participation by low-income people.

The success of Bolivia's social movements in occupying the spaces created by decentralization, however, is not unique. Heller (2002) describes how the combination of strong left-of-center governments, robust civil societies and political decentralization initiatives has combined to generate opportunities for social movements in the state of Kerala, India, the city of Porto Alegre, Brazil, and South Africa.

In Brazil, Latin America's best-known case of devolving authority to the municipal level, several hundred left-wing local governments have used decentralization, promoted decades earlier by local elites to consolidate their power in the face of a modernizing military, to institute participatory budgeting (Abers 2000; Goldsmith and Vainer, 2001). In a trajectory that echoes the MAS but on a much larger scale, the Brazilian Workers' Party (PT) gained experience through years of governing first municipal and then state governments as they built a political party that, with a coalition government, won the presidency in 2002 and again in 2006.

In Guatemala, left-of-center civic fronts and indigenous organizations have formed a network to support participation in municipal planning by the poor in fourteen of twenty-two departments and to establish a presence in fifty-five municipalities (Puente and Molina 2000). Fernando Espinoza describes how, in Ecuador, "indigenous peoples and organizations consider local spaces as strategic terrain in the construction of a plurinational state and the exercise of radical democracy" (2003: 198). And, in Chiapas, Mexico, indigenous groups have taken control of municipalities abandoned during the 1990s (Rombera and Luévano (2003). The trend of building progressive movements on local foundations continues throughout much of Latin America, as reflected in political groupings such as *Causa R* in Venezuela, *Frente Amplio* in Uruguay and FREPASO in Argentina (Oxhorn 2004).

Conclusions

The processes of change in Bolivia illustrate a particular synergy between decentralization, political restructuring and social movements, reflecting the importance of the social mobilization strand of planning theory in understanding planning processes in countries with strong histories of contentious politics. The LPP, although fundamentally a reform measure incapable of changing the basic material conditions of the majority of Bolivians, did serve as a catalyst to mobilize a marginalized population to adopt a re-energized repertoire of political actions. However, even as the government prescribed spaces of action, it also introduced a new rhetoric of citizenship and participation in planning, as well as creating new expectations of the state.

Political decentralization made municipal planning and electoral politics a proving ground for a growing grassroots democratic opposition to traditional urban political parties. Bolivian opposition movements, centered on the coca producers, consolidated a hold on a small territory before forming broader alliances. Building on initial successes in 1995 and 1999, the opposition movements became increasingly self-assured and effectively combined an indigenous, nationalist and anti-neoliberal discourse to propel the MAS to electoral victory.

Over the short term, decentralization channeled the attention of political groups to the local arena, a strategy similarly used by elites in both Mexico and Kenya seeking to shore up their own legitimacy while simultaneously attempting to prevent greater democratic participation at a national level (Tulchin and Selee 2004). In Bolivia, decentralization enabled groups that could not successfully compete on a national or departmental scale to occupy new political spaces in the local arena, creating hundreds of laboratories that enabled a largely male leadership to develop. The coca producers in the Chapare gained control of their municipalities and planning early on, but, because of their powerful identification with a long history of *campesino* and miner struggles, they always sought national support—and supported broader calls for social justice—as well.

Heller (2002) argues that such historical and political circumstances can determine when popular movements will be able to take advantage of political decentralization. In Bolivia, well-organized and combative social movements, built on a trajectory of resistance that reaches back to the Spanish Conquest, were key elements in enabling the poor to assume a greater role in both local planning and politics. The social movements' ability to nurture astute leaders was also of critical importance. The spiraling economic and political crisis that confronted Bolivia from 1999 on created important political opportunities that these leaders recognized and exploited. All these factors were fundamental in facilitating Bolivians' appropriation of political decentralization for their own ends, rather than those envisioned by national elites and international financial institutions.

Notes

1   There are over thirty lowland indigenous groups, with a total population of about 600,000, with the Guaraní accounting for about 300,000 of them.
2   *Campesinos*, literally, are people who live in the countryside. The word is commonly translated as peasants, but includes both landowning and landless people of rural origin, who participate in commodity production and urban labor markets to different degrees.
3   The majority of the population lived outside established municipalities, which were administered by officials appointed at the departmental level.
4   The *ayllu* and *capitanía* are both pre-Conquest organizational structures that persist until today, the *ayllus* in the western highland areas, and *capitanías* among the eastern lowland groups, most importantly the Guaraní. As Jojola (1998) found in Pueblo Indian nations of the American southwest, they both represent indigenous planning traditions that have played an important role in centuries of survival and resistance. The *ayllu* is a nested moeity structure that provides local governance (Platt 1982). *Campesino* unions arose after the 1952 revolution, when a modernizing government changed the perjorative "*indio*" to "*campesino*" as the nomenclature to describe rural indigenous people. The *campesino* union model is based on the organizational forms of the labor movement in Bolivia. In many areas of Bolivia, existing *ayllu* and *capitanía* structures compete for the authority to represent local communities with either urban neighborhood organizations or campesino unions. As resources are often allocated on a per capita basis, this has become an increasing source of conflict.
5   German technical assistance provided support for drafting the legislation.
6   See Platt (1982, 1999) and Albó *et al.* (1990) for a discussion of these and other indigenous forms of organization.
7   Although electoral laws call for including higher percentages of women, and indeed more women appear on ballots, they do not specify how women are to be ranked on electoral lists, of key importance in determining who actually enters office in a proportional electoral system. The number of women mayors and municipal council presidents declined in the 2004 municipal election.
8   Bolivian law stipulates that municipal elections be held every five years, throughout the country. These elections have come at the midpoint of a presidential term, although it is not clear what will happen as the presidential elections, scheduled for June 2007 were held in December 2005.

References

Abers, R.N. (2000) *Inventing Local Democracy: Grassroots Politics in Brazil*, Boulder, CO: Lynne Rienner.
Ahumanda Beltrán, C. and Velasco Jaramillo, M. (2000) "Colombia: Decentralización, poder local y participación comunitaria," in M. Huerta Malbrán, C.F. Presacco Chávez, C. Ahumanda Beltrán, M. Velasco Jaramillo, J. Puente Alcaraz and J.F. Molina Meza (eds) *Decentralización, municipio y participación ciudadana: Chile Colombia y Guatemala*, Bogotá: Central Editorial Javeriano, pp. 159–226.
Albó, X. (1996) "Making the leap from local mobilization to national politics," *NACLA Report on the Americas* 29: 15–20.
Albó, X., Libermann, K., Pifarro, F. and Gondinez, A. (1990) *Para comprender las culturas rurales en Bolivia*, La Paz: UNICEF.

Albro, R. (2005) "The water is ours, carajo!: Deep citizenship in Bolivia's water war," in J. Nash (ed.) *Social Movements: An Anthropological Reader*, Oxford and Cambridge: Basil Blackwell, pp. 249–71.

Angeles, L.C. and Magno, F.A. (2004) "The Philippines: Decentralization, local governments and citizen action," in P. Oxhorn, J. Tulchin and A. Selee (eds) *Decentralization, Democratic Governance and Civil Society in Comparative Perspective*, Washington, DC: Woodrow Wilson Center, pp. 211–57.

Assies, W. and Salman, T. (2003) "Bolivian democracy: Consolidating or disintegrating?," *Focaal—European Journal of Anthropology* (Netherlands) 42: 141–60.

Beard, V.A. (2003) "Learning radical planning: The power of collective action," *Planning Theory and Practice* 2: 13–35.

Bienen, H., Kapur, D., Parks, J. and Riedinger, J. (1990) "Decentralization in Nepal," *World Development* 18: 61–75.

Bush, G. (2002) "National security strategy of the United States, September 2002." Available online at www.whitehouse.gov/ncs/nss.pdf, July 16, 2006.

CIPCA (1991) *Por una Bolivia diferente*, La Paz: CIPCA.

Domingo, P. (2001) "Party politics, intermediation and representation," in J. Crabtree and L. Whitehead (eds) *Towards Democratic Viability: The Bolivian Experience*, Basingstoke; New York: Palgrave, pp. 141–59.

Douglass, M. and Friedmann, J. (1998) *Cities for Citizens: Planning and the Rise of Civil Society in a Global Age*, Chichester: John Wiley & Sons.

Ducci, M.E. (2004) "Local governance and democratization," in P. Oxhorn, J. Tulchin and A. Selee (eds) *Decentralization, Democractic Governance and Civil Society in Comparative Perspective*, Washington, DC: Woodrow Wilson Center, pp. 119–38.

Ejdesgaard Jeppesen, A.M. (2002) "Reading the Bolivian landscape of exclusion and inclusion: The law of popular participation," in N. Webster and L.E. Pedersen (eds) *In the Name of the Poor*, London: Zed, pp. 30–52.

Farthing, L. and Kohl, B. (2001) "Bolivia's new wave of protest," *NACLA Report on the Americas* 34: 8–11.

Farthing, L. and Kohl, B. (2005) "Conflicting agendas: The politics of development aid in drug producing areas," *Development Policy Review* 23: 183–98.

Fernando Espinoza, M. (2003) "Descentralización, poderes locales indígenas y manejo de recursos naturales en Ecuador," in W. Assies (ed.) *Gobiernos locales y reforma del Estado en América Latina*, Zamora: El Colegio de Michoacán.

Friedmann, J. (1987) *Planning in the Public Domain*, Princeton, NJ: Princeton University Press.

Gamarra, E.A. (1996) "Bolivia: Managing democracy in the 1990s," in J. Dominguez and A. Lowenthal (eds) *Constructing Democratic Governance: South America in the 1990s*, Baltimore, MD: Johns Hopkins University Press.

Gill, S. (2002) "Constitutionalizing inequality and the clash of globalizations," *The International Studies Review* 4 (2): 47–65.

Goldsmith, W. and Vainer, C.V. (2001) "Participatory budgeting and power politics in Porto Alegre," *Lincoln Land Institute: Landlines* 13: 1.

Gray Molina, G. (2003) "The offspring of 1952: Poverty, exclusion and the promise of popular participation," in M. Grindle and P. Domingo (eds) *Proclaiming Revolution: Bolivia in Comparative Perspective*, London: Institute for Latin American Studies, pp. 345–63.

Grindle, M.S. (2000) *Audacious Reforms: Institutional Invention and Democracy in Latin America*. Baltimore, MD: Johns Hopkins University Press.

Healey, S. (2005) "Rural social movements and the prospects for sustainable rural communities: Evidence from Bolivia," *Canadian Journal of Development Studies* 26: 151–74.

Heller, P. (2002) "Moving the state: The politics of democratic decentralization in Kerala, South Africa and Porto Alegre," *Peripherie, Germany*: 337–77.

Holston, J. (1998) "Spaces of insurgent citizenship," in L. Sandercock (ed.) *Making the Invisible Visible: A Multicultural Planning History*, Berkeley, CA: University of California Press, pp. 37–56.

Huerta Malbrán, M., Presacco Chávez, C.F., Ahumanda Beltrán, C., Velasco Jaramillo, M., Puente Alcaraz, J. and J.F. Molina Meza (2000) *Decentralización, municipio y participación ciudadana: Chile Colombia y Guatemala*, Bogotá: Central Editorial Javeriano.

Hutchcroft, P.D. (2001) "Centralization and decentralization in administration and politics: Assessing territorial dimensions of authority and power," *Governance* 14: 23–53.

Huther, J. and Shah, A. (1998) "Applying a simple measure of good governance to the debate on fiscal decentralization." Available online at http://wb-cu.car.chula.ac.th/Papers/world bank/wps1894.pdf, accessed July 7, 2006, vol. 2006, World Bank.

Hylton, F. and Thomson, S. (2004) "The roots of rebellion," *Nacla Report on the Americas* 38: 15–19.

Hylton, F. and Thomson, S. (2005) "The chequered rainbow," *New Left Review* 35: 40–66.

Jojola, T. (1998) "Indigenous planning: Clans, intertribal confederations, and the history of the All Indian Pueblo Council," in L. Sandercock (ed.) *Making the Invisible Visible: A Multicultural Planning History*, Berkeley, CA: University of California Press, pp. 37–56.

Klein, H.S. (1998) *The American Finances of the Spanish Empire: Royal Income and Expenditures in Colonial Mexico, Peru, and Bolivia, 1680–1809*, Albuquerque, NM: University of New Mexico Press.

Kohl, B. (2002) "Stabilizing neoliberalism in Bolivia: Privatization and participation in Bolivia," *Political Geography* 21: 449–72.

Kohl, B. (2003a) "Restructuring citizenship in Bolivia: *El Plan de Todos*," *International Journal of Urban and Regional Research* 27: 337–51.

Kohl, B. (2003b) "Democratizing decentralization in Bolivia: The law of popular participation," *Journal of Planning Education and Research* 23: 153–64.

Kohl, B. (2006) "Challenges to neoliberal hegemony in Bolivia," *Antipode* 38: 304–26.

Kohl, B. and Farthing, L. (2006) *Impasse in Bolivia: Neoliberal Hegemony and Popular Resistance*, London: Zed.

Kymlicka, W. (1995) *Multicultural Citizenship: A Liberal Theory of Minority Rights*, New York: Clarendon Press.

Ley 1551 (1994) Law of Popular Participation 1994, Bolivia modified by Law 1702/96.

MDH-SNPP (Ministerio de Desarrollo Humano & Secretaría de Participación Popular) (1996) *La Participación Popular en Cifras: resultados y proyecciones para analizar un proceso de cambio*, La Paz: MDH-SNPP.

Medeiros, C. (2001) "Civilizing the popular: The law of popular participation and the design of a new civil society in 1990s Bolivia," *Critique of Anthropology* 21: 401–25.

Medina, J. (1997) *Poderes locales: implementando la Bolivia del próximo milenio, protocolos de gestión de un Subsecretario*, La Paz: FIA/Semilla/CEBIAE.

Molina Monasterios, F. (1997) *Historia de la Participación Popular*, La Paz: MDH-SNPP.

Morales, W.Q. (1992) *Bolivia: Land of Struggle*, Boulder, CO: Westview Press.

Nickson, R.A. (1995) *Local Government in Latin America*, Boulder, CO: Lynne Rienner.

Olivera, O. (2004) *Cochabamba! Water War in Bolivia* (translated by T. Lewis), Boston, MA: South End Press.

Oxhorn, P. (2004) "Unraveling the puzzle of decentralization," in P. Oxhorn, J. Tulchin and A. Selee (eds) *Decentralization, Democratic Governance and Civil Society in Comparative Perspective*, Washington, DC: Woodrow Wilson Center, pp. 3–30.

Oxhorn, P., Tulchin, J. and Selee, A. (2004) *Decentralization, Democractic Governance and Civil Society in Comparative Perspective*, Washington, DC: Woodrow Wilson Center.

Oyugi, W.O. (2000) "Decentralization for good governance and development: The unending debate," *Regional Development Dialogue* 21: iii–xix.

Peck, J. (2001) "Neoliberalizing states: Thin policies/hard outcomes," *Progress in Human Geography* 25: 445–55.

Peet, R. (2003) *Unholy Trinity: The IMF, World Bank and WTO*, New York: Zed Books.

Platt, T. (1982) "The role of the Andean *Ayllu* in the reproduction of the petty commodity regime in Northern Potosi (Bolivia)," in D. Lehman (ed.) *Ecology and Exchange in the Andes*, Cambridge: Cambridge University Press, pp. 27–69.

Platt, T. (1999) *La persistencia de los ayllus en el norte del Potosí: de la invasión europea a la República de Bolivia*, La Paz: Fundación Diálogo.

Popular Participation Law (1994) N. 1551/94, modified by Law 1702/96.

Pressacco, C.F. and Huerta, M.A. (2000) "Chile: Descentralización, municipio y participación ciudana" in M. Huerta Malbrán, C.F. Presacco Chávez, C. Ahumanda Beltrán, M. Velasco Jaramillo, J. Puente Alcaraz and J.F. Molina Meza (eds) *Descentralización, municipio y participación ciudadana: Chile Colombia y Guatemala*, Bogotá: Central Editorial Javeriano.

Puente, J. and Molina, J.F. (2000) "Descentralización y democracia: Gobierno local y participación ciudana" in M. Huerta Malbrán, C.F. Presacco Chávez, C. Ahumanda Beltrán, M. Velasco Jaramillo, J. Puente Alcaraz and J.F. Molina Meza (eds) *Descentralización, municipio y participación ciudadana: Chile Colombia y Guatemala*, Bogotá: Central Editorial Javeriano.

Robinson, W.I. (1996) *Promoting Polyarchy: Globalization, US Intervention, and Hegemony*, Cambridge: Cambridge University Press.

Robinson, W.I. (2003) *Transnational Conflicts: Central America, Social Change, and Globalization*, London: Verso.

Rombera, R. and Luévano, A. (2003) "Construyendo democracia y poder local: Apuntes sobre los retos y perspectivas de la gestión local democrática," in W. Assies (ed.) *Gobiernos locales y reforma del Estado en América Latina*, Zamora: El Colegio de Michoacán.

Sachs, J. (1987) "The Bolivian hyperinflation and stabilization," *American Economic Review* 77: 279–83.

Sachs, J. and Warner, A. (1999) "The big push, natural resource booms and growth," *Journal of Development Economics* 59: 43–76.

Samoff, J. (1979) "The bureaucracy and the bourgeoisie: Decentralization and class structure in Tanzania," *Society for the Comparative Study of Society and History* 21: 30–62.

Sandercock, L. (1998) *Making the Invisible Visible: A Multicultural Planning History*, Berkeley, CA: University of California Press.

Schönwälder, G. (1997) "New democratic spaces at the grassroots? Popular participation in Latin American local governments," *Development and Change* 28: 753–70.

Shultz, J. (2003) "Bolivia's war over water." Cochabamba: Democracy Center. Available online at http://democracyctr.org/bolivia/investigations/water/the_water_war.htm, accessed February 28, 2008.

Slater, D. (1989) "Territorial power and the peripheral state: The issue of decentralization," *Development and Change* 20: 501–31.

Tarrow, S.G. (1998) *Power in Movement: Social Movements and Contentious Politics*, Cambridge and New York: Cambridge University Press.

Tulchin, J. and Selee, A. (2004) "Decentralization and democratic governance," in P. Oxhorn, J. Tulchin and A. Selee (eds) *Decentralization, Democratic Governance and Civil Society in Comparative Perspective*, Washington, DC: Woodrow Wilson Center, pp. 295–319.

Van Cott, D.L. (2003) "From exclusion to inclusion: Bolivia's 2002 election," *Journal of Latin American Studies* 34: 751–75.

Wanyande, P. (2004) "Decentralization and local governance: A conceptual and theoretical discourse," *Regional Development Dialogue* 25: 1–13.

Werlin, H. (1992) "Linking decentralization and centralization: A critique of the new development administration," *Public Administration and Development* 12: 223–35.

World Bank (1997) *The State in a Changing World: World Development Report 1997*, New York: Oxford University Press.

World Bank (2000) *Decentralization: Rethinking Government World Development Report 1999/2000*, New York: Oxford University Press.

Wunsch, J. (2001) "Decentralization, local governance and 'recentralization' in Africa," *Public Administration and Development* 21: 277–88.

Section Two
The challenges of fiscal and administrative
decentralization

Chapter 6

The evolution of subnational development planning under decentralization reforms in Kenya and Uganda

Paul Smoke

Introduction

Although planning has been a cornerstone of international development through-out the past half century, it has changed dramatically over time as development paradigms have shifted.[1] The original focus on economy-oriented, technical, centralized planning has evolved into an activity that is generally broader in scope (focusing more on human development), more process-oriented (embedded more within political and institutional reforms), and often at least partially decentralized.

Perhaps the most striking change in planning in recent years has been the great effort to move it closer to citizens, both through the adoption of formal techniques and processes for subnational government planning and through efforts of various actors to nurture civil society development.[2] These trends have resulted in part from disappointing progress in meeting national goals through centralized or centrally dominated processes. Rapid political, economic and technological changes have also fueled the trend to rely more heavily on subnational governments and local communities.

Although decentralization is common, there is uncertainty about its benefits—empirical evidence on if and how best to pursue it is limited and mixed.[3] The lack of strong evidence in part reflects great contextual variations across countries. The frameworks and approaches used to design and evaluate decentral-ization and subnational planning are normative and relatively standardized, but countries differ in many respects—the structures, rights, responsibilities and interrelationships of government institutions; subnational government capacity; strength of civil society; etc. Such factors can be targets of decentralization reform, but not all reforms can occur at the same time.

Even if a decision is made to decentralize, obstacles abound. National agen-cies are often reluctant to act in ways that reduce their powers. In addition, giving new responsibilities and resources to subnational governments that are politically, managerially and technically unprepared to use them is problematic. Perhaps the greatest challenge is enabling meaningful local participation, particularly where civil society is unprepared to take advantage of formal participatory mechanisms, and central governments are not serious about encouraging genuine citizen engagement.

Although generalization about ideal systems and how to approach reform is difficult, a few features suggest whether a subnational planning system can facilitate the typically broader objectives of decentralization—citizen empowerment, better public services, and ultimately the improved well-being of citizens, including marginalized groups. First, a decentralized planning system needs to be appropriately *linked to the larger government system* of planning, resourcing, budgeting and implementation, and, as needed, to non-governmental actors who may play a productive role. Second, the system requires *sustainable capacity to perform its functions*—adequate financial and human resources and the autonomy on which the intended benefits of decentralization depend. Third, the *governance system must be sufficiently deep and inclusive*, adequately representing the interests of all citizens in the planning jurisdiction.[4]

This chapter considers decentralized planning, primarily from a national reform perspective, in two African countries, Kenya and Uganda. Both have enjoyed a reputation in different ways as relatively successful cases of African decentralization and local government reforms.[5] The comparison is built around the three principles noted above, but the focus is on the institutional design of the decentralized planning system and the degree to which it is capacitated. Governance development, of course, is equally critical to meet decentralization goals, but central governments, assuming they genuinely support such reforms, can play only a partial role in promoting citizen engagement—establishing and enforcing legal rights and frameworks, making information available, providing civic education, and so on. Such activities need to be supported by efforts at the grassroots level that emerge locally or with external support. Unfortunately, evidence on citizen empowerment related to subnational planning reform in the two countries under consideration is limited and far from definitive.

The next section introduces the two countries, followed by a section that briefly compares their inter-governmental structures. The fourth section describes the planning systems embedded in these broader structures, followed by an analysis of key positive and negative features in each country. Finally, a few summary comments about the state of decentralized planning in the two countries are presented.

The evolution of current decentralization reforms

Kenya has a substantial history of local decision-making, both from the self-governance traditions of its many ethnic groups and from the local government system set up during British colonial rule.[6] Although the latter was established to meet the needs of European settlers, colonial local governments were fairly autonomous and had significant sources of revenue, unusual features of formal subnational institutions relative to much of the developing world. Local governments were weakened after independence under the rhetoric of "national unity" promotion in the ethnically diverse state, but they continued to provide key services, collect revenues and be governed by elected councils. Elite capture and other governance problems common in post-colonial states constrained local governments, but they long performed better than those in many developing countries. Kenyan local governments have historically been among the most fiscally independent in Africa, with limited fiscal transfers provided after independence until just a few years ago.

Unfortunately, relative to their legal powers and long history, local governments have performed well below their potential in recent years, inadequately responding to the growing needs of a progressively more informed population. Central officials blamed poor performance on local incompetence and corruption, but seemed powerless or unwilling to help. Local officials claimed they could not improve without a reduction of excessive central interference and an increase in resources. Local citizens, of course, were the losers in this situation, but were not in a strong position to effect meaningful change.

This deterioration of local authorities largely resulted from the evolution of political dynamics. Power consolidation after Kenya's independence in 1963 and reinforced after a 1982 coup attempt included public-sector restructuring efforts that significantly undermined the link between local authorities and their constituents. The erosion of that link intensified over time, with increasingly poor local performance, reinforcing the central view of local authorities as problematic entities to be controlled rather than key developmental entities to be supported. Many citizens, if they thought about local government at all, surely felt that they were being asked to participate in local elections and to pay local taxes without being provided with adequate basic services.

Several conditions provided opportunities for reform in the 1990s. First, local service delivery declined to a point where it was broadly unacceptable, and the impact of poor services on development was increasingly recognized and highlighted through growing protests by citizens and business organizations. Second, rapidly changing central fiscal conditions sharply focused attention on the burden imposed on the central budget by local governments, which had for years failed to repay international donor loans to Kenya that were onlent to them by the central Local Government Loans Authority. Third, the political environment has been shifting substantially. A freer press that emerged with a political crisis in the early 1990s and the resulting reinstitution of a multi-party political system raised public awareness, and national scandals weakened the legitimacy of the center in calling local authorities corrupt. Genuine political opposition parties emerged during the 1990s, and their success in winning local elections and a voice in parliament confronted the ruling party with new demands, which were reinforced by pressure from major donors. An opposition party candidate won the presidency in 2003, further bolstering a climate for reform.

Uganda did not have as elaborately developed a local government system as Kenya during the colonial era.[7] The powers that local governments did enjoy were reduced by the 1967 republican constitution, and the system suffered from some of the same types of central manipulation and local elite capture problem that plagued Kenya in the post-colonial period. The entire system was substantially weakened as Uganda was enveloped in oppressive regimes with little interest in modern conventions of governance. The Idi Amin era saw the effective marginalization of the local government system. When Yoweri Museveni became President in 1986, he presided over a gradual public-sector resurrection that eventually involved local governments. There was, as in Kenya after independence, a perceived need to improve national cohesion, but there was also some motivation to improve responsiveness to citizens and enhance development. Unlike Kenya, Uganda does not enjoy a multi-party system, a situation that has both its critics and supporters.[8] The political support for decentralization, however, was relatively broad and strong. The desire to bring the country back from a long period of conflict and underdevelopment meant that Uganda, unlike many developing countries, did not make the mistake of moving decentralization forward without building a relatively broad-based consensus on the general value of reform and the eventual shape the inter-governmental system should take. In addition, decentralization was substantially home grown—as early reforms were being developed, the Ugandan government requested donor support for decentralization only selectively.

In this self-driven, pro-reform environment, the government was able to develop a fairly robust formal framework for decentralization. The Local Governments Statute of 1993, 1995 Ugandan Constitution and Local Governments Act of 1997 provide considerable detail about local government powers and responsibilities. In addition, institutional innovations created atypical checks and balances in the management of decentralization. The Local Government Finance Commission (LGFC), for example, which helps frame revenue policy, is a broad-based, independent body (defined by the Constitution and legislation) that reports directly to the President and helps somewhat to moderate the effects of central institutional self-interested behavior and power struggles over control of the decentralization agenda. As discussed below, however, the implementation of reforms has faced serious challenges.

The broad national and inter-governmental context

Kenya and Uganda share a number of socio-economic characteristics and have similar colonial heritages. They are ethnically and environmentally diverse nations, both were originally part of a unified British East African Protectorate, and they share a common border. The economies of both countries are substantially agricultural. Their public sectors are both of moderate size (about 30 percent of GDP in Kenya and 25 percent in Uganda) and both run moderate public-sector deficits (13.2 percent in Kenya and 10.1 percent in Uganda in 2000).[9]

At the same time, the two countries have inter-governmental systems that differ in important ways (Table 6.1). Kenya has both a provincial/district system

Table 6.1 Structure of decentralization in Kenya and Uganda

	Kenya	*Uganda*
Structure of subnational government	Deconcentrated provincial/district system reports to central government; separate elected local governments (LG—municipal, town, urban and county councils)	Elected local governments (districts and four levels below, separate municipalities in urban areas); no separate, competing system of subnational administration
Subnational government fiscal role	LGs make 6% of public expenditures and generate 5% of revenues; provinces/districts dominate subnational expenditures	LGs make 28% of public expenditures and generate 8% of public revenues
Subnational expenditures	Local services and infrastructure; social services (health and education) in a few colonial-era municipalities	Social services (health and education); some infrastructure and local services
Subnational own-source revenues	Provinces/districts under central budget; LGs have property tax, user charges, licenses, agricultural cess (rural); mixed performance	Graduated personal tax, property tax, user charges, licenses; generally weak performance
Inter-governmental tax sharing	Personal income tax (instituted fiscal year 2000 to replace local authority service charge)	None (all transfers are allocated by formulae)
Inter-governmental transfers	Block transfers (formula-based distribution of a share of the personal income tax share)	Recurrent unconditional, equalization, conditional (separate formulae); in practice, substantial restrictions on all transfer use; separate capital transfers unconditional but largely donor-funded
Subnational borrowing	Once significant via LG Loans Authority, now virtually gone because of poor performance	None
Central oversight agencies	Ministry of Local Government; Ministry of Finance	Ministry of Local Government; Ministry of Finance, Planning and Economic Development
Subnational autonomy	LGs relatively empowered, but some central control over revenues and sectors and some reform conditions placed on use of new transfers	Strong legally for expenditures, but weaker in practice owing to restrictions on LG budgeting/ use of "unconditional" transfers; weak revenue autonomy
Subnational capacity	Mixed across urban and rural	Mixed across levels, generally better in urban areas
Donor role in decentralizing	Longstanding system with ongoing reform of various types both donor and domestic driven	Home grown but donor influence and financing became more substantial after basic framework developed

that reports to the center (deconcentration) *and* a semi-independent system of elected local authorities (devolution). The provinces/districts and local governments have separate planning and budgeting systems, as explained below. In contrast, Uganda's subnational government activity functions through a unified system of elected authorities at district level, which has primary local planning and budgeting responsibility, and four elected lower levels.

The relative importance and fiscal independence of elected local governments vary considerably. In Kenya they account for less than 6 percent of expenditures and raise about 5 percent of revenues (in 2000). (This excludes provinces and districts, which are incorporated under the national budget.) In Uganda, they account for 28 percent of expenditures (in 2000), but they raise less than 8 percent of revenues.[10]

Local governments in both cases have major responsibilities for infrastructure (roads, water, and so on), although exact functions depend to some extent on higher-level decisions, local capacity and rural versus urban location. In Kenya, only a few large colonial-era municipalities provide social services (health and education)—these are mostly covered by the deconcentrated system outlined above and NGOs. In Uganda, local governments have legal responsibility for health and education, but many have been unable to deliver services adequately owing to capacity constraints and subnational accountability problems that are not unexpected in an immature local democratic environment. Weak performance in local service delivery led to the imposition of new conditions on local government use of inter-governmental transfers (discussed below), reducing subnational autonomy.

The two countries have dissimilar local revenue structures. Kenya has relied heavily on property rates and, from the late 1980s, a local authority service charge (LASC) that was abolished in 2000 and replaced by an inter-governmental transfer system (explained below). In Uganda, the major local revenue (and dominant outside Kampala, accounting on average for 70 percent of local revenues) is the graduated personal tax (GPT), an unusual and complex hybrid of a PAYE income tax, a presumptive income tax, a wealth tax and a poll tax. Uganda local governments have access to the property tax, but few use it effectively, and it is significant only in large cities. Both countries use various local fees, licenses and other minor revenues.

Finally, the two countries use different approaches to inter-governmental transfers. After post-colonial recentralization, Kenya eliminated all transfers except limited education grants to a few municipalities and small grants to poor councils. A new transfer system was adopted in fiscal year 2000. This has initially accounted for about 11 to 12 percent of local revenues, and it is largely earmarked for development expenditures. Uganda has three types of recurrent transfer: block, equalization and conditional. The system is not fully implemented, but it already represents nearly 24 percent of the national budget and an average of nearly 80 percent of local government revenues (less in urban municipalities). A separate transfer system discussed below is devoted to subnational development expenditures and is directly linked to the local government planning process.

In summary, Kenyan local governments, which in effect compete with deconcentrated central administrative units, account for a smaller percentage of public activity than those in Uganda, and Uganda's local governments have stronger constitutional and legal powers. In practice, however, Kenyan local governments are subject to fewer restrictions since the recent imposition of conditions on the use of inter-governmental transfers in Uganda, and they have historically been considerably less financially dependent on the center.

Overview of the planning systems

Planning has been a government activity in both Kenya and Uganda since the colonial period. Although the countries, as noted above, took different paths after independence, both continue to prepare medium-term national plans that have evolved in purpose and form with international planning conventions. Major differences in subnational political and institutional structures, however, have resulted in dissimilar decentralized planning mechanisms.

Kenya has a bifurcated system of subnational planning that reflects the dichotomy between the deconcentrated provincial/district system and the semi-autonomous elected local authority system summarized above.[11] National development planning conducted under the Ministry of Planning and National Development (MPND) reaches down to the administrative units at provincial and district level. Provincial and District Development Plans (PDPs and DDPs) are prepared under the direction of MPND field staff. The subnational process, however, is essentially simultaneous with the national process, such that it neither flows directly from the national plan nor substantially influences it. At all levels, there is only a weak linkage to the annual budgeting process. Participation is largely limited to deliberations of District Development Committees (DDCs), which are chaired by a District Commissioner (DC) appointed by the office of the president. DDC membership is dominated by district-level staff of national ministries, with only a few representatives from elected local governments and local NGOs based in the district.[12]

The local government planning system is essentially separate. Local Authority Development Plans (LADPs) were initiated in the early 1980s by the Ministry of Local Government (MLG) to program donor funding for local government investments. "Coordination" with the DDP is limited to the empowerment of DDCs to approve LADP projects. As with DDPs, LADPs are poorly linked to local budgets, and formal popular participation mechanisms are weak and essentially voluntary. A separate Local Authority Service Delivery Action Plan (LASDAP) was initiated in 2000 to allocate resources from the new transfer program noted above, providing a partial linkage to the local budget and mandating participatory planning, but it is in effect independent of the LADP.

Uganda has a unified subnational planning system anchored at the district council and financed by dedicated funding allocations.[13] Levels of government below that (there are four additional levels, the lowest of which is the village) have a less formal planning process that feeds into the formulation of DDPs. Thus, Ugandan DDPs, unlike those in Kenya, are linked to elected local governments, with no parallel deconcentrated administrative units or plans. Planning-process supervision comes from a single national agency, the MLG, and participatory planning mechanisms are more clearly elaborated than in Kenya. DDPs have evolved over time, both in terms of technical content and connection to citizens, with considerable support from international donors and pressure in some areas from NGOs and community-based organizations. There are, however, substantial limitations to the system, as discussed below.

Assessing the planning systems in the larger inter-governmental reform context

Both Kenya and Uganda show strengths and weaknesses in their approach to decentralization and subnational planning. These in part derive from differences in basic context. Kenya is trying to revitalize existing and legally empowered, but long semi-dysfunctional local governments, whereas Uganda is trying to develop a new system to replace what was destroyed during turbulent times between the 1960s and 1980s.

Kenya

Kenya's local government revitalization efforts are still in a relatively early stage.[14] Many reforms adopted to date are technocratic in nature, and they do not directly improve citizen engagement. Many of them, however, are important for good governance because they promote rule-based, transparent behavior on the part of local governments and help to clarify the rights of citizens to place demands on their elected councils.

A key achevement has been an increase in the willingness of the central government to reduce control over local governments. Particularly noteworthy in this area is the gradual movement to transform the main role of the MLG from control and regulation to technical assistance and performance-enhancement support.

Major inter-governmental fiscal reforms have also been underway since the late 1990s. The Ministry of Finance (MOF) has been harmonizing problematic central and local revenues,[15] and objectively defined inter-governmental transfers, as noted above, have been re-established. The Local Authority Transfer Fund (LATF) is legally required to be capitalized with 5 percent of personal income taxes.[16] Allocations have been below that to date, but the fund has grown annually; a special Treasury account was created to protect LATF funds; a broad-based advisory committee led by non-governmental actors was formed to manage transfers, and clear fund disbursement rules have been issued.

The government has instituted significant measures to enhance local authority revenue generation and financial management. The initial effort is on property rates, the uniquely local source with the greatest unmet potential. The Rates Administration Management System (RAMS), which initially involves updating of fiscal cadastres and appropriately simple computer-assisted mass appraisal systems, is being piloted and will eventually be replicated across the country. An Integrated Financial Management System (IFMS) is being developed to enhance procedures and incentives for recurrent and capital budgeting, cash-flow management, and revenue and expenditure control. Other efforts to improve internal auditing and local employment management are being designed and tested.

Finally, there is an atypical degree of effort to integrate reforms. The property rates reform is being carried out with complementary financial management reforms. The LATF replaced the administratively difficult and politically unpopular Local Authority Service Charge and is being implemented along with central/local revenue harmonization reforms, thereby improving the overall inter-governmental revenue system. The transfer formula provides incentives for improved revenue generation and, unusually, also requires the adoption of managerial and operational reforms. All of these efforts are embedded in the broad-based Kenya Local Government Reform Program (KLGRP), which is also supporting efforts to build local accountability and capacity.

Despite these noteworthy technical and bureaucratic reforms to strengthen local governments, the problematic planning system outlined above has received scant attention. The bifurcated provincial administration–local government system persists, with continued poor coordination between DDPs and LADPs/LASDAPs. Ongoing efforts to merge subnational administration and government through constitutional reform have not yet gained political traction. Both systems produce plans that are closer to wish lists than true development plans because of the weak linkage to a budget envelope/resource constraint, a key basis for meaningful planning; in addition, there is also a poor linkage to the budget cycle, such that project priorities are often defined too late to be funded.

The Kenyan system is particularly deficient with respect to citizen engagement. Local elections have become more competitive in recent years, and this may contribute to a broad ability of the public to remove non-responsive politicians from office. Planning, however, suffers from weak participatory mechanisms, and the development of civil society to drive more meaningful participation from below is hampered by central regulation and is highly uneven across the country, although some potentially promising improvements have been documented.[17] With respect to DDPs, there is a process for villages to make project requests up through sub-locations and locations to the DDCs, but lower levels have poor DDC representation and no effective recourse if ignored. At the local government level, the LADP seems to have become almost irrelevant. The LASDAP mandates participation and has been formalized with better guidelines and support in recent years, but the quality of participation and the performance of the process have not yet been well evaluated.[18]

Uganda

The relatively robust inter-governmental framework—and the fact that it was prepared with support from donors only when requested by the government—is a strong achievement in the developing-country context. Despite the positive features outlined above, serious problems remain.[19] Although decentralization enjoys a strong legal basis, implementation was poorly planned. Too many functions were officially transferred simultaneously to local governments. In practice, decentralization in some sectors has been slow because reluctant ministries have impeded progress. In others, ministries attempting to comply with the law devolved functions too rapidly and overwhelmed limited local capacity. Moreover, coordination of the multiple, complex aspects of reform has been difficult—a now defunct Decentralization Secretariat was set up under MLG, which is not a sufficiently powerful ministry to play a coordination role. In the absence of effective leadership and in response to the often poor performance of weak local governments in service provision, the Ministry of Finance, Planning and Economic Development (MFPED) began to play a stronger role. Restrictions were placed on the use of "unconditional" inter-governmental transfers, as noted above, and stronger financial oversight was adopted. These actions have probably contributed to improved upward accountability (in terms of enforcing financial responsibility and local government support of national poverty reduction strategy objectives/Millennium Development Goals), but they have surely compromised decentralization and local autonomy.

Other important concerns relate to the structure of decentralization reforms. Formal efforts have focused exclusively on recurrent budgets, probably as a result of limited government resources for local development spending rather than as part of a reform strategy to get one major part of the budget functioning before decentralizing the other. International donors took responsibility for developing local capital "budgets," but, as explained below, in ways that created significant problems as well as supporting noteworthy reform. Another key concern is the heavy emphasis given to developing inter-governmental transfers relative to improving own-source revenues. Local revenues have performed poorly under decentralization—transfers still dominate (typically above 80 percent of local revenues outside a few municipalities).

Conditions on the use of transfers and poor own-source revenue performance limit the ability of local governments to respond directly to locally expressed needs, and, in the relatively immature governance environment of Uganda, the resources that are available are often captured by local elites and used for patronage purposes.[20] Indeed, despite progress, linkages between the development of local administration and the development of local democracy remain limited. Participation and other accountability mechanisms have been formally adopted, and citizen awareness and levels of engagement are certainly improving. Genuine civil society empowerment with respect to local governments, however, needs to evolve at the grassroots level and still requires extensive non-governmental and external support.[21]

These general decentralization issues have great implications for planning in Uganda, all the more so as development planning has essentially been a separate, donor-dependent exercise. The system originated with a small pilot Local Development Fund (LDF) financed by the UN Capital Development Fund[22] under the District Development Program (DDPR). The DDPR provided districts with small, unconditional transfers for local public investments that had to be developed through participatory planning and service delivery processes supported by well-designed and -resourced capacity building and performance incentives. The success of this initiative led to the development of the much larger Local Government Development Program (LGDP), an umbrella program funded by World Bank loans and other donor support. LGDP has replaced the original DDPR and has been mainstreamed across local governments.

LGDP has in many respects been very successful in funding development expenditures within a true, budget-constrained planning framework, in building some local capacity, and in adopting and enforcing an element of meaningful participation and performance review from above and below. This development planning mechanism, however, remains entirely separate from the recurrent budget. Thus, the restrictive budgeting regulations introduced by MFPED (noted above) have considerably reduced local government flexibility for programming recurrent resources to finance the operating expenses of new infrastructure developed through the district planning process. This situation, in turn, further exacerbates the above-noted constraints on the ability of local governments to be accountable to their constituents, even if local civil society is powerful in a particular jurisdiction and local officials genuinely wish to be responsive.

Concluding comments

Relative to many African countries, Kenya and Uganda have made solid progress with recent decentralization and local government reforms. Major problems remain, but both countries have improved at least some elements of their local government and decentralized planning systems. The development of an empowered civil society has been more elusive, but progress has been made even in this challenging area, mostly through activities beyond the scope of the central government-led decentralization reforms covered here. Table 6.2 summarizes key features of the planning systems in the two countries.

How do the Kenyan and Ugandan systems measure up to the three broad principles for subnational planning effectiveness outlined above in the introduction? Neither is fully *linked to the larger government system* of planning, resourcing, budgeting and implementation. Uganda has a relatively strong system for local development planning and financing, but it remains somewhat isolated as a donor-supported effort and needs to be institutionalized in a way that is consistent with broader decentralization reforms. The weak linkage of the DDP to the recurrent budget, generally poor local revenue generation, and the imposition of central restrictions on the use of "unconditional" recurrent transfers collectively raise concerns over the ability of local governments to be genuinely responsive to their constituents and to sustain the operation of infrastructure resulting from the local development planning process.

The Kenya situation is different, but even more problematic, with a stark bifurcation and lack of functional clarity between the district administration and local authority governance and bureaucratic processes, including the DDP and LADP. This situation creates possibilities for redundancy between the two systems and for potentially significant resource allocation inefficiencies. It also undermines basic accountability linkages to local citizens, who have little influence over district activities and are also unclear about what they can legitimately demand from their elected local officials. A further major concern is that LADPs are inadequately resourced and remain more like "wish lists" than true development plans. One potentially promising improvement is the linkage established between the recently adopted LASDAP and the resources provided by the new LATF. The status of LADP relative to LASDAP, however, has not been clarified.

The systems are mixed in terms of having the *institutionalized capacity to perform their functions.* The Ugandan decentralization reforms are relatively new, and so capacity development has been a major challenge in many areas. In terms of financial capacity, the Ugandan DDP has its own, relatively discretionary budget allocation for development expenditures. These resources, however, are largely externally funded, and own source revenues are extremely weak, so that the financial sustainability of the system is far from certain. In terms of other areas, there have been extensive support activities and incentives imbedded in the planning system in order gradually to develop human resource capacity and improve performance, including capacity building grants to local governments that are unable to meet preconditions for receiving development funding allocations. Many Ugandan local governments, however, started relatively recently from a weak

Table 6.2 Decentralized planning in Kenya and Uganda

	Kenya	*Uganda*
Planning levels	National/provincial/district (DDP); LADP; and new LASDAP linked to transfers	National and district (DDP) with informal planning below districts (down to village level)
Supervision and support	Ministry of Planning and National Development supervises provincial/district plans; Ministry of Local Government supports LADP/LASDAP	Ministry of Local Government supervises and supports DDPs, the only subnational development plans
Integration and coordination	Province/district plans integrated but not well timed to national plans or coordinated with budgets; LADP/LASDAP separate from DDP	National plan separate; DDPs subject to central guidance, but fairly autonomous; main issue is separation of subnational budgeting and planning
Capacity	Human resource capacity varies and capacity building limited; fiscal capacity relatively strong	Human resource capacity weak but growing and fairly well supported; fiscal capacity relatively weak
Participation	Limited and informal, but increasing through civil society pressure and LASDAP process	Substantial but uneven and not directly binding; in some areas substantial donor or NGO support for participation
Civil society	Relatively long history of NGOs, community-based organizations and fund raising for community projects, but subject to central regulation and uneven across the country	Civil society greatly weakened during extended periods of conflict; improving but still limited, and unable to function in areas of continuing conflict
Noteworthy feature(s)	Failure to blend deconcentrated and devolved subnational units and plans (DDP vs LADP/LASDAP) despite long history of local government	Strong commitment in a low capacity environment, but some serious problems, especially the division between recurrent and capital budgets and heavy donor dependence for latter

base, and there is still a long way to go before the human resource capacity needed to perform reliably is broadly in place.

Kenyan local governments have been functioning for much longer, so that more of them have at least a minimum of technical and administrative capacity. They also have stronger sources of recurrent local revenue and are much less dependent on resources transferred from the central government. They do not, however, have independent resources for development activities beyond the LATF allocations, which often get diverted for other purposes, and the central government devotes most of its development resources to the separate provincial/district planning system. As LADP priorities often remain unimplemented, there has been little incentive to develop further the type of capacity needed for effective local government development planning. There is some reason for hope that the introduction of LATF/LASDAP linkages could begin to turn this situation around, but this is not yet clear.

The *governance systems underlying the planning process* must be given mixed reviews. Democratic, relatively competitive (although not multi-party in Uganda) local elections are now conducted in both countries, and some evidence of councilor turnover between election cycles suggests a basic public appreciation of the meaning of the vote. However, in both cases, colonial experiences certainly did not encourage inclusive local governance, and local elite capture has been a significant ongoing problem in the post-colonial and recent reform periods.

Ongoing government efforts to broaden civic participation in development planning are potentially important and more serious than past participation schemes. Uganda is more advanced than Kenya in providing formal avenues for participatory planning and budgeting, but implementation remains problematic, in part owing to the technical and capacity issues raised above and in part owing to the still limited strength of civil society. Kenya's introduction of the LASDAP is a positive step, but the degree of its inclusiveness and influence has not been adequately studied. In both countries, weaknesses in civil society hamper genuine and adequately influential participation.

It is not possible to draw definitive or comprehensive conclusions from this broad overview of two highly complex reforms, but it is clear that Kenya and Uganda still suffer from significant weaknesses in their subnational planning systems. In a technical sense, many of these problems can be relatively easily fixed, and specific needs in this respect are indicated or implied in the analysis provided above. Additional work is needed to explain more fully the political dynamics that have facilitated the development and obstructed the correction of these weaknesses in the system and to inform the development of potential steps towards improving the situation that could be undertaken realistically within prevailing political and institutional constraints. At the same time, it is critical to emphasize that the reform of formal institutional structures and processes for subnational planning will not be sufficient to realize the potential benefits of decentralization.

Independent, more locally grounded and often externally supported efforts to develop civic awareness and governance capacity are also needed.

Decentralization is clearly a complex process, and the various reform efforts intended to create an appropriate intergovernmental system and to empower local citizens will require time to take root, interact and produce broader improvements in governance. Moreover, the specific steps to further reform are context-dependent. Kenya and Uganda, despite their proximity and some important similarities, also have considerable differences in terms of institutional and political realities, paths in public sector decentralization reform, and degrees of citizen empowerment. These differences need to be reflected in future efforts to improve the subnational planning system and to build a stronger and more engaged citizenry.

Notes

1   The evolution of planning is reviewed, for example, in: Conyers and Hills (1984); Healy (1997); Ingham (1993); Rodwin and Sanyal (2000); and Sundaram (1997).
2   Decentralization trends are reviewed, for example, in World Bank (1999; 2005).
3   Much of the literature is reviewed, for example, in: Bardhan and Mookerjee (2006); Cheema and Rondinelli (2007); Litvack *et al.* (1998); Smoke (2001); and Smoke *et al.* (2006).
4   Much has been written about these issues, either broadly regarding decentralization or more specifically with respect to development planning. The extensive literature includes many of the references provided in notes 1–3 above. It is not possible to include a comprehensive review of the literature here, but ideas from it will be incorporated in the review of the two countries considered in the rest of the paper.
5   African decentralization is reviewed, for example, in: Millet *et al.* (2006); Smoke (2003a); UNCDF (2002); UNDESA (2005); and Wunsch and Olowu (2003).
6   See Smoke (1993; 1994; 2003b) and Steffensen *et al.* (2004) for details on the evolution of Kenya's local government system.
7   See Francis and James (2003); Government of Uganda (2001); Onyach-Olaa (2003); and Steffensen *et al.* (2004) for more information on decentralization in Uganda.
8   Francis and James (2003) provide a useful discussion of Museveni's "non-party" system, known as the National Resistance Movement.
9   Data were taken from country budget documents and the *IMF Government Finance Statistics Yearbook*.
10   Ugandan data include only recurrent expenditures, as the development budget is not formally decentralized.
11   The system is summarized in Cohen and Peterson (1999) and Government of Kenya (2005).
12   This system emerged under the District Focus for Rural Development Strategy (DFRD) of 1983, a reform portrayed as returning "power to the people" in response to a coup d'état attempt. Many critics, however, saw DFRD as an attempt to reinforce central control and further weaken local governments.
13   Onyach-Olaa (2003) summarizes the system.
14   See Smoke (2003b) and Steffensen *et al.* (2004) for a summary of recent Kenyan reforms and the Kenya Local Government Reform Program.

15   Devas and Kelly (2001) provide details on business licensing harmonization reform.
16   Local Authority Transfer Fund Law, Government of Kenya, Law No. 8 of 1998.
17   For useful discussions of civil society development in Kenya, see Nyamu-Musembi and Musyoki (2004) and Orvis (2003).
18   See Government of Kenya (2005) for more details on LASDAP.
19   See Smoke (2002) and Steffensen *et al.* (2004) for more information on Ugandan local government reforms and the LGDP.
20   Francis and James provide an interesting discussion on what they call a dual-mode system of "technocratic" and "patronage" driven governance in Uganda, and they also provide a more general review of developments in local democracy and participation.
21   Assessments of the state of civil society in Uganda and efforts to support its development are provided in DENIVA (2006), Robinson and Friedman (2005) and Thue *et al.* (2002).
22   See Romeo (1996) on the LDF and Onyach-Olaa (2003) for details of the Ugandan experience.

References

Bardhan, P. and D. Mookerjee (eds) (2006) *Decentralization and Local Governance in Developing Countries: A Comparative Perspective*, Cambridge, MA: MIT Press.

Cheema, G.S. and Rondinelli, D. (eds) (2007) *Decentralized Governance: Emerging Concepts and Practices*, Washington, DC: Brookings.

Cohen, J. and Peterson, S. (1999) *Administrative Decentralization in Developing Countries*, Boulder, CO: Lynne Reinner.

Conyers, D. and Hills, P. (1984) *An Introduction to Development Planning in the Third World*, Chichester: John Wiley & Sons.

Devas, N. and Kelly, R. (2001) "Regulation or revenues: Analysis of local business licenses, with a case study of the single business permit in Kenya," *Public Administration and Development* 21 (5): 381–91.

Development Network of Indigenous Voluntary Associations (DENIVA) and CIVICUS World Alliance for Citizen Participation (2006) *Civil Society in Uganda: At the Crossroads?*, Kampala: DENIVA.

Francis, P. and James, R. (2003) "Balancing Rural Poverty Reduction and Citizen Participation: The Contradictions of Uganda's Decentralization Program," *World Development* 31 (2): 325–37.

Government of Kenya (2005) "Guidelines for the preparation, implementation and monitoring of local authority service delivery action plan," Nairobi: Ministry of Local Government.

Government of Uganda (2001) "Fiscal decentralization in Uganda: Draft strategy paper," Kampala: Decentralization Coordination Group.

Healey, P. (1997) *Collaborative Planning*, Vancouver, BC: University of British Columbia Press.

Ingham, B. (1993) "The meaning of development: Interactions between 'new' and 'old' ideas," *World Development* 21 (11): 1803–21.

Litvack, J., Ahmad, J. and Bird, R. (1998) *Rethinking Decentralization in Developing Countries*, Washington, DC: World Bank.

Millet, K., Olowu, D. and Cameron, R. (2006) *Local Governance for Poverty Reduction in Africa*, Tunis: Joint Africa Institute.

Nyamu-Musembi, C. and Musyoki, S. (2004) "Kenya civil society: Perspectives on rights-based approaches to development and participation," IDS Working Paper No. 236, Brighton: Institute of Development Studies, University of Sussex.

Onyach-Olaa, M. (2003) "The challenges of implementing decentralization: Recent experiences in Uganda," *Public Administration and Development* 23 (1): 105–13.

Orvis, S. (2003) "Kenyan civil society: Bridging the rural–urban divide," *Journal of Modern African Studies* 41: 247–68.

Robinson, M. and Friedman, S. (2005) "Civil society, democracy and foreign aid in Africa," IDS Working Paper No. 383, Brighton: Institute of Development Studies, University of Sussex.

Rodwin, L. and Sanyal, B. (eds) (2000) *The Profession of City Planning: Changes, Images and Challenges*, New Brunswick, NJ: Center for Urban Policy Research, Rutgers University.

Romeo L. (1996) *Local Development Funds: Promoting Decentralized Participatory and Planning and Finance*, New York: United Nations Capital Development Fund.

Smoke, P. (1993) "Local government fiscal reform in developing countries: Lessons from Kenya," *World Development* 21 (6): 901–23.

Smoke, P. (1994) *Local Government Finance in Developing Countries: The Case of Kenya*, Oxford University Press.

Smoke, P. (2001) *Fiscal Decentralization in Developing Countries: A Review of Current Concepts and Practice*, Geneva: United Nations Research Institute for Social Development.

Smoke, P. (2002) "Fiscal decentralization in east and southern Africa: A selective review of experience and thoughts on moving forward," prepared for the International Monetary Fund.

Smoke, P. (2003a) "Decentralization in Africa: Goals, dimensions, myths and challenges," *Public Administration and Development* 23 (1): 1–17.

Smoke, P. (2003b) "Erosion and reform from the center in Kenya," in J. Wunsch and D. Olowu (eds) *Local Governance in Africa: The Challenge of Decentralization*, Boulder, CO: Lynne Reinner.

Smoke, P., Gomez, E. and Peterson, G. (eds) (2006) *Decentralization in Asia and Latin America: Towards a Comparative Interdisciplinary Perspective*, Chichester: Edward Elgar.

Steffensen, J., Naitore, H. and Tideman, P. (2004) "A comparative analysis of decentralization in Kenya, Tanzania and Uganda," Report by Nordic Consulting Group for the World Bank.

Sundaram, K.V. (1997) *Decentralized Multilevel Planning: Principles and Practice*, New Delhi: Concept Publishing Company.

Thue, N., Makubuye, A. and Nakirunda, N. (2002) *Report of a Study on the Civil Society in Uganda*, Kampala: Norwegian Agency for Development (NORAD), Royal Norwegian Embassy.

United Nations Capital Development Fund (UNCDF) (2002) *Decentralization and Local Governance in Africa: Proceedings from the Cape Town Symposium*, New York: UNCDF.

United Nations Department for Economic and Social Affairs (UNDESA) (2005) *Decentralized Governance*, New York: UNDESA.

World Bank (1999) *Entering the 21st Century: 1999–2000 World Development Report*, Washington, DC: World Bank.

World Bank (2005) *Decentralization in East Asia and the Pacific: Making Local Government Work*, Washington, DC: World Bank.

Wunsch, J. and Olowu, D. (eds) (2003) *Local Governance in Africa: The Challenge of Decentralization*, Boulder, CO: Lynne Reinner.

Chapter 7

Decentralization and planning in Vietnam's water sector

Community level privatization in the Mekong Delta

James H. Spencer

This chapter reviews some of the existing literature on urban water supply in developing countries that points towards the importance of PPPs and decentralization in financing and planning urban water systems, as well as to the dependence of these relationships on local leadership. It then describes an innovative system of local water service delivery developed in a rapidly urbanizing area of Vietnam to illustrate how decentralization and market reform have stimulated innovative state, private-sector and community partnerships in the absence of large-scale external capital investment in water supply. This case calls for a better understanding on the part of planners of how decentralization and market reform may affect the provision of basic urban services—especially in the fast-developing areas of Asia —as well as pointing out alternative ways in which "community" planning might be defined. In particular, it calls for an examination of the relationship between community residents and profit-motivated community entrepreneurial activities surrounding public goods provision. By doing so, this chapter suggests that, under the conditions of weak private-sector community structures, community planning may actually be the privatization of social responsibilities to community-based individuals.

The field of urban planning has long focused on studies of housing, social policy, transportation, economic development and other areas in which urban spatial configurations influence state responsibilities for the provision of public goods. Such studies have frequently had important planning and policy implications that incorporate both market principles and state incentives and regulation. Much of this literature has focused on industrial countries, where basic public infrastructure is already in place and current issues focus on *efficiency, maintenance* and *water source protection* (e.g. Dziegielewski and Baumann 1992; Platt 1995; Sauri 2003), rather than the *creation* of water systems able to support urban centers to accommodate urban lifestyles. Where there is attention paid by planners to the creation of water supply systems in industrial countries is in areas undergoing rapid growth and urbanization, such as the western American states (Hanak and Browne 2006). Thus—with a few notable exceptions (e.g. Crane 1994; Crane *et al.* 1997) —the field has not been strong on urban water supply in developing countries. However, in poor countries currently experiencing an urban transition, the creation of new water supply systems is a central urban need requiring further examination from a spatial planning perspective.

What planning literature does exist on water supply in developing countries suggests that analysis of residential water use is limited to those places where urban growth has accelerated rapidly, such as in Beijing and Tianjin, China, where urban growth has boomed since the 1980s (Zhang and Brown 2005) or in Kenya, where informal rural–urban migration has placed massive demands on existing urban water infrastructure (Gulyani et al. 2005). It is such conditions of rapid urban development—especially in Asia and Africa—that call for a better understanding of the relative strength of municipal governments, through urban consolidation and decentralization, to make decisions independent of national objectives (Laquian 2005a).

The decentralization literature has examined water supply in developing cities and generally found that greater municipal autonomy through decentralization can lead to improvements in urban water supply (Memon et al. 2006), and that a lack of decentralized authority can be a barrier to improved water supply (Haq 2006). Such improvements, however, do have costs, as seen in the creation of tensions between municipal and central authorities (Beyer 2006; Laquian 2005b) and should not be seen as simply the result of the superiority of local decisions over non-local ones (Purcell and Brown 2005; Asthana 2003). What seem to be most important to the success of such decentralization initiatives in rapidly developing urban areas are trust and meaningful community-level participation in decision-making (Lemos and De Oliveira 2005).

Many efforts to provide greater municipal autonomy in the provision of water supply, however, are linked to larger market reforms calling for PPPs in financing water supply (e.g. Sahooly 2003), which comprise the bulk of the literature on water supply in developing countries.

Because it is a public good, often seen as a natural monopoly, the question of domestic water and sanitation provision is embedded within the larger question of the appropriate role of the state and differences in these roles at different administrative levels. Research on the variety of complex institutional structures dominating the water sector in industrial countries has sparked important debates on the *Pareto-optimal* structure for state–private relations of water production in Europe and other wealthy nations (Warner and Bel forthcoming). Such institutional analyses of water provision in developing countries, however, have not yet adequately explored administrative structures and how rapid urbanization, global integration and the creation of new water infrastructure have evolved in poor countries. In many developing countries, the state has difficulty providing adequate services such as water, especially in the low-wealth countries of sub-Saharan Africa and Asia. In such countries, privatization and market reform are a question of development finance, rather than simply one of making a public service more efficient.

The literature on privatization in water provision suggests that it can either increase or decrease access to clean water (Budds and McGranahan 2003; Olmstead 2003). Since the 1980s, international institutions have promoted the privatization and market allocation of water, suggesting that it should be treated as a commodity subject to private competition in its provision and management (Nickson 1996, 1998). However, there is little evidence supporting the hypothesis that the private sector is more efficient at providing clean water access to citizens. Empirical studies show that public enterprises are no less efficient at providing water than private ones (Lobina and Hall 2000), and that private and public entities both fail to provide adequate services to the poor and those most in need of clean water (Budds and McGranahan 2003). Such findings, however, also suggest that privatization does not serve to disenfranchise a previously empowered poor (Olmstead 2003), but that the debates about privatization of the water supply may not be as important as other socio-political developments (O'Riordan 2003) such as spatial scale. There are few studies, however, of small-scale private-sector providers of water; what literature exists on water and sanitation services in the developing world focuses on corporate privatization, leaving other forms of state–private sector–civil society partnerships relatively unexamined.

Places where decentralization is combining with market reform and privatization provide interesting case studies of new institutional arrangements in the developing world surrounding water supply. Because there is mutual suspicion between non-market states and corporate investors in the water sector, municipalities in such contexts are environments within which alternative forms of private-sector participation have space to evolve. Such conditions exist in Vietnam, where the post-socialist transition state is undergoing reform of state-owned enterprises (e.g. Knutsen and Nguyen 2004), trade integration (e.g. Arkadie and Mallon 2003) and the rapidly growing need to finance urban infrastructure.

The case of water supply in Can Tho City, in the Mekong Delta of Vietnam, is illustrative of how the implementation of privatization and decentralization efforts can create unexpected institutional forms based on local leadership, community-level entrepreneurs and complex forms of state–community collaboration.

Community-level water entrepreneurs in a transitional setting: the case of Can Tho

The linked processes of privatization and decentralization in Vietnam have somewhat unique characteristics that have prompted new institutional forms as they are implemented within a strongly socialist state. The two trends are liberalizing forces rather than conservative ones. Since 1986, Vietnam has followed a strategy of reducing state management of the economy while maintaining control over basic flows of information and politics, which has been well described elsewhere (e.g. Arkadie and Mallon 2003). Termed *Doi Moi*, this strategy was developed with the intention of helping the country make a gradual transition to a market economy without the political turmoil and uncertainty associated with the free market. Land reform and the establishment of secure property rights were early steps in *Doi Moi* that have been associated with significant increases in agricultural and industrial production, as well as a boom in construction, services and other private-sector enterprises. A second shift enabled by *Doi Moi* was the opening up of state-owned enterprises to competition and possible dissolution if they are not able to compete. This process has led to significant turmoil, corruption and management changes in much of Vietnam's industry (Gainsborough 1998). To date, however, water management has not been treated as a wholly private-sector enterprise, and many Vietnamese water companies, while being opened up to market-based management regimes, remain protected by the state in a way not done for industrial products and manufacturing (Fontenelle 2003). Moreover, in the Mekong Delta region of Vietnam, local community structures—another form of social regulation (O'Rourke 2003)—have historically been weaker than in other parts of the country (Beresford 2003; Li 1998; Luong 2003).

Evidence from Can Tho, however, suggests that state protection may be weakening, creating new opportunities for corruption. This protection is in part due to a vision of clean water as a right rather than a commodity, and in part due to the fact that, in very rapidly urbanizing countries and in transition economies, urban water provision cannot be assumed to be a natural monopoly. In 2004, the Vietnamese National Assembly developed a strategy to turn Can Tho City into the fifth municipality in the country and invest in infrastructure that would turn it into a regional growth pole for the Mekong Delta. In effect, this strategy divorced the City of Can Tho from Can Tho Province and significantly increased its governmental autonomy. The decision had several important material outcomes. First, it meant that the national government would prioritize the construction of major infrastructure for Can Tho City that would link it more directly to external markets. Thus, for example, an international airport is to be constructed in Can Tho over the next several years, and the final section of a major highway linking Can Tho to Ho Chi Minh City, the country's most dynamic economic center, is likely to be completed within two years, despite a delay because of a major accident in late 2007 prior to its completion date. More locally, the plans mean that every ward in Can Tho must have a market to facilitate local trading, and the City's population is planned to grow from about 1.3 million in 2004 to about 3 million by 2010. This doubling of the size of the city in six years will bring major changes to the current residents of Can Tho. One such change is the way that residents secure clean water and sanitation.

There is currently no centralized water system serving the whole city, other than that serving a small neighborhood in the central part of the city. Before 2000, most water for domestic use was, as is common practice throughout the Mekong Delta, taken from the extensive rivers and canals, as well as from rain catchment off roofs (Le 2003). Some residents had wells they had dug themselves, but these wells usually only lasted a short period before they became polluted by groundwater contaminated with agricultural runoff and human waste. In 1989–90, UNICEF had co-financed a number of deeper wells dug 80 meters below the surface, but residents say that, when the equipment broke down, no one was able fix the wells, and they fell into disuse. Thus, Can Tho faces a major challenge in the provision of adequate water and sanitation services if its population is to roughly double in size, and if it is to make a rapid shift from a rural water system to an urban one over the next six years.

The strategy that Can Tho has adopted is based on a kind of localized privatization scheme that fits neither into the current model of corporate participation in water services (e.g. Simonson 2003; Barlow and Clarke 2004), state-run systems (e.g. Gutierrez 2003), nor local community control and management of water resources (e.g. Yeung and McGee 1986) . Instead, it is based on a complex system of local entrepreneurs working together with an entrepreneurial state-owned enterprise above them and entrepreneurial households beneath them. This quasi-private model for water management is not obviously better or worse for local residents and in particular the poor, but the structure of the system argues for a closer examination of how decentralization leads to new institutional forms of state collaboration.

Local-level interviews with staff from the Can Tho City water company, local managers of neighborhood water stations, user households and other residents provided an overview of how the system works.

The Can Tho Center for Water Supply and Sanitation (CTCWSS) was established in 1989 with substantial support of UNICEF. It used to operate and provide support for a number of provinces surrounding Can Tho City by coordinating and assisting external funders of water supply and sanitation projects for all the communities, most of which were primarily rural at the time. UNICEF provided funds to dig wells, and manual pumps for households, while local communities provided labor, and the CTCWSS coordinated the projects. In addition to coordinating these technical aspects, the CTCWSS provided information and raised awareness of local residents about the importance of the protection of water sources, pollution and which sources of water were clean.

The CTWSS significantly expanded its scope of activities in 1998, when it began to collaborate formally with some other provinces in the Mekong Delta region to implement a small water provision network. The rationale for this approach was that, rather than provide a small well and individual pump to each household, UNICEF would support the construction of a station with a much larger well run by an electronic pump and a water filter treatment system. This solution, the center's staff believed, would solve some of the problems faced by individual households using only a small well: how to treat water properly before use and how to test its quality. Thus, new water supply stations were built in coordination with UNICEF and linked to a new network of pipes that would be able to connect each household to a central neighborhood station that could monitor and control water quality. Each station provided enough water for the daily needs of 100–150 households—a total of 5–6 m^3 of water per hour—within 1,500–2,000 m of the station. At that time, the cost of construction was about 100 m (US$6,452) Viet Nam Dong (VND) per station, which had increased to 180 m VND ($11,613) by 2005, averaging 1.2 m VND (US$77.42) per household served.

In 2000, however, owing to a reorientation of UNICEF's funding priorities, the CTCWSS lost its support, and became dependent on the Can Tho provincial budget. The rationale for this decision was that funding would be withdrawn from those areas likely to be able to mobilize internal financial resources. However, this hope was only partly realized, and, recently, the Center received some support from the World Bank as part of a larger Mekong Delta regional initiative.

In 2004, there were 358 stations in Can Tho Province, most of which had 4–6 m^3 per hour capacity, but a few had 19 m^3 per hour capacity. The CTCWSS planned to build an additional sixty stations in 2005, fifty with 4–6 m^3 capacity and ten with 10 m^3 capacity. The process for selecting which wards receive funding to provide a station is a competitive one. The CTWSS asks local ward people's committee officials to compile a set of proposals for the construction of wells in their area and justify them according to the needs of the local communities. The CTCWSS then consults with the City's Department of Planning and Investment to allocate funding. Because one of their major concerns is the pollution of natural sources, they prioritize areas subject to flooding.

The Director of the CTCWSS describes this system as one of state–community collaboration, in which the state sector invests in the primary capital, the station and the baseline pipes, and the households only need to invest in the connection from the system to the home, which includes some piping and a water meter. This model mirrors what some entrepreneurial individuals did in the past, digging smaller stations and networks of pipes, selling water to users. Such enterprises in the Mekong Delta, he believed, were only financially sustainable in densely populated areas and where residents had no alternative, natural sources to use. The wards that the CTCWSS serves, on the other hand, are in those areas recently redesignated from rural commune to urban ward. Thus, although they are part of the newly designated municipality of Can Tho, they retain much of their rural character and are unable to achieve such an economy of scale to prove profitable for water station providers. Rather, he sees the company as a "business that generates many social benefits: a better health situation and reduction in the illness rate rather than economic profits."

At the ward level, there is significant participation by officials and local residents. According to the CTCWSS director, state agencies and the local community cooperate to operate, maintain and manage the station. However, such a description takes a loose, but conceptually and spatially relevant definition of both "community" and "participation." In reality, cooperation exists between the CTCWSS, ward people's committees and a local landowner.[1] The total land required for a 4–6 m^3 station is 48 m^2, and the CTCWSS will not take action if there is no one willing to donate the land, which must be located in the center of a population cluster to provide sufficient water pressure. In addition, the person who donates the land must be willing to learn how to manage and maintain the water station. Once the station is constructed, it is the responsibility of the landowner to manage, monitor and repair the station, along with technical assistance from the CTCWSS. For this reason, although the relationship is called a community–state partnership, it is more accurately described as a PPP at the community level. The landowner invests land as capital and manages the production and distribution of water as a subcontractor for the water company in their effort to recoup costs. In the words of one of the station managers, "my contract is signed every year . . . I don't think I am a permanent staff of the company." For this service, he or she takes advantage of several incentives provided for his/her management role. Station managers sign an agreed-upon contract with the Center stipulating their incentives. The first incentive is a basic management stipend for collection of bills and payment to the CTCWSS. However, the main incentive for the land-owner lies in helping the CTCWSS recover the cost of its investments rather than in the management stipend. The CTCWSS generally loses money at the beginning of its investment owing, first, to the relatively low population density and the availability of alternative water sources. Second, users are economical with their use of piped water, especially as they are not familiar with using water meters to manage their daily use. Thus, the only stations that are profitable for the company are those where a natural monopoly exists.

In order for a station to be profitable, it must sell at least 500 m^3 per month, or between 4 and 5 m^3 per household per month. For the time being, support from the World Bank and other international donors covers the shortfall, but, once this support disappears, the CTCWSS will not be able to maintain the program. For this reason the landowners receive a second kind of incentive. The contract also encourages them to mobilize neighborhood residents to connect to the system by stating that they will receive the monetary equivalent of a cubic meter of water (roughly VND2,500, or US$0.16) for every 3 m^3 of water used through the installed meters. Thus, they will receive higher incomes the greater the number of connections into the system that they manage. Along with this incentive, however, comes the typical risk of a privately contracted subcontractor. According to one of the station managers:

> yes, I collect water fees from the users. I have to pay the bill to the company based on the numbers of cubic meters showing up on the master water meter in the station. If users for some reason have not paid their fee, I have to advance my [own] money to the company. Users [currently] owe me around VND 1.7–1.8 m (US$109–116).

Although this manager recognizes that some of these households have explanations such as a disability, when he submitted a list of the non-payers and their explanations, the CTCWSS refused to assume the debt.

The difficulty that managers have in collecting is partly due to connected households acting as secondary water station managers as well. A legal meter for a household to connect to the system costs about VND340,000 (US$21.94). However, this cost can be quite high for the poorer members of the ward, and some ward residents have connected to the system by installing semi-legal meters to their neighbors' connections. Such informal connections cost only VND22,000 (US$1.42), and in some cases three or four submeters are connected to a main, legal meter. Like the station managers, the households with submeter spokes assume a management role regarding their neighbors' domestic water, collecting payments for their use and paying out to the station manager, who in turn pays out to the City water company. These households manage their family and friends' water use through this system and sometimes provide credit when payments are burdensome for the poorer members on the spoke. However, if they are unable to collect regular payments from the spokes on their system, they may pass on the cost to the station manager through non- or under-payment.

Usage rates vary widely, with one manager stating that sixty-four of a possible 100 households had signed up to use the system, while another reported that ninety of a possible 200 had connected. In addition, interviews with several managers revealed some differences in the amounts paid out per household connected, and in the company's treatment of who assumes responsibility for non-payment. In any case, however, the station manager does take on the general financial responsibility for billing and collecting, as well as for signing up greater numbers of users.

This case of water provision in the context of a weak private sector and weak community structures suggests that the role of community planning may take the form of privatized social responsibilities at the local level.

Decentralization, market transition and changing state–society relations

Given the very tight social relationships present in Can Tho's wards, the relationship between the CTCWSS, local officials and well managers is a complex one. On the one hand, officials probably turn to well-connected and influential private residents to provide land. On the other hand, those private managers probably provide favors in water provision and other arenas to local officials, as has traditionally been the practice in southern Vietnam regarding local state officials (Li 1998). Similar to critiques of corporate privatization efforts that describe an overly cozy relationship between private providers and government regulators of water, these local and decentralized politico-economic relationships mirror close relationships between state officials and state-owned enterprises (Gainsborough 1998), and state officials and non-government organizations (Salemink 2003) in Vietnam. Contrary to findings from corporate privatization of the water sector in other developing countries, however, this tight relationship between private investors and officials has not yet led to water overpricing. In part, this is because water provision for domestic use in Can Tho is not yet a natural monopoly, thereby precluding a significant temptation for inflated water tariffs. In fact, the CTCWSS has a difficult time recouping its investment costs, farming some of that cost out to the station managers. However, as natural sources and private wells become polluted with industrialization, agricultural intensification and aquacultural development in Can Tho, these PPPs may gradually become a natural monopoly. If this environmental change does occur, then the case represents a transitional community-entrepreneurial model of privatized social responsibilities at the community scale, similar to that discussed by Crane (1994) for Indonesia.

This new transitional institutional arrangement for the provision of water supply infrastructure in Can Tho is the result of greater autonomy of municipal governments and entrepreneurs. It clearly shows that, in a nominally socialist state, market principles of private-sector participation have, paradoxically, taken a strong hold in the provision of public services. Since at least 2000, the Can Tho City Water Company, the primary provider of clean household water and sanitation, has developed a market-based, semi-privatized scheme to provide water to all the urban wards. Although somewhat successful at increasing coverage of the households within the urban wards, the changes have led to a three-tiered, semi-privatized structure that uses local entrepreneurs to manage delivery, payment and repairs, and opens multiple possibilities to increase coverage, while simultaneously opening up multiple opportunities for corruption and price-gouging in the absence of strict and enforced regulation by the City authorities, as competitive pressures within and for the ward-level water markets decrease.

It is difficult to measure whether such a system is better at providing access to clean water than a simple state-run system. Nevertheless, this illustrative story does indicate that an innovative PPP at the community level for good water supply and sanitation has been created over the past five years in Can Tho, in part due to the greater automomy offered by the City's recent designation as an independent municipality. Whether this transitional model evolves into a more stable one or not, Can Tho's attempts to provide clean, piped water to its growing population base point towards an important cautionary response to the current debates about privatization in the water sector: is the concept of privatization a robust one, where infrastructure concerns center on development finance rather than efficiency of existing systems. More specifically, to what degree are such conceptual dichotomies useful for planners and policymakers?

Concluding thoughts: recognizing community-level privatization

The main contribution of this chapter towards community planning is in its description of an evolving, potentially transitional model for water provision. In the Can Tho case, decentralization has contributed to privatization through local individuals rather than privatization through corporate entities. In doing so, it challenges some potentially important implicit assumptions about which actors represent communities, which the private sector, and which government.

The use of general descriptions of decentralized versus centralized financing, private versus public management, and community versus local, although useful as general ideal types, can often mask important ad hoc, transitional arrangements that point towards the importance of local pragmatism, leadership and institutional collaboration. The case of water provision in Can Tho does not conform neatly to a public–private dichotomy. More important for understanding water supply provision in Vietnam are the issues of scale, both geographic and organizational, that are enabled by decentralization of authority and financing. As Bakker (2003) points out, private water providers range from small water vendors to multinational corporations, and state providers range from local water coops to municipal and national corporations. From her point of view, the complexity of the organization and the scale at which it operates are central sources of variation in the alternative ways water is provided.

Figure 7.1 provides, from a water user's standpoint, a stylized scatter plot of the various institutions providing domestic water along public/private and more/less competition gradients. In doing so, it also provides a preliminary heuristic framework for a better understanding of the complexity of private and public institutions in the water sector. The general neoliberal assumption that lies behind efforts to privatize water services is represented by the dotted line running from the origin, where private entities are associated with modes of production that are more competitive, to the upper right corner, where purely state-run institutions are associated with monopolistic modes of production. From a water user's perspective, few of the institutions lie along the stereotypical relationship, let alone at either end. The City of Can Tho water company, for example, is generally monopolistic, yet only quasi-governmental, and the two subcontractor levels tend more towards private entities, yet remain somewhat monopolistic in their mode of water production. Moreover, private and state-owned bottlers also vie for the local user market and represent a production mode that is highly competitive.

This heuristic framework of privatization in the water sector provides some structure to the complexities of institutions and competition enabled by decentralization in Vietnam and points out how important it is for community planners and national policymakers better to understand the various mechanisms

A decentralized understanding of local PPPs for water provision

7.1 A decentralized understanding of local PPPs for water provision.

for water service delivery in rapidly urbanizing areas where little or no infrastructure currently exists.

In this context, the use of simple private/public or centralized/decentralized distinctions may not be appropriate. If organizational and geographic scale are indeed central issues in the provision of clean water under the current conditions in Vietnam, then planning and policy scholars might best ascertain whether the theoretical and empirical understanding of water provision described above applies to processes of decentralization and privatization elsewhere. If it does, then planners might best consider how both communities and government agencies act as coordinated entrepreneurs in the provision of public services, and how such arrangements perform in providing for the basic needs of the urban poor, one of the field's historic concerns.

Acknowledgement

The author would like to thank the University of Hawaii's Globalization Research Center for its generous support of this research, as well as two anonymous reviewers.

Note

1   Technically, the government of Vietnam does not recognize private property rights. However, under *Doi Moi* reforms, urban land law has allowed for exclusive and transferable use rights for urban land that can be inherited.

References

Arkadie, B.V. and Mallon, R. (2003) *Viet Nam: A Transition Tiger?*, Canberra: ANU Press.

Asthana, A.N. (2003) "Decentralization and supply efficiency: The case of rural water supply in central India," *Journal of Development Studies* 39 (4): 148–60.

Bakker, K. (2003) "Archipelagos and networks: Urbanization and water privatization in the south," *The Geographic Journal* 169 (4): 328–41.

Barlow, M. and Clarke, T. (2004) "The struggle for Latin America's water," North American Congress on Latin America 38 (1). Available online at www.Nacla.Org/Art_Display. Php?Art=2450

Beresford, M. (2003) "Economic rransition, uneven development, and the impact of reform on regional inequality," in H.V. Luong (ed.) *Postwar Vietnam: Dynamics of a Transforming Society*, New York: Rowman & Littlefield.

Beyer, S. (2006) "Environmental law and policy in the People's Republic of China," *Chinese Journal of International Law* 5 (1): 185–211.

Budds, J. and McGranahan, G. (2003) "Are the debates on water privatization missing the point? Experiences from Africa, Asia and Latin America," in *Environment and Urbanization* 15 (2): 87–113.

Crane, R. (1994) "Water markets, market reform and the urban poor: Results from Jakarta, Indonesia," in *World Development* 22 (1): 71–83.

Crane, R., Daniere, A. and Harwood, S. (1997) "The contribution of environmental amenities to low-income housing: A comparative study of Bangkok and Jakarta," in *Urban Studies* 34 (9): 1495–512.

Dziegielewski, B. and Baumann, D.B. (1992) "The benefits of managing urban water demands," *Environment* 34 (9): 6–11, 35–41.

Fontenelle, J.P. (2001) "Water management decentralisation in the Red River Delta, Vietnam: An uncompleted transition process towards local governance," *International Journal of Water* 3 (4): 380–96.

Gainsborough, M. (1998) *Changing Political Economy of Vietnam—The Case of Ho Chi Minh City*, Oxford: RoutledgeCurzon.

Gulyani, S., Talukdar, D. and Kariuki, R. (2005) "Universal (non)service? Water markets, household demand and the poor in urban Kenya," *Urban Studies* 42 (8): 1247–74.

Gutierrez, E. (2003) "Privatization and the failed promise of free market theory in water services provision: Towards developing an alternative theoretical framework," paper presented at Mexico City Conference, April 2–3, 2003. Retrieved September 22, 2004, from http://users.ox.ac.uk/~prinwass/PDFs/Gutierrez1.pdf.

Hanak, E. and Browne, M.K. (2006) "Linking housing growth to water supply," *Journal of the American Planning Association* 72 (2): 154–66.

Haq, K.A. (2006) "Water management in Dhaka," *International Journal of Water Resources Development* 22 (2): 291–311.

Knutsen, H.M. and Nguyen, C.M. (2004) "Preferential treatment in a transition economy: The case of state-owned enterprises in the textile and garment industry in Vietnam," *Norwegian Journal of Geography* 58 (3): 125–35.

Laquian, A.A. (2005a) "Metropolitan governance reform in Asia," *Public Administration and Development* 25 (4): 307–15.

Laquian, A.A. (2005b) *Beyond Metropolis: The Planning and Governance of Asia's Mega-Urban Regions*, Baltimore, MD: Johns Hopkins University Press.

Le, T.A. (2003) *Technical Report on Water Supply in the Mekong Delta*, Viet Nam: Can Tho University.

Lemos, M.C. and De Oliveira, J.L.F. (2005) "Water reform across the state/society divide: The case of Ceará, Brazil," *International Journal of Water Resources Development* 21 (1): 133–47.

Li, T. (1998) *Nguyen Cochinchina: Southern Vietnam in the Seventeenth and Eighteenth Centuries*, Monograph, Southeast Asia Program Publications, Ithaca, NY: Cornell University.

Lobina, E. and Hall, D. (2000) "Public sector alternatives to water supply and sewerage privatization: Case studies," *Water Resources Development* 16 (1): 35–55.

Luong, H.V. (2003) "Wealth, power and inequality: Global market, the state, and local sociocultural dynamics," in H.V. Luong (ed.) *Postwar Vietnam: Dynamics of a Transforming Society*, New York: Rowman & Littlefield.

Memon, M.A., Imura, H. and Shirakawa, H. (2006) "Reforms for managing urban environmental infrastructure and services in Asia," *Journal of Environment and Development* 15 (2): 138–58.

Nickson, A. (1996) *Urban Water Supply: Sector Review*, University of Birmingham: School of Public Policy, Papers in the Role of Government in Adjusting Economies, No. 7, January.

Nickson, A. (1998) "Organizational structure and performance in urban water supply: The case of the SAGUAPAC cooperative in Santa Cruz, Bolivia," paper presented at 3rd CLAD Inter-American Conference, Madrid, October 14–17.

O'Riordan, T. (2003) "Rethinking water provision," *Environment* 45 (10).

O'Rourke, D. (2003) *Community-Driven Regulation: Balancing Development and the Environment in Vietnam*, Cambridge, MA: The MIT Press.

Olmstead, S.M. (2003) "Water supply and poor communities: What's price got to do with It?," *Environment* 45 (10).

Platt, R.H. (1995) "The 2020 water supply study for Metropolitan Boston," *Journal of the American Planning Association* 61 (2): 185–200.

Purcell, M. and Brown, C.J. (2005) "Against the local trap: Scale and the study of environment and development," *Progress in Development Studies* 5 (4): 279–97.

Sahooly, A. (2003) "Public–private partnership in the water supply and sanitation sector: The experience of the Republic of Yemen," *International Journal of Water Resources Development* 19 (2): 139–53.

Salemink, O. (2003) "Disjunctive developments: The politics of good governance and civil society in Vietnam," unpublished manuscript. Available online at www.soas.ac.uk/eidosfiles/conferencepapers/salemink/pdf, last accessed August 14, 2006.

Satterthwaite, D., McGranahan, G. and Mitlin, D. (2005) *Community-Driven Development for Water and Sanitation in Urban Areas: Its Contribution to Meeting the Millennium Development Goal Target*, Report to the Water Supply and Sanitation Collaborative Council, London: IIED.

Saurí, D. (2003) "Lights and shadows of urban water demand management: The case of the metropolitan region of Barcelona," *European Planning Studies* 11 (3): 229–44.

Simonson, K. (2003) *The Global Water Crisis: NGO and Civil Society Perspectives*, Geneva: CASIN.

Warner, M.E. and Bel, G. (forthcoming) "Competition or monopoly? Comparing US and Spanish privatization," *Public Administration*.

Yeung, Y.M. and McGee, T.G. (eds) (1986) *Community Participation in Delivering Urban Services in Asia*, Ottawa, ON: International Development Research Centre.

Zhang, H.H. and Brown, D.F. (2005) "Understanding urban residential water use in Beijing and Tianjin, China," *Habitat International* 29 (3): 469–91.

Chapter 8
Decentralization and local democracy in Chile
Two active communities and two models of local governance

Anny Rivera-Ottenberger

During the 1990s, Chile was a showcase of economic reform, with a well-functioning but "low-intensity" democracy that curbed social mobilization and kept redistributive issues off the political agenda (Mainwaring and Torcal 1998; Posner 1999). Great hopes were pinned, however, on the potential of local governments for channeling the participation of the organized urban poor and for addressing their demands. Since the early 1980s, decentralization had endowed the municipalities[1] with fresh resources, enhanced authority, and the administration of key social services such as primary health and education.

Grassroots organizations of the poor in urban municipalities were numerous and active. Most were part of a social movement of urban squatters, the *pobladores*. The *pobladores* were territorially based and were uniquely suited to act at the local level. Throughout three decades of sustained collective action, they had amassed a rich experience of self-government and delivery of social services (Espinoza 1988; Oxhorn 1995).

This chapter argues that neither decentralization nor the re-establishment of elections has been sufficient to fulfill the democratic potential that the municipality seemed to open for the organized urban poor. Instead, the design of municipal institutions, inherited from the authoritarian government of General Pinochet, has combined with neoliberal social policies to restrict both grassroots participation and the accountability and responsiveness of local governments. However, in studying in depth two poor municipalities in Santiago, I found that a model of local governance structured around participatory planning can counteract the dire effects of institutional design and neoliberal policies on local democracy. This model was implemented in the municipality of El Bosque. I contrast its experience with that of Peñalolén, which has been faithful to the dominant institutional design.[2]

The winding road to decentralization

The military government (1973–90) set the main pillars of state decentralization. In 1973, the government appointed new mayors, created planning offices and hand-picked social leaders to join councils for local development in all Chilean municipalities. In 1975, the country was divided into thirteen regions with ad hoc administrations, and central ministries opened regional offices. Fiscal decentralization got an early start with the National Fund for Regional Development in 1976. The Municipal Common Fund followed in 1979. A year later, the military government redefined municipal boundaries and transferred the administration of primary health and educational services to the municipalities. These reforms acquired a coherent legal form in the 1988 Law of Municipalities.

Decentralization was not an obvious reform choice for the military. Chile had been historically highly centralized, and the municipality was hardly more than the last link in the state administrative chain (Nickson 1995; Valenzuela 1977). Despite this tradition, decentralization fulfilled disparate but ultimately converging ends. Decentralization enhanced governmental control over regions and communes and, particularly, over territorially based movements such as the *pobladores*, who largely opposed military rule. The subsequent transfer of education and health to municipal administration fragmented the formerly powerful unions of education and health workers (Morales and Rojas 1987). In addition to enhancing social control, decentralization fit nicely the neoliberal pursuit of reducing the role of the central state, granting greater autonomy to subnational units while opening an avenue for the private sector to participate in service provision. Chilean decentralization thus reflected the influence of the two cornerstones of the authoritarian regime: the military and the emerging "new right." The former was mainly concerned with maintaining order by extricating politics from Chilean society, whereas the latter embraced free-market economics and a technocratic model of governance to "depoliticize" public decision-making. The resulting municipality was authoritarian insofar as it concentrated power in the mayors and linked them, through a hierarchical chain of command, to the head of state. It was also "managerial," in that it aimed at efficient service provision by technical, not political, decision-making. These mutually reinforcing features of the authoritarian municipality—concentration of power in the executive (mayor) and managerialism—were to survive regime change.[3]

Upon the return to democracy in 1990, decentralization had gained new advocates, both among progressive movements, which saw its potential to nurture democracy from the grassroots, and among multilateral agencies, which promoted decentralizing as a modernization strategy for making more efficient the delivery of public services, in tune with the new managerial paradigm that came to dominate public administration in Chile (Garretón and Cáceres 2003).

Despite the fact that the center-left governing coalition, *Concertación*, did not have a model of governance for the young municipalities, it called for elections of municipal authorities in 1992, eager to challenge the right's stronghold on local governments.[4] Municipal government was equipped with a Communal Council (*Concejo Comunal*), consisting of elected representatives nominated by the political parties, with limited powers to oversee the mayor, and an advisory council with direct representation of community organizations (Economic and Social Council (CESCO)). However, these minor institutional reforms left unchanged the main features of its authoritarian predecessor: a powerful mayor and a managerial model.

By the second round of municipal elections in 1996, local political institutions were already displaying a handful of worrisome traits. The unfettered power of the mayor forced political parties to concentrate votes in the mayoralty, a move that in turn enhanced political personalism and eroded the programmatic profile of the parties. Managerialism, with its stress on decision-making and accountability, has further promoted power concentration in the mayor's office. Mayoral preeminence and its monopoly over political resources have also created fertile grounds for clientelism,[5] with the other local politicians forming clientelistic ties with community organizations in order to ensure their political survival. Managerial emphasis on a technical rather than political rationale for decision making encouraged local politicians to resort to "non-ideological" problem-solving in lieu of political discussion of viable alternatives.

Ironically, then, open political competition increased the concentration of power in the executive. It has done little to restrict the reliance on non-deliberative mechanisms of local decision-making in the local scene. In addition, clientelism has put down roots in municipal politics, generating divisive dynamics among the organized poor and further depriving citizens of their capacity to hold politicians and parties accountable.

Participatory social policies: empowerment or control?

The *Concertación* maintained the focus of social policies on the provision of targeted assistance to the needy, but sought to increase equity and social justice (Castiglioni 2005). President Aylwin created the Ministry of Planning and Cooperation (MIDEPLAN), to fight poverty and to incorporate the active participation of the citizenry in the provision of social services, particularly at the local (municipal) level. Some of MIDEPLAN's social programs displayed innovative and participatory approaches that seemed ideal to channel both the NGOs' knowledge and the grassroots organizations' self-help practices, nurtured by years of state neglect. These policies ranged from programs in traditional social areas such as education or health, which involved beneficiaries in their execution and monitoring, to small grants for community groups to carry out their own projects on a competitive basis.

Participatory policies, however, were handled with great caution to smother even the dimmest spark of social mobilization, lest it destabilize the fragile post-authoritarian democracy. These concerns had a decisive influence on the NGOs that had supported grassroots organizations. When the return to democracy in Chile radically diminished the flow of international aid to the non-profit sector, many surviving NGOs reoriented their work to implementing public programs.

NGO reliance on state funding deprived the organizations of the urban poor of one of their main sources of independent technical support and intermediation with public bureaucracies (Clewett 1998; Delamaza 2005).

Despite languishing NGO support, the *pobladores* were able and willing to participate in state social programs. The *pobladores'* lengthy experience designing and implementing social policies, as well as their savvy in dealing with local governments, raised hopes for "associative networks" sprouting in urban municipalities across Chile, as happened throughout Latin America in the 1990s. These "non-hierarchical structures formed through decisions by multiple actors who come together to shape public policy" (Chalmers *et al.* 1997: 567) had proven an effective empowerment path for the organized poor (Tendler 1997).

Participatory social policies, however, offered few opportunities for establishing the connections to create an effective network to shape policy. Social participation in most programs was restricted to fund-raising, service co-production and monitoring performance (Noé 1998). The programs where grassroots organizations had a larger role in diagnosing needs and designing interventions were typically micro-projects with very limited impact. These micro-projects provided resources to thousands of community groups (Delamaza 2005), but did not generate any connections between them. In addition, fund allocation to these micro-projects was done thorough competitive bidding. Competition required from leaders and community organizations technical know-how and energy, assets the poorest often lack. Competition also tested solidarity in poor communities, while discouraging community groups from negotiating with each other on the distribution of funds. Finally, social policy design preempted "scaling-up" policy chains by increasing the technical knowledge needed to access higher levels, making it difficult for grassroots organizations to reach the apex of policies. Therefore, policy fragmentation and the absence of mediators such as political parties or NGOs that could link social organizations to higher levels of policy-making conspired against the building of effective social policy networks.

Managerial emphasis on technical rationale limits the potential of democratic deepening in the municipality in two ways. First, by restricting decision-makers to those endowed with the technical expertise in the matter at hand, it effectively marginalizes the poor and the disadvantaged. Second, application of technical rationale to public policies narrows the scope of issues that are subjected to the deliberation and consent of the citizens. Fragmented social policies and programs offer the poor the chance to become active participants in the provision of services that will benefit them and their communities, but do not open avenues for empowerment. The question is whether it is possible, within this institutional design, to recreate a more participatory polity able to incorporate the organizations of the urban poor in the decision-making of their local government.

Paradoxically, the concentration of power in the executive can configure a positive political opportunity structure for the urban poor in some municipalities.

Table 8.1 Chile: models of local governance

Model			
Relationship of organizations to municipality	*Structure of decision-making*	*Focus of citizen participation*	*Connectedness (associative networking)*
Managerial-elitist (dominant)			
Narrow and functional to meet precise goals (Performance efficiency) Clients	Mayor-centric Centralized decision-making and decentralized execution of policies Strong emphasis on technical/managerial expertise	Individual Collective input limited to very specific projects Voting	Parceled specialization of organizations Little or no horizontalism
Deliberative-participatory (emergent)			
Diverse and multi-faceted, seeking to create an active public arena Partners	Mayor-centric Decentralized decision-making and fully participatory at all stages of policy process Citizen input a major component of policymaking	Collective Individual and collective input in several stages of policymaking Voting	Associative interaction and linkages among organizations Strong horizontalism

Even sharing the same managerially driven blueprint, the mayor can divest power for the purpose of allowing organized participation. The dominant "managerial elitist" model, which favors technical/centralized decision-making and precludes public deliberation, is not the only option. The alternative is the "participatory–deliberative" model, which relies on mayoral willingness to incorporate organized participation in local government and local social programs. It can foster articulation and deflect the damaging effects of the design of local political institutions. The model combines innovative adaptation of public policies to "fit" local demand, extensive use of networks, and public forums (see Table 8.1). The following section examines these models in two poor municipalities: Peñalolén and El Bosque.

El Bosque: building community and deliberative democracy

When he was elected mayor in 1992, Sadi Melo, a socialist educator and urban planner, hoped to build in El Bosque a "democratic model of local govern-ance" (interview 1999). The poor municipality in southern Santiago appeared a good match for the task at hand. Melo had served as interim mayor since 1990 and he brought with him a team of over thirty professionals experienced in NGO or community work. In turn, the community of 173,000[6] was highly organized. Traditional grassroots organizations such as the neighborhood councils (*juntas de vecinos*), mothers' centers and sports clubs were active and widespread, and a large number of autonomous organizations of women, youth and housing or health activists continued advocating and providing a variety of community services.[7]

El Bosque's model of democratic governance relied on two main pillars. The first was community involvement in planning and decision-making, which required carving participatory spaces in public policies and programs to complement the weak mechanism for incorporating organized participation into the local government (CESCO). The second was increasing the effectiveness and responsive-ness of the municipality to the community needs and demands. The mayor was adamant that good government, good management and participation were not in contradiction.

Weaving participation and deliberation

Social policies were the natural starting point for the strategy of participatory planning. Improving social services ranked high among community demands; service provision was a main expertise of the organized poor. The municipal team structured its work to include participation but also to link policy areas into networks.

A brief account of the health network will illustrate the workings of the participatory planning strategy. Dr Angélica Verdugo became Director of Health in 1992, determined to turn around the local health system, which topped the list of complaints regarding municipal services. The plan aimed at improving coverage and quality while incorporating local organizations into the planning, execution and evaluation of health policy. El Bosque had a solid organizational foundation of women's health groups, which were invited to join a health network. Sweeping changes in the practices and organizational culture were implemented in the clinics, organizing health workers into teams that ventured regularly into the neighborhoods they served. In 1995, the municipality created territorial health Coordinators, linking health personnel, community groups, NGOs and medical administrators. Each Coordinator drafts an annual plan for its territory (with goals, health targets and interventions), which it monitors in monthly meetings.

Community organizations have brought their expertise and creativity to local health, presenting, in one year alone (1999), seventeen projects to the public fund *Salud con la Gente*. El Bosque's achievements in health coverage and reduction of infant mortality earned the municipality a special incentive from the Ministry of Health (IMEB 1998: 7).

The most encompassing instance of community incorporation into decision-making is participatory budgeting, where the community discusses and sets priorities for the municipal development plan (PLADECO) The municipality has implemented a PLADECO every three years since 1994. The first PLADECO created six planning territories, where 750 community leaders and neighbors detected problems, set priorities and proposed solutions. Parallel planning meetings were held by policy areas. In the second PLADECO held in 1999, 9,000 participants held meetings in their neighborhoods, determining three problems the municipality promised to address. The most recent PLADECO was held in 2003, with the participation of 4,000 neighbors and 600 social leaders.

Without doubt, the most powerful instances of community participation are found not in the traditional political institutions but in the policy networks. The municipality has increased the number and the diversity of the organizations represented in the Social and Economic Council, CESCO, and has requested it to evaluate local services and budgetary, zoning and local development matters. However, the advisory nature of the CESCO limits its impact on local politics, even though many of its suggestions have found their way into public policy (José Miguel Vergara, CESCO, interview 1999). Local political institutions have failed fully to incorporate organized participation, a vacuum that policy networks have partially filled.

Networks have become spaces of community encounter and debate, well beyond a planning instrument to detect needs accurately, coordinate solutions and maximize resources. The "connectedness" provided by the networks has been a counterforce to the fragmentary nature of social policies. By creating spaces for publicly presenting and debating policy alternatives and allocation of resources, networks have laid the foundations for a sense of community to reemerge and for a public view to resettle in El Bosque. In this sense, these policy networks have

8.1 Mayor Melo and a health committee discuss "problem health spots" in their neighborhood.
Source: Photo by Manuel Carvallo, Municipality of El Bosque.
© Kumala Sari

recreated a public space for social actors to discuss matters that are politically relevant to their daily lives (see Figure 8.1).

Flexibility in practice

In a context of limited resources, good government and managerial effectiveness rely mainly on the capacity of the municipal team creatively to adapt existing programs, to devise new practices, and to find synergy among programs. The following illustrate the creative practices devised by the municipal team and community organizations to maximize scarce resources with institutional innovation.

In 1996, the Women's Office (WO) of El Bosque and women's groups devoted a great deal of their efforts to organizing a series of meetings, workshops and research to make a participatory diagnosis of the condition of women in the commune. In the process, one grassroots organization made a startling discovery: almost 30 percent of women in two neighborhoods were functionally illiterate, and there was no program to meet their needs. A year later, and after several failed attempts to obtain support from the central state agencies, an adult education school named Elena Caffarena opened, with a gender-based curriculum, an afternoon schedule, on-site health and childcare services and a staff of volunteers recruited among municipal workers, community activists and pedagogy students.

In its first two years, sixty women graduated from literacy classes; 101 completed primary studies, ninety completed secondary studies, and six graduates continued into higher education. By the third year, the school had eleven teachers, and the WO had secured resources from the Education Department and the Ministry of Health. In 2000, this experiment received a prize for innovation from the Ford Foundation.

The capacity of the team to generate solutions and adapt programs to the needs of the community is also reflected in the municipality's management of housing programs. Overcrowding was significant in the early 1990s, but municipal planners lacked the data to assess the extent of the problem. Knowing that unauthorized construction was an indicator of overcrowding, the municipality approved a "sketch law," which granted permits to existing additions with a handmade sketch of the works. This allowed for a more adequate diagnosis of the quality of dwellings and of overcrowding. The 1994 PLADECO worked with the community, offering a varied mix of housing options, ranging from basic construction to be finished by the owners, to repairs and building upgrades in older *poblaciones.*

The team of the Youth Office (YO) did not hesitate to work some days from 11:00 p.m. to 3:00 a.m. to reach an important segment of the youth that had fallen into a marginalizing path. The office also supported the public expression of this marginal culture, earning enough trust among youth groups that several of them developed a project to safeguard the public spaces of their neighborhood.

Policy networks have created synergy between the local state and the organized citizenry. These collaborative enterprises generate trust, adding to the stock of social capital (Fox 1996). The local state, with its creative adaptation of programs and its search for resources, has become an apt mediator between the community and higher levels of policy chains. This is a key role in light of the relative weakness of other possible mediators, such as political parties or NGOs. As an indicator of the effectiveness of the El Bosque approach, in 2000 the commune showed the highest drop in the percentage of poverty (–9.3 percent) in the metropolitan region.

In summary, networks and other public forums have nurtured an emerging public, collective vision of the needs of El Bosque through deliberation. The participatory and inclusionary local policy has opened a space for democracy.

Peñalolén: a municipality out of reach

Peñalolén is a poor to middle-income municipality, southeast of the metropolitan region. The commune had a population of 214,000 people in 2000. Several waves of land invasions in the decade 1960–70 were followed by new settlers of middle- and upper-class status in the 1980s, resulting in high socio-economic polarization. In 1999, 47 percent of the population were middle- or upper-class, with a median family income of over US$3,000 per month, while 24 percent were poor or extremely poor, with a median family income of US$150 per month (IMP 1999).

In 1996, Carlos Alarcón (1996–2004), representing the rightist coalition, became the second elected mayor of Peñalolén. Alarcón had been involved in local politics since the times when Peñalolén was one of the experiments of new right in poor municipalities. Consistent with the managerial style, his government clearly delimited functions and concentrated power in the executive. The community's input was sought via polls, in which neighbors chose between policy options. Major plans, including the PLADECO, were drafted by the mayor and the municipal directors and later opened to the suggestions and approval of the Communal Council. Organized participation in public policy areas was not encouraged (Interview 1999)

Organized participation was channeled by the Directorate of Community Development (DIDECO), which handled only public subsidies and small community projects. Main social policy decisions were left to the Planning Secretariat, Secplac (SECPLAC), in tune with the municipality's highly hierarchical and function-specific organizational design that reserved major decisions to the higher executive levels. Constrained to an implementation role, DIDECO's staff efficiently administered centrally designed programs, but could do little to adapt them to the local reality, only "catering" to those groups targeted by official social programs.

A strictly managerial model of governance is not conducive to organized participation in social policy design, and does not allow for the flexibility to incorporate grassroots organizational knowledge into social programs. Social organizations in Peñalolén were as active as their counterparts in El Bosque. However, the limited and relatively rigid programmatic offer of the municipality attracted mostly traditional organizations, which came exclusively searching for resources channeled by DIDECO. The *Juntas* (neighborhood councils) were the most assiduous clients. Multi-service organizations such as development committees, women's groups or youth groups found it difficult to engage with the municipality because of the limited supply of programs and the perceived clientelism in grant allocations. These autonomous organizations resorted to "flexibilizing" the central state offer on their own. Miguel Huenul, president of the ethnic organization *Revnu Mapu*, opted for pulling resources from competitive central state funds, notwithstanding that DIDECO has a program for native peoples. The same strategy of self-reliance based on constant applications to central state funding was adopted by the Centro Cultural REM, an organization of thirty young *pobladores* who work on family and childhood issues (interviews 1999)

The net effect of this pattern of incorporation was sustained organizational activity, but absence of synergy. These organizations tend to become self-contained and isolated. Lack of participation and of policy networks fostered vital but highly fragmented organizational activity.

The managerial model of governance can be successful in pooling resources to improve the quality of services when this requires "rationalizing" organizations and where organized participation plays a minor role. This is allegedly the case with the municipal corporation for health and education, which achieved financial self-sufficiency thanks to aggressive fund-raising and the finding of alternative funding sources. The same managerial techniques were extended to the schools.[8] The managerial model requires insulation from social pressures in the name of ensuring the best possible technical solution; thereby, the model can serve the citizens of Peñalolén well as clients, but cannot open participatory and deliberative spaces.

Closed to deliberation

The CESCO in Peñalolén had minimal influence on the spheres of power. This fact, paired with the absence of participatory spaces in policy arenas, left the *pobladores'* organizations without relevant spaces in which to express themselves collectively.

Clientelism in Peñalolén exerted a particularly pervasive and destructive effect on the social fabric. The concentration of power in the executive precluded public discussion when contradictory interests clashed over policy alternatives. Faced with "correct technical solutions," members of the unusually activist and partisan Communal council have resorted to mobilizing their clienteles in order to push for their alternatives. This transferred political conflicts to the social realm and turned grassroots organizations into stages for partisan contests: The *Juntas* in Peñalolén were pawns in a bitter political battle between forces of the right and the *Concertación*. The *Juntas* split into two communal unions, and an unworkable number of *Juntas* emerged in each neighborhood (Guillermo Navarro, interview 1999).

Extreme shifts in the political allegiances of social leaders are common in Peñalolén, attesting to the vulnerability of the social sphere to the political one when clientelism predominates.

The lack of public spaces to discuss contentious matters has stressed the social fabric. Nowhere was this more evident than in the treatment of housing problems. Since the late 1980s, Peñalolén witnessed seven illegal land occupations involving about 12,000 families; another 2,000 had invaded a privately owned parcel, and yet another movement occupied piedmont lands in the year 2000. These movements reflected a decade of persistent overcrowding, with no subsidized public housing being built from 1992 to 1998, compounded by a hot housing market that increased land prices.

The community was divided regarding the housing problem. Some justified the market allocation of housing, which would likely expel a significant number of the *pobladores* from their neighborhood; others saw housing as a right and a matter of public responsibility. However, rather than encouraging public discussion, local politicians used the movements to their advantage, supporting or opposing the invasions. Mayor Alarcón exerted pressure on the central state to provide a solution, but the municipal development plan for 2001 recommended building more middle- and upper-class housing. The lack of public discussion brought the problem back to the community and pitted those who opted for the official housing programs against those who had occupied land, opening deep rifts among the *pobladores*. Land invasions and violent confrontations were still happening in 2006.

Conclusions

El Bosque is unique in its innovative way of overcoming the sterile terrain for deliberation that is provided by Chile's low-intensity democracy. The strategies devised to piece together public policies and programs have fended off the fragmentary forces of neoliberal social policies with a project of rational discussion around public policies. Participation and deliberation became powerful forces against the second nemesis of the local polity: clientelism. Indeed, El Bosque's model of governance resembles what Fung and Wright (2001: 17–24) called "Empowered deliberative democracy," a progressive institutional reform strategy that advances the democratic values of participation, deliberation and empowerment with a practical orientation, bottom-up participation and deliberative solutions.

The managerial/elitist model is often able to deliver benefits to its citizens. However, without participation, the *pobladores* become citizen–clients, non-political consumers of policies. Social organizations, unable to reach local resources, resort to a myriad of projects from other state agencies, which maintain their activity but lack the capacity to produce synergy and a public space.

The effect of both models on the organizations of the *pobladores* is stunning. Networks in El Bosque allow organizations to connect with each other, so that collective action is facilitated. Insofar as they expose organizations to different policy outlets, networks have increased organizational autonomy, while avoiding fragmentation. Conflict is played out within deliberative spaces, and so the social fabric is strengthened.

In Peñalolén there is no such reinforcing effect on the social fabric. On the contrary, the de-politicizing effect of managerialism and power concentration opened the door to aggressive clientelism. Lacking public forums, the rampant intervention of politicians in the *pobladores'* organizations has transferred conflicts to the community. The most telling sign of the lack of deliberative spaces is the persistent and unaddressed problem of socio-economic disparities in housing in Peñalolén. Peñalolén is exemplary of the virtues of the managerial model and of its limitations in creating participatory and deliberative spaces.

The model of participatory planning also has limitations. Traditional policy areas, with well-established bureaucratic structures and procedures, limit the ability of local actors to innovate and to adapt these policies to local reality. Translating networks and participatory practices into the political arena is not easy. Widespread clientelism has been kept at bay in El Bosque because of the strong relations between the mayor, the municipal team and the organized community. However, this model has limited the role of mediators between the community and other political or policy arenas. Political parties and NGOs languish in a polity where all the roads lead to the municipality. Expanding the deliberative model would mean addressing the development of links with other local and non-local actors. In 2006, El Bosque joined the Local Observatory for Participatory Democracy, and it is leading ten progressive southern metropolitan municipalities to enact participatory democracy on a larger territorial scale.

Perhaps El Bosque will help advance an agenda of social justice and dignity. The subsidiary state radically questioned the identity of the *pobladores*: from bearers of rights, to recipients of subsidized privileges; from having a voice and a place in the public space, to clients and quiet co-producers of their own services. The participatory model of El Bosque captures the need for a place where rights are not only abstract principles, but offer a tangible social space in which to recover a sense of continuity, of community and of worth.

Interviews

- Sadi Melo, Mayor of the Ilustre Municipalidad El Bosque (IMEB), interviews 6/10/94, 8/25/99 and 7/2/2006.
- Carlos Alarcón, Mayor of the Ilustre Municipalidad Municipalidad de Peñalolén (IMP), interview 9/10/99.
- Guillermo Navarro, President of the Union of Juntas de Vecinos de Peñalolén, interview 9/20/99.
- José Miguel Vergara, Community Council (Cesco) IMEB, interview 9/14/99.
- Loreto Cisternas and Víctor Olmedo, Centro Cultural REM (Renovación en Masa) Peñalolén, interview 9/22/99.
- Miguel Huenul, Revnu Mapu Cultural Centre, Peñalolén, interview 9/23/99.
- Angélica Verdugo, Director of Health, IMEB, interview 9/13/99.
- Paulina Araneda, Director of Educational Corporation IMP, interview 6/30/2006.
- Andrés Castillo, Director of Director Educational Technical Unit, Educational Corporation IMP, 9/27/99.

Notes

1   Even though "commune" denotes primarily territory and "municipality" refers to local government, both terms are considered synonyms in common use.
2   Case studies were built with eighty-five interviews with grassroots organizations, NGOs, unions, state officials and political party officers, plus municipal laws, electoral statistics, and data on social policies, community organizations and political parties, all 1990–2000.
3   According to Nickson (1998: 2), Chilean decentralization is one of the few in Latin America that conforms to the "economic model," whereby efficient delivery of services is the primary goal for decentralizing. The central government allocates services and distributes responsibilities among tiers of government. Local governments fulfill an administrative role under a principal/agent model.
4   The new right made strategic use of the municipalities to gather political support among the urban poor. Their involvement paid off: twenty-three of the forty-eight representatives of the rightist coalition elected to the Congress in 1990 had been mayors during the military government (Morales and Bugueño 2001).
5   Clientelism is an exchange between individuals of unequal power where support (electoral or otherwise) is given in exchange for particularistic favors.
6   In 2000, around 21.5 percent of the communal population was poor, with a monthly household income below US$200. The remaining population was largely middle–low income (MIDEPLAN, 2000).
7   In 1968, the law of Neighborhood Councils and Other Community Organizations (Law 16,880) created four types of territorially based and functionally defined organization: Neighborhood Councils, Mothers' Centers, Sport Clubs and Youth Centers (*Juntas de Vecinos, Centros de Madres, Clubes Deportivos* and *Centros Juveniles*). The purpose of these organizations was to represent the interests of their respective constituencies and to mediate between the community and state authorities.
8   Andrés Castillo, Director of Education (interview 1999). In spite of this claim, an independent audit in 2005 found a large financial deficit and no measure of educational improvement. Interview 1906 with Paulina Araneda, Director of Education, Peñalolén.

References

Castiglioni, R. (2005) *The Politics of Social Policy Change in Chile and Uruguay*, New York: Routledge.

Chalmers, D., Martin, S. and Piester, K. (1997) "Associative networks: New structures of representation for the popular sectors?" in D. Chalmers, C. Vilas, K. Hite, S. Martin, K. Piester and M. Segarra (eds) *The New Politics of Inequality in Latin America*, Oxford; NY: Oxford University Press.

Clewett, E. (1998) "The development of civil society in Chile in the1990s and the role of the NGO sector," paper presented at the XXI meeting of LASA, Chicago, September, 24–6.

Delamaza, G. (2005) *Políticas públicas y sociedad civil en Chile*, Santiago: LOM Ediciones.

Espinoza, V. (1988) *Para una historia de los pobres de la ciudad*, Santiago: Sur Ediciones.

Fox, J. (1996) "How does civil society thicken? The political construction of social capital in rural Mexico," *World Development* 24(6).

Fung, A. and Wright E. (2001) "Deepening democracy: Innovations in empowered participatory governance," *Politics & Society* 29 (1): 5–41.

Garretón, M. and Cáceres, G. (2003) "From the disarticulation of the state to the modernization of public management in Chile: Administrative reform without a state project," in B. Schneider and B. Heredia (eds), *Reinventing Leviathan: The Politics of Administrative Reform in Developing Countries*, Miami: North South Center Press.

IMEB Ilustre Municipalidad El Bosque (1998) *Cuenta Pública 1998*, Santiago: Secretaría Comunal de Planificación.

IMP Ilustre Municipalidad de Peñalolén (1999) *Diagnóstico Comunal de Peñalolén 1998*, Santiago: Secretaría Comunal de Planificación.

Mainwaring, S. and Torcal, M. (1998) "Social cleavages, political heritages, and post-authoritarian party systems: Chile in the 1990s," paper presented at the meeting of the Latin American Studies Association, Chicago, September 24–6.

MIDEPLAN (Ministerio de Planificación y Cooperación) (2000) "Indicadores Económico-Sociales 1990–2000," Santiago: Mideplan. Available online at www.mideplan.cl/sitio/Sitio/indicadores/htm/indicadores_impacto.htm.

Morales, E. and Rojas, S. (1987) "Relocalización socio-espacial de la pobreza," in J. Chateau, B. Gallardo, E. Morales, C. Piña, H. Pozo, S. Rojas, D. Sánchez and T. Valdés, *Espacio y Poder. Los Pobladores*, Santiago: FLACSO.

Morales, M. and Bugueño, R. (2001) "La UDI como expresión de la Nueva Derecha en Chile," *Americas Forum*, OAS. Available online at www.oas.org/Seine/ezine6/art4.htm.

Nickson, A. (1995) *Local Government in Latin America*, Boulder, CO; London: Lynne Rienner Publishers.

Nickson, A. (1998) "Where is local government going in Latin America? A comparative perspective," paper presented at the Annual Conference of the Society of Latin American Studies, University of Liverpool, April 17–19.

Noé, M. (1998) "Ciudadanía y políticas públicas," in E. Correa and M. Noé (eds) *Nociones de una Ciudadanía que Crece*, Santiago: FLACSO.

Oxhorn, P. (1995) *Organizing Civil Society. The Popular Sectors and the Struggle for Democracy in Chile*, University Park, PA: Pennsylvania State University Press.

Posner, P. (1999) "Popular representation and political dissatisfaction in Chile's new democracy," *Journal of InterAmerican Studies and World Affairs*, 41 (1): 59–85.

Tendler, J. (1997) *Good Government in the Tropics*, Baltimore, MD: Johns Hopkins University Press.

Valenzuela, A. (1977) *Political Brokers in Chile: Local Government in a Centralized Polity*, Durham, NC: Duke University Press.

Section Three

The role of civil society and community actors in decentralization

Chapter 9

Community-driven development and elite capture

Microcredit and community board participation in Indonesia

Victoria A. Beard, Menno Pradhan, Vijayendra Rao, Randi S. Cartmill and Rivayani

Introduction[1]

In the late 1990s, a series of events occurred that would change the course of Indonesian history in dramatic and irreversible ways. The Asian economic crisis resulted in months of runaway inflation followed by civil unrest in Indonesia's major urban centers. Many observers concur that the turning point was on May 12, 1998, when four Indonesian university students were killed by Indonesian security forces (Bird 1999: 29). These and other closely related events, such as violent attacks on Indonesians of Chinese descent and the occupation of the National Assembly building by university students, led ultimately to the resignation of President Suharto (Siegel 1998). The resignation was followed by a period of consolidation of the pro-democracy and political reform movements. This consolidation encompassed a national dialogue about the need for clean government, an opening up of the news media and civil society in unprecedented ways and a series of electoral reforms. Another significant event in the late 1990s was the passing of two pieces of decentralization legislation, Law 22/1999 and Law 25/1999, that began to reverse a thirty-year process of centralization and that gave substantial political and fiscal power to local, municipal-level governments. These events presented incredible challenges and opportunities for Indonesia's national development.[2] One challenge was dealing with the rise in urban poverty rates spurred by the crisis. Another major challenge was sustaining the national momentum for more democratic, transparent and accountable governance from the village to the national level. Finally, there was the question of how successful state and civil society actors would be in using the new political spaces created by these events while also protecting them from elite capture.

At the nexus of these opportunities and challenges, the World Bank implemented the Urban Poverty Program (UPP), which relied on local residents to conduct a deliberative planning process at the community level.[3] This chapter uses data from an evaluation of UPP to examine how the opportunities and challenges outlined above are unfolding at the community level. The program is worth examining for a number of reasons. First, it is one of the World Bank's most ambitious, community-driven development (CDD) efforts, a strategy increasingly popular internationally, although there is little robust examination of its foundational assumptions (Mansuri and Rao 2004). One assumption is that the deliberative planning process inherent in CDD will be able to identify worthy program beneficiaries—in this case, the urban poor. It is assumed that CDD also empowers the poor because well-designed efforts ". . . are inclusive of the poor and vulnerable groups, build positive social capital, and give them [the poor] greater voice both in their community and with government entities" (Dongier *et al.* 2002: 304). UPP is Indonesia's largest internationally supported poverty alleviation effort and is now being adopted by the Indonesian government and implemented nationally. As a result, it is an opportune time for rigorous empirical evaluation of UPP and its underlying assumptions.

The analyses in this chapter interrogate a series of assumptions about the presumed relationship between decentralization, CDD, poverty alleviation and elite capture. The first assumption is that the poor and vulnerable benefit from CDD efforts. Testing this assumption requires examining how well UPP is reaching the poor and disadvantaged and to what extent it may reinforce patterns of poverty and social exclusion. The second assumption tested by the chapter is that CDD empowers local community members rather than reinforcing patterns of elite capture. Examining that assumption means asking who is likely to play a leadership role, who makes key decisions and who controls program resources at the local level. The chapter begins with background information about Indonesia's decentralization legislation, CDD, patterns of elite capture and UPP. The chapter then explains how the data set and variables were constructed. Descriptive statistics present the employment and age distributions of members of the microcredit groups and community boards.[4] Next, the chapter turns to descriptive statistics and logistic regression analyses of the individual characteristics that are expected to predict membership in both the microcredit groups and the community boards. Finally, conclusions are drawn based on the analyses.

Decentralization, community-driven development and elite capture[5]

In 2001, Indonesia enacted two pieces of decentralization legislation.[6] Law 22/1999 gave greater "authority" (*kewenangan*) to lower levels of government, thus weakening the central government's control over provinces and districts. The law sought to bring the state closer to the people and create more transparent governance, particularly at the municipal level (Nordholt 2004: 37). The enactment of this legislation shifted the pressure for accountability from the central government to local and provincial legislatures. For example, local parliaments (*Dewan Perwakilan Rakyat Daerah*—DPRD) were given new powers to dismiss the head of the province, approve annual local budgets and authorize local laws and regulations (Kaiser *et al.* 2006: 168). Law 22/1999 also increased local government responsibility for delivering health, educational, environmental and infrastructure services (Kaiser *et al.* 2006: 167). Law 25/1999 reconstituted the fiscal relationship between the central government and the regions by replacing earmarked funds with grants (*dana alokasi umum*).[7]

Much of the driving force behind the decentralization legislation was political pressure for local autonomy (*otonomi daerah*). The first source of pressure was the outer provinces, those outside Java, because many of these provinces were resource-rich, and President Suharto's regime had a long history of suppressing local needs and aspirations for self-governance (Turner *et al.* 2003). Pressure was also exerted by civil society and community actors. By dismantling Law 5/1979, which defined rural villages (*Desa*) and urban sub-districts (*Kelurahan*) as the lowest political–administrative level, the 1999 decentralization law also increased the power and autonomy of community-level governance bodies (Antlöv 2003). The decentralization legislation mandates that village/sub-district-level governance focus on "diversity, participation, genuine autonomy, democratization and people's empowerment" (Antlöv 2003: 197). According to Antlöv (2003: 200) the effects of the legislation

> constitute nothing less than a quiet revolution in the countryside, not only providing a mechanism for checks and balances in village government, but also revising the old paradigm of villagers as objects of development to one in which villagers have the right to exercise their democratic authority and autonomy over public matters.

Although the mandates of the decentralization legislation complement the objectives of the political reform movement as well as the objectives of CDD, in many places the legislation's implementation has been uneven. In the worst cases, for example, community-level government has been hijacked by predatory local elites (Hadiz 2003; McCarthy 2002).

Similar to decentralization, CDD is vulnerable to elite capture, because participants enter the process from unequal power positions. For example, they have asymmetrical social standings, disparate access to economic resources, differing literacy rates and varying levels of familiarity with political protocols and procedures (Abraham and Platteau 2000; Fung and Wright 2003: 33). Elite power at the community level derives from many sources: social, cultural, religious, political and economic. Specific examples of its sources may include land holdings, kinship, lineage, employment status, political party affiliation, educational attainment, religious affiliation, tenure or other less tangible bases of popularity. CDD is also vulnerable to elite capture, because the impetus for participation is motivated locally and the process is intentionally flexible to work in the diverse community contexts where it is implemented.

The literature suggests several institutional arrangements and mechanisms that may protect CDD from elite capture. For example, supervised and enforced rules of conduct can help achieve internal accountability. External accountability can be checked through mechanisms that facilitate exit and voice, such as elections, conflict resolution agencies and participatory budgeting (Hirschman 1970; 1984; Olowu 2003: 47). Other factors that affect elite capture are the frequency and intensity with which elites participate compared with non-elites, the capacity of elites to advance special interests, and the extent of their power to exclude other participants and issues (Fung and Wright 2003: 34–5).

The fall of Suharto's New Order regime and the transitions to competitive elections in 1999 provided new opportunities for civil society actors; however, these changes have opened new ways for local elites to consolidate power. Hadiz (2003: 124) describes the new elites in Indonesia as "ambitious political fixers and entrepreneurs, wily and still-predatory state bureaucrats, and aspiring and newly ascendant business groups, as well as a wide range of political gangsters, thugs, and civilian militia." Sidel finds that ". . . economic and political power at the regency, municipal, and provincial levels in Indonesia appears to be associated with loosely defined, somewhat shadowy, and rather fluid clusters and cliques of businessmen, politicians and officials" (Sidel 2004: 69). He goes on to state that, at the village level, "power-sharing arrangements, contestation between rival families and factions, and high turnover appear to be the norm" (Sidel 2004: 70). Given the diverse set of actors vying for power, UPP's formidable challenge is to open up the deliberative planning process to broad-based participation while simultaneously protecting program resources from elite capture.

Hypotheses

The chapter tests two foundational assumptions that support arguments in favor of both decentralization and CDD. The first is that, when governance and planning are decentralized and community actors are given more control over the development process, project planning will become more accountable and transparent, and as a result the benefits of development (e.g., project resources) will be more likely to reach appropriate beneficiaries—in this case the urban poor. This hypothesis is tested here by examining the extent to which individual characteristics predict microcredit group membership—specifically gender, educational attainment, per capita expenditures, employment and access to social networks. The second assumption is that decentralization and CDD empower local actors because those processes encourage broad-based participation and give local residents voice and control over development outcomes. This hypothesis, too, is tested by examining the extent to which individual characteristics predict participation in the community boards that undertake planning, implementation and allocation of program resources. Again, we look at gender, educational attainment, per capita expenditures, employment and access to social networks to determine who fills these leadership positions. The alternative to the second hypothesis is that CDD further empowers local elites.

The Urban Poverty Program in Indonesia

The chapter uses UPP baseline and midterm evaluation data to examine critically the foundational assumptions that underlie arguments in favor of decentralization and CDD. UPP began in 1999 as a response to the economic crisis in Indonesia. The program was introduced by the central government in consultation with local governments; however, because of the desire for the program to be community-driven, the program was introduced to communities by independent, program-funded and -trained facilitators who usually came from their respective regions. Implementation in the first phase of the program focused on dense urban corridors in fifty-nine sub-districts (*Kecamatan*) and 1,298 villages (*Kelurahan*) in northern Java, Yogyakarta and Malang (World Bank 1999: 4). The second phase of the program was implemented in approximately 289 sub-districts and 3,150 villages in Java, Sulawesi, Kalimantan and Lombok. During the first years, some communities received approximately 1 bn Rupiah, and smaller communities received 250 m Rupiah. In later years, the allocation was reduced to 250–500 m Rupiah.[8]

There are some other important differences between the earlier years of the program and its more recent implementation. In the early years, when the program was implemented on Java, the majority of communities allocated their grants to microcredit groups (*Kelompok Swadaya Masyarakat*—KSM). It was soon understood by those evaluating the program that microcredit has a limited ability to help the poorest of the poor. So, in the later years when the program expanded beyond Java to the outer islands, approximately 50 percent of funds were allocated to infrastructure development, and roughly 15 percent of funds were allocated to fulfill basic needs. The funds allocated for basic needs provide support for housing rehabilitation, health care expenses and other assistance to help the poorest households. The reader should note that the chapter only evaluates membership in microcredit groups, which represents about 35 percent of the program's funds, as well as membership in community boards, which are responsible for overseeing all aspects of the program.

As part of the program's introduction, the facilitator explained that the program was to be implemented through a community-based organization. In most communities, this required establishing a new community board (*Badan Keswadayaan Masyarakat*—BKM) or strengthening an existing organization to receive and administer the program funds. This process usually took 4–6 months and unfolded with a high degree of variation from one community to the next. The length of

9.1 A microcredit recipient making palm sugar for her new business in Lombok, Indonesia.
© Kumala Sari

time depended on the introduction of a poverty awareness raising campaign, dialogue about what the desirable qualities are in a local leader and how to select the BKM members. In all communities, the BKM exists at the same level as the *Kelurahan*, the lowest level of the state's political administrative hierarchy, although it purposely seeks to set itself apart from that structure. The BKM is managed by community volunteers who are selected by local residents through a deliberative process.

The program was introduced in generally the same way in each community. Faciliators underscored the importance of open public participation, with emphasis placed on the participation of poor residents. For selecting program leaders, the use of a "democratic" process, defined as everyone in the community having an equal voice, was stressed. Also highlighted was the importance of transparency and accountability in resource allocation decisions. These general guidelines were communicated during the program's introduction. In addition, some specific mechanisms for applying the guidelines in practice were also suggested: for example, establishing groups of borrowers comprised of both successful entrepreneurs and poor community members, using secret ballots for leader selection, and displaying program information in public areas in ways that were easy for non-elites to access and understand. However, no mechanisms existed to guarantee that

9.2 A program facilitator introducing a community board in West Java, Indonesia.
© Kumala Sari

the guidelines were followed. Ultimately, residents determined how the program would be implemented in their community, such as the qualities leaders should possess, the detailed protocol for their selection, and the criteria for judging proposals, and that flexibility allowed significant variation in program outcomes.

Data

This section explains how the data set was constructed using data from four surveys. The first source is the UPP2 baseline survey, which collected data between February and March 2004 from all members of a random selection of households in 159 "treatment" and ninety-seven "control" villages. The second source is a midterm survey conducted outside Java between August and November 2005 and on Java between April and June 2006, in which the same households were contacted again in 154 of the "treatment" villages. The sample of the third survey, the "KSM survey," was randomly selected from all households that contained a microedit group member in the treatment villages. Similarly, the respondents in the fourth survey, the "BKM survey," were randomly selected from all BKM members in the treatment villages. The KSM and BKM surveys were conducted at the same time as the midterm survey.

The sample for the baseline survey comprised 37,335 individuals. The midterm survey data were collected from 9,279 individuals. Key variables for the analyses here were created using data from both the baseline and midterm surveys; thus, only respondents who were successfully contacted again in the midterm survey are analyzed. Also, the analyses examine only adults aged twenty years or older. Finally, the sample is limited in different ways for each survey. The baseline–midterm data include an important social network variable for only two respondents per household, one male and one female respondent who are considered to have the most knowledge of participatory development activities in the period prior to the baseline survey. The final baseline–midterm sample thus comprises 8,018 individual respondents from 4,883 households. The KSM and BKM survey respondents included in the data set are the 2,277 microcredit group members and twenty-four community board members from the KSM survey, and the 462 community board members from the BKM survey. The final data set thus has 10,757 individual observations. Table 9.1 illustrates how the various data sources were combined to create the data set analyzed in the chapter.

Variables

The analyses in Table 9.2 describe the sectors and status of employment for program participants and non-participants at the time of the survey. These data were measured at the time of the baseline for the baseline–midterm sample and at the midterm for the KSM and BKM samples, as were the "employment" and "hours worked" variables used in the other analyses. The employment sector variable was divided into ten categories: agriculture; mining and excavation; industry; electricity, gas and water; construction; commerce; transportation and communication; finance; service; and others. Employment status was divided into seven categories: self-employed; government employee; private-sector employee; own-account worker in agriculture; own-account worker outside agriculture; unpaid family worker; and others. Own-account workers differ from the self-employed in that they work alone in their business or with a small number of partners who are also own-account workers.

The descriptive analyses in Tables 9.3 and 9.5 and two regression models in Tables 9.4 and 9.6 identify the individual characteristics likely to predict microcredit and community board membership. In both regression models, the dependent variables are dichotomous indicators of group or board membership. The variables used in the descriptive analyses are the same as the explanatory variables in the models and are divided into three categories. The first category of variables represents an individual's demographic and socio-economic status: gender, educational attainment, per capita expenditures, employment and hours worked in the last seven days. Education is divided into three categories: no education or primary education;

Table 9.1 Construction of UPP evaluation data set

	Individuals	Individuals < 20 years	KSM member	Non-KSM member	KSM member < 20 years	BKM member	Non-BKM member	BKM member < 20 years	Final sample
Baseline survey									
Household survey	37,335 (16,883)	12,683	—	—	—	—	—	—	—
Primary male and female respondent	15,295 (12,343)	129	—	—	—	—	—	—	—
Midterm survey									
Household	9,279 (4,922)	—	—	—	—	—	—	—	—
Baseline-midterm combined	8,055 (4,883)	37	2,124	5,931	5	160	7,895	0	8,018
KSM	2,292 (2,292)	15	2,292	0	15	24	2,268	0	2,277
BKM	462 (462)	0	0	462	0	462	0	0	462
N	10,809	52	4,416	6,393	20	646	10,163	0	10,757

Household numbers are stated in parentheses.

junior high school or senior high school education (omitted in the regression models); and attainment above the senior high school level. Per capita expenditures were measured at the time of the baseline survey and are also divided into three categories: the first to the twenty-fifth percentile, the twenty-sixth to the seventy-fifth percentile (omitted in the models), and the seventy-sixth to the hundredth percentile. Because per capita expenditure data were not available for respondents from the KSM and BKM surveys at the time of the baseline, their expenditures were predicted by regressing the assets of the baseline sample on expenditures for that sample. The estimated coefficients from this model are used to predict per capita expenditures of the KSM and BKM samples, using their asset data. A dichotomous measure of employment indicates whether respondents:

1   worked for, or helped to earn, income in the last seven days; or
2   were not working because they were looking for a job, still in school, working as a housewife, retired or unemployed.

A continuous measure indicates the number of hours an individual has worked in the seven days prior to the survey.

The second set of independent variables measures an individual's access to social networks and social capital. The first variable is a dichotomous measure of the individual's religious affiliation, specifically Muslim or non-Muslim, which includes Christian, Catholic, Hindu, Buddhist and Kong Hu Chu. The second variable is a continuous measure of how many types of government official and activist an individual knows personally. The types of official and activist that a respondent was asked about were the head of the village, head of the village administration, village officials, leaders of the other village governance organizations (e.g., *LPM*, *LKMK* or *LKMD*)[9] and representatives from the Women's Family Welfare Organization (*Wanita PKK*). This variable was created using data from the midterm, KSM or BKM surveys; thus, it was not measured prior to the start of the program. However, the types of official in question are not directly involved in UPP, which is designed to be independent of the village governance structure.

The analyses also include a number of control variables. These are the respondent's age in years; number of household members; and marital status, which is a dichotomous variable indicating that the respondent is married as opposed to single, divorced or widowed. The household size variable was measured at each data collection period, but the age and marital status variables were measured at the baseline for the baseline–midterm sample and at the midterm for the KSM and BKM samples. The age variable was corrected to adjust for the elapsed time between the data collection periods. Finally, all the regression analyses include province fixed effects to control for geographic heterogeneity.

Findings

To examine the relationship between decentralization, CDD, poverty alleviation and elite capture, the findings are divided into three parts. The first part compares the employment patterns and age distributions of KSM and BKM members with those of non-members. Second, descriptive analyses compare several other characteristics of micro-finance members with characteristics of non-members, and regression analyses show which of these characteristics predict participation. Similarly, in the third set of findings, descriptive and regression analyses compare the characteristics of community board members with those of non-members and predict participation on the boards.

In Table 9.2, the first set of analyses describes individual participation by employment sector, employment status and age. All comparisons are statistically significant, indicating that, for example, microcredit group members have patterns of employment significantly different than those who did not participate in the program. More specifically, microcredit group members are significantly more likely than non-members to work in the commerce and industrial sectors, and non-members more often work in the agricultural and service sectors. Community board members are significantly more likely to be employed in the financial and service sectors, and non-members work more often in agriculture, industry or commerce.

As for employment status, microcredit members are significantly more likely than non-members to be self-employed. This finding suggests that participation in the program appeals to individuals who have prior entrepreneurial experience. Community board members are significantly less likely to be self-employed or own-account workers and more likely to work as government or private-sector employees. The higher representation of community board members in the civil service and the formal private sector indicates that board members are more likely than non-members to be socio-economic elites. The age distributions show that microcredit participants are less likely to be elderly (aged 60 or older), and that community board members are more likely to be between the ages of 30 and 49, as compared with non-members.

The next set of descriptive analyses, in Table 9.3, compares the characteristics of individuals who joined a microcredit group with those of individuals who did not. Microcredit members are more likely to be men and also more likely to have junior or senior high school education. KSM members and non-members are equally distributed across the three expenditures categories, although the results of the regression models show that, net of the effects of the other variables, poor individuals are more likely to participate (see Table 9.4 for details). Members are employed more often than non-members are, and members work significantly more hours than non-members do, averaging nearly forty hours per week. The high number of average hours worked by program participants may indicate that the program is serving employed individuals as a secondary means of income. The

Table 9.2 Employment sector, employment status and age distributions of microcredit and community board members and non-members

	KSM (%)	Non-KSM (%)	BKM (%)	Non-BKM (%)
Employment sector				
Agriculture	14.45*	19.25*	10.07*	17.12*
Mining and excavation	0.82*	0.96*	0.37*	0.90*
Industry	9.82*	7.79*	5.41*	8.84*
Electricity, gas and water	0.40*	0.79*	0.19*	0.62*
Construction	3.49*	3.36*	3.17*	3.40*
Commerce	40.70*	26.35*	16.79*	33.21*
Transportation and communication	3.35*	4.45*	1.87*	4.00*
Finance	0.34*	0.54*	2.24*	0.44*
Service	26.43*	35.96*	59.70*	31.09*
Others	0.20*	0.54*	0.19*	0.38*
N	3,523	4,046	536	7,431
Employment status				
Self-employed	67.71*	50.41*	41.64*	58.63*
Government employee	9.60*	17.40*	35.50*	13.41*
Private-sector employee	13.23*	19.60*	17.84*	16.75*
Own-account worker in agriculture	4.48*	6.84*	1.12*	5.79*
Own-account worker outside agriculture	3.54*	4.39*	2.97*	4.02*
Unpaid family worker	1.19*	1.09*	0.56*	1.14*
Others	0.25*	0.27*	0.37*	0.26*
N	3,530	4,051	538	7,443
Age distribution				
20–29 years	10.91*	10.95*	6.74*	11.03*
30–39 years	30.75*	24.60*	32.16*	26.88*
40–49 years	30.07*	27.98*	32.62*	28.80*
50–59 years	19.03*	19.45*	18.07*	19.30*
60–69 years	6.92*	10.45*	8.27*	9.07*
70 years or older	2.32*	6.56*	2.14*	4.92*
N	4,336	6,361	646	10,111

* Variables are significantly different at $p < 0.05$.

Table 9.3 Individual characteristics of microcredit group members and non-members

	KSM	Non-KSM
Individual characteristics		
Female	45.96*	55.12*
Low education	37.19*	44.05*
Medium education	54.59*	46.28*
High education	8.23*	9.67*
Low expenditure (1–25th percentile)	22.06	22.19
Medium expenditure (26–75th percentile)	53.09	50.97
High expenditure (76–100th percentile)	24.85	26.84
Employed	77.64*	59.47*
Hours worked in the last 7 days, mean	37.08*	26.24*
Social networks and social capital		
Non-Muslim	10.95*	7.79*
Number of officials known, mean	4.05*	2.96*
Control variables		
Age, mean	42.89*	45.32*
Household size, mean	4.68*	4.57*
Married	88.71*	90.40*

* Variables are significant at $p < 0.05$.

All figures in the table are percentages except where labeled as mean.

measures of social networks indicate that members are more likely than non-members to identify as being non-Muslim, and that, on average, group members know more government officials. Group members are also significantly younger on average, live in slightly larger households and are less likely to be married.

Table 9.4 shows the results of a logistic regression predicting microcredit group membership. Women are significantly less likely than men to become microcredit group members. Interestingly, education does not predict microcredit group membership. One interpretation of this pattern is that the program is not overly bureaucratic or complex and does not inhibit participation by those with less education. Individuals in the low expenditures category are significantly more likely to become microcredit group members, and individuals in the high expenditure category are significantly less likely to become microcredit group members than are those with moderate expenditures. This finding may indicate that the program is indeed reaching those who need it the most—the urban poor in the lowest per capita expenditure quartile. Moreover, individuals in the highest expenditure quartile are not capturing program resources, though they may not be seeking participation in the program because they have access to other forms of credit. Employment status and hours worked do not significantly affect an individual's likelihood of becoming a microcredit group member. As for the indicators of social networks and social capital, religious affiliation does not predict program participation, but knowing more government officials is positively associated with group membership. One interpretation of this finding is that the program is not as independent from the state governance structure as it sought to be. Turning to the control variables, older respondents are less likely to participate. Household size and marital status have no significant effect on microcredit group membership.

Table 9.4 Logistic regression models predicting microcredit group membership

	Odds ratio	*P*
Individual characteristics		
Female	0.587*	0.000
	(0.041)	
Low education	0.887	0.072
	(0.059)	
High education	0.977	0.811
	(0.095)	
Low expenditure (1–25th percentile)	1.236*	0.006
	(0.095)	
High expenditure (76–100th percentile)	0.805*	0.003
	(0.059)	
Employment status	1.010	0.380
	(0.119)	
Hours worked in the last 7 days	0.999	0.799
	(0.002)	
Social networks and social capital		
Non-Muslim	1.089	0.589
	(0.171)	
Knowledge of government officials	1.880*	0.000
	(0.042)	
Control variables		
Age	0.991*	0.001
	(0.003)	
Household size	0.984	0.385
	(0.018)	
Married	1.212	0.088
	(0.136)	
N		7,942

* Variables are significant at p < 0.05.

All regression models include province fixed effects.

Table 9.5 Individual characteristics of community board members and non-members

	BKM	Non-BKM
Individual characteristics		
Female	25.23*	52.05*
Low education	4.02*	41.92*
Medium education	46.44	49.40
High education	49.54*	8.67*
Low expenditure (1–25th percentile)	9.38*	22.39*
Medium expenditure (26–75th percentile)	46.88	51.55
High expenditure (76–100th percentile)	43.75*	26.05*
Employed	76.16*	66.43*
Hours worked in the last 7 days, mean	33.40*	30.45*
Social networks and social capital		
Non-Muslim	9.44	8.94
Number of officials known, mean	5.46*	3.39*
Control variables		
Age, mean	43.82	44.36
Household size, mean	4.69	4.60
Married	90.08	89.70

* Variables are significant at $p < 0.05$.

All figures in the table are percentages except where labeled as mean.

Table 9.5 compares the individual characteristics of community board members with those of non-members. Interestingly, only 25 percent of the board members are female, whereas 52 percent of non-members are female. Board members are much less likely than non-members to have low educational attainment and much more likely to have post-secondary education. A similar pattern was found for per capita expenditures. Few community board members are from the low expenditure category. The majority of board members are from the high expenditure category. These findings indicate that community boards tend to be dominated by elites defined in terms of gender, educational attainment and economic status. Community board members are more likely to be employed, and they worked more hours on average in the week prior to the survey. The effects of social networks and social capital are consistent with the findings for microcredit group membership. No significant differences were found in the religious affiliations of community board members, but, on average, community board members know more government officials. As for the control variables, board members do not differ from non-members in their average age, household size or marital status.

The final model, Table 9.6, examines the relationships between individual characteristics and community board membership. As in the findings for microcredit group membership, women are significantly less likely to become community board members. Interpreting the microcredit and community board membership findings together, gender barriers seem to exclude some women from receiving microcredit resources and to exclude a much larger group of women from assuming leadership roles as community board members.[10] Compared with respondents with junior and senior high education, those without education or with only primary-

Table 9.6 Logistic regression models predicting community board membership

	Odds ratio	*P*
Individual characteristics		
Female	0.265*	0.000
	(0.068)	
Low education	0.394*	0.002
	(0.117)	
High education	2.771*	0.000
	(0.545)	
Low expenditure (1–25th percentile)	0.903	0.739
	(0.277)	
High expenditure (76–100th percentile)	1.348	0.124
	(0.261)	
Employment status	0.588	0.115
	(0.198)	
Hours worked in the last 7 days	0.997	0.573
	(0.006)	
Social networks and social capital		
Non-Muslim	1.248	0.596
	(0.523)	
Knowledge of government officials	3.113*	0.000
	(0.297)	
Control variables		
Age	0.988	0.161
	(0.009)	
Household size	1.017	0.762
	(0.057)	
Married	1.317	0.478
	(0.511)	
N		7,850

* Variables are significant at p < 0.05.

All regression models include province fixed effects.

level attainment are less likely to be board members; individuals with post-secondary education are more likely to hold these positions. Interestingly, an individual's per capita expenditures, employment status and hours worked do not affect board membership. Turning to the social networks and social capital variables, an individual's religious affiliation has no significant effect, but, as expected, knowing more officials is positively associated with community board membership. This finding in both the microcredit and community board models suggests that, despite UPP's efforts to distance itself from previously established state governance structures, these social networks still have a powerful impact on individual participation. As for the control variables, an individual's age, living in a larger household and being married have no significant effect on community board membership.

Conclusion

In Indonesia, recent historical events have created both opportunities and challenges for the implementation of community-driven poverty alleviation efforts. These events include, but are not limited to, the rise in poverty resulting from the economic crisis, the political reform and pro-democracy movements, and the enactment of national decentralization legislation. The analyses in this chapter tested a series of assumptions that are foundational to decentralization and community-driven development and the opportunities they provide to local residents. The chapter sought to examine whether these efforts reach the poor and to what extent the leadership and decision-making roles are open to non-elites. These questions were addressed through an examination of membership in two groups that are central to UPP:

1   micro-finance groups; and
2   community boards.

In summary, the microcredit resources seem to be reaching more individuals than average in two employment sectors: industry and commerce. As one might expect, the microcredit portion of the program is helping those who have some experience with owning a business. As evident from both the descriptive statistics and regression model, gender barriers are inhibiting women from accessing microcredit resources. A positive finding about the program is that an individual's low educational attainment does not inhibit receipt of microcredit. Another positive finding is that resources are more often reaching individuals who are in the bottom quartile of the per capita expenditure distribution and less often helping those who are in the highest quartile of the expenditure distribution, thus indicating limited "leakage" of program benefits.

In some areas, UPP has the potential to reinforce patterns of social exclusion and inequality. For example, the fact that those who own their own business are more likely to participate in the microcredit portion of the program could make it difficult for those without prior entrepreneurial experience to take full advantage of the program. Also, individuals who know more government officials personally are more likely to receive microcredit resources and assume a leadership role. It is difficult to suggest ways that UPP might address these two findings. One reason is that someone who is currently running a business is in a better position to borrow money for a business venture than is someone who is unemployed or working in an unrelated sector such as agriculture. The second reason is that the microcredit program design encourages individuals to apply for loans in small groups that share responsibility for debt repayment. In other words, all individuals in these small groups assume the debt burden of the other group members. The design helps ensure repayment, but it also helps ensure the exclusion of individuals who are viewed as economically unreliable or inexperienced. These individuals are excluded to protect other participants from personally having to repay part of the microcredit debt of a failed business.

Turning to the problem of elite capture via community board membership: members are more likely to be civil servants or private sector employees, and they more often work in the finance and service sectors. Community board membership is more likely among individuals who are male, who are highly educated and who are well-connected to government officials. From these empirical findings it is easy to conclude that only socially and politically well-connected elites have control over program resources and decision-making. However, when these findings are viewed in light of the microcredit membership, it appears that these elites are delivering program resources to appropriate beneficiaries. It is therefore concluded that the findings point to a pattern of *elite control*, but not of elite capture of resources, with the attendant corruption and misuse of power. These findings are also consistent with earlier evaluations of the first phase of UPP (Beard and Dasgupta 2006; Dasgupta and Beard 2007). The findings thus indicate that, although the program is fulfilling CDD's first assumption by successfully delivering resources to the poor, it is falling short of its potential to empower the poor and socially excluded. For the program to achieve this objective in the future, it must make further efforts to diversify its leadership by including more women and non-elites.

Notes

1   The opinions expressed in the chapter are solely the views of the authors and should not be attributed to the World Bank, its executive directors and member countries, or any affiliated organization. The authors thank George Soraya for his support of the evaluation and comments on the chapter and Yulia Herawati for her help with the analyses. The authors gratefully acknowledge the funding from the World Bank's research support budget and the Trust Fund for Environmentally and Socially Sustainable Development (TFESSD).

2   The events briefly described in the introduction are the culmination of a longer period of complex, more covert movements for social and political transformation, which included but are not limited to the separatist movements in East Timor and Aceh, diverse labor movements and the growth and momentum of the Indonesian Democratic Party; see Aspinall (2005) or Bertrand (2004). A detailed history of this period is beyond the scope of the chapter. The point is, however, that decentralization and CDD efforts need to be interpreted in the context of broader social and political change that is occurring in Indonesia.

3 Throughout the chapter, the term community and village are used interchangeably to refer to a *Kelurahan*, the smallest political–administrative unit in urban areas.

4 When the term microcredit is used in reference to UPP it refers to a revolving fund (*dana bergulir*). In a limited number of cases, the fund and the profit from the fund were used for purposes other than providing credit to entrepreneurs, such as building infrastructure or making scholarships available, respectively.

5 The section entitled "Decentralization, community-driven development and elite capture" and the section entitled "The Urban Poverty Program in Indonesia" borrow from Dasgupta and Beard (2007), published by the Institute of Social Studies and Blackwell Publishing. The remainder of the chapter is original.

6 For more information about decentralization in Indonesia see Booth (2003); Crane (1995); Fane (2003); Ferrazzi (2000); Silver (2003); Smoke and Lewis (1996); USAID Democratic Reform Support Program (2006); and World Bank (2003).

7 Revisions were made to the key decentralization laws in 2004, specifically concerning the role of regional governance and its finances. For a comprehensive update of this ongoing process, see USAID Democratic Reform Support Program (2006).

8 The exchange rate at the time was approximately US$1 per 9,300 Rupiah.

9 LPM—*Lembaga Pemberdayaan Masyarakat* (People's Empowerment Organization); LKMK—*Lembaga Ketahanan Masyarakat Kelurahan* (Community Welfare Organization); LKMD—*Lembaga Ketahanan Masyarakat Desa* (Village Welfare Organization).

10 For additional analyses of the relationship between gender and participatory development in Indonesia, see Beard and Cartmill 2007.

Appendix

Table 9.7 Descriptive statistics for the variables included in the regression models

	Mean	*SD*
Dependent variables		
KSM membership	0.265	(0.441)
BKM memberships	0.020	(0.141)
Individual characteristics		
Female	0.515	(0.500)
Low education	0.427	(0.495)
Medium education[a]	0.472	(0.499)
High education	0.100	(0.300)
Low expenditure (1–25th percentile)	0.222	(0.416)
Medium expenditure (26–75th percentile)[a]	0.515	(0.500)
High expenditure (76–100th percentile)	0.262	(0.440)
Employed	0.618	(0.486)
Hours worked in the last 7 days	27.377	(26.34)
Social network and social capital		
Non-Muslim	0.095	(0.293)
Knowledge of government officials	3.308	(1.546)
Control variables		
Age	45.37	(12.26)
Household size	4.610	(1.670)
Married	0.916	(0.277)

a This category is omitted in the models.

References

Abraham, A. and Platteau, J.P. (2000) "The dilemma of participation with endogenous community imperfections," Department of Economics and CRED (Centre de Recherche en Economie du Développement), Namur, Belgium: University of Namur.

Antlöv, H. (2003) "Village government and rural development in Indonesia: The new democratic framework," *Bulletin of Indonesian Economic Studies* 39 (2): 193–214.

Aspinall, E. (2005) *Opposing Suharto: Compromise, Resistance and Regime Change in Indonesia*, Stanford, CA: Stanford University Press.

Beard, V.A. and Dasgupta, A. (2006) "Collective action and community-driven development in rural and urban Indonesia," *Urban Studies* 43 (9): 1451–68.

Beard, V.A. and Cartmill, R.S. (2007) "Gender, collective action and participatory development in Indonesia," *International Development Planning Review* 29 (2): 185–214.

Bertrand, J. (2004) *Nationalism and Ethnic Conflict in Indonesia*, Cambridge: Cambridge University Press.

Bird, J. (1999) "Indonesia in 1998: The pot boils over," *Asian Survey* 39 (1): 27–37.

Booth, A. (2003) "Decentralisation and poverty alleviation in Indonesia," *Environment and Planning C* 21 (2): 181–202.

Crane, R. (1995) "The practice of regional development in Indonesia: Resolving central–local coordination issues in planning and finance," *Public Administration and Development* 15 (2): 139–49.

Dasgupta, A. and Beard, V.A. (2007) "Community driven development, collective action and elite capture in Indonesia," *Development and Change* 38 (2): 229–49.

Dongier, P., Van Domelen, J., Ostrom, E., Rizvi, A., Wakeman, W., Bebbington, A., Alkire, S., Esmail, T. and Polski, M. (2002) "Community-driven development," in J. Klugman (ed.) *A Sourcebook for Poverty Reduction Strategies*, Vol. 1, Washington, DC: World Bank, pp. 301–11.

Fane, G. (2003) "Change and continuity in Indonesia's new fiscal decentralisation arrangements," *Bulletin of Indonesian Economic Studies* 39 (2): 159–76.

Ferrazzi G. (2000) "Using the 'f' word: Federalism in Indonesia's decentralization discourse," *Publius* 30 (2): 63–85.

Fung, A. and Wright, E.O. (eds) (2003) *Deepening Democracy: Institutional Innovations in Empowered Participatory Governance*, London: Verso.

Hadiz, V.R. (2003) "Power and politics in North Sumatra: The uncompleted *reformasi*," in E. Aspinall and G. Fealy (eds) *Local Power and Politics in Indonesia: Democratisation and Decentralisation*, Singapore: Institute of Southeast Asian Studies, pp. 119–31.

Hirschman, A.O. (1970) *Exit, Voice, and Loyalty: Responses to Decline in Firms, Organizations, and States*, Cambridge, MA: Harvard University Press.

Hirschman, A.O. (1984) *Getting Ahead Collectively: Grassroots Experiences in Latin America*, New York: Pergamon Press.

Kaiser, K., Pattinasarany, D. and Schulze, G.G. (2006) "Decentralization, governance and public services in Indonesia," in P. Smoke, E.J. Gomez and G.E. Peterson (eds) *Decentralization in Asia and Latin America: Towards a Comparative Interdisciplinary Perspective*, Cheltenham: Edward Elgar, pp. 164–207.

Mansuri, G. and Rao, V. (2004) "Community-based and -driven development: A critical review," *The World Bank Research Observer* 19 (1): 1–39.

McCarthy, J.F. (2002) "Turning in circles: District governance, illegal logging, and environmental decline in Sumatra, Indonesia," *Society and Natural Resources* 15 (10): 867–86.

Nordholt, H.S. (2004) "Decentralisation in Indonesia: Less state, more democracy?", in J. Harris, K. Stokke and O. Törnquist (eds) *Politicising Democracy: The New Local Politics of Democratisation*, New York: Palgrave Macmillan, pp. 29–50.

Olowu, D. (2003) "Local institutional and political structures and processes: Recent experience in Africa," *Public Administration and Development* 23 (1): 41–52.

Sidel, J.T. (2004) "Bossism and democracy in the Philippines, Thailand and Indonesia: Towards an alternative framework for the study of 'local strongmen,'" in J. Harris, K. Stokke and O. Törnquist (eds) *Politicising Democracy: The New Local Politics of Democratisation*, New York: Palgrave Macmillan, pp. 51–74.

Siegel, J.T. (1998) "Early thoughts on the violence of May 13 and 14, 1998 in Jakarta," *Indonesia* 66: 74–108.

Silver, C. (2003) "Do the donors have it right? Decentralization and changing local governance in Indonesia," *The Annals of Regional Science* 37 (3): 421–34.

Smoke, P. and Lewis, B.D. (1996) "Fiscal decentralization in Indonesia: A new approach to an old idea," *World Development* 24 (8): 1281–99.

Turner, M., Podger, O., Sumardjono, M. and Tirthayasa, W.K. (2003) *Decentralisation in Indonesia: Redesigning the State*, Canberra: Asia Pacific Press.

USAID Democratic Reform Support Program (2006) *Decentralization 2006: Stock Taking on Indonesia's Recent Decentralization Reforms*, Jakarta: Democratic Reform Support Program.

World Bank (1999) *Program Appraisal Document: Indonesia Urban Poverty Program*, Urban Development Sector Unit, Indonesia Country Department, East Asia and Pacific Region, Jakarta: World Bank.

World Bank (2003) *Decentralizing Indonesia: A Regional Public Expenditure Review Overview Report*, Report No. 26191-IND, Jakarta: World Bank.

Chapter 10

University–community partnership

Institutionalizing empowered participatory planning in Indonesia

Christopher Silver and Tubagus Furqon Sofhani

Introduction

The past decade has witnessed first the rise and then the fall of market liberalism orthodoxy in development economics. In the early 1990s, development economics based upon market liberalism challenged the interventionist state as an impediment to growth and promoted privatization of service delivery and social welfare programs through non-governmental entities as the answer. Yet the market approach failed to acknowledge the necessity of civil and political institutions to counter the tendency of autocratic states to use privatization to enhance the control and power of entrenched interests. Privatization in regimes where power remained vested in the hands of a minority of economic elites further distorted the existing system. In those developing nations that were able to shake off autocratic regimes (most notably in Indonesia, South Africa, the Philippines and recently in Mexico), the following factors were present to some degree: a move to restructure governmental institutions through decentralization; strengthening and broadening political participation through the introduction of democratic practices; and encouraging non-governmental, civic institutions to sustain and consolidate political and governmental reforms (Pycroft 1994). Although democratization and decentralization have had relatively long gestation periods in several of these cases, what is distinctive about the successes is the focus on strengthening social capital as a complement to institutional change (Wunsch 1998). International organizations such as the World Bank and the Ford Foundation have made social capital formation programs a priority in their assistance to developing nations. The changing institutional forms of local planning tied to national political and administrative reform also have connections to social capital formation and represent a shift from state-dominated decision and planning processes to a locally focused participatory structure that promotes accountability. As Mohan and Stokke observe, civil society institutions can also be vehicles for participation in development programming and empowerment of target groups of poor people. In short, social capital formation has invigorated a planning approach that directly involves a variety of local stakeholders and a significantly greater level of responsibility at the local level (2000: 248).

This case study examines the links between decentralization and a changing planning paradigm in Indonesia's emerging democratic society. A new paradigm in local planning processes, known widely as participatory planning, emerged from the decentralization movement in Indonesia following the fall of the New Order government in 1998. In Indonesia's development efforts over the previous three decades, the rhetoric of participatory planning (typically referred to as planning from the bottom upward) and decentralization was advanced as an objective of the New Order government. In fact, local administrators and planners (supported by consultants) were not accountable to the communities that they served, but only to their superiors in central government in Jakarta. Local non-governmental stakeholders had little freedom to express political preferences and played a negligible role in the process of planning. The proliferation of participatory processes in Indonesian localities since 1998 transformed planning into a process to reach a collective agreement among a greater number of potential stakeholders and shifted the role of planners from that of technician to facilitator and mediator to reach collective agreement among the stakeholders. The proliferation of local stakeholder groups, generally referred to as "forums," introduced a new community-focused institution into local government. Although varying in their effectiveness across Indonesia's vast urban landscape, these forums constitute a key component of the participatory processes that are transforming planning at the local level. Antlov (2003: 77) argued that the citizen forum has provided an opportunity for disadvantaged groups to play a larger role in the decision-making process at the local level.

This study examines a model of participatory planning that emerged in the Sumedang district of West Java, Indonesia. The emergence of participatory planning in Sumedang since 1998 not only exemplifies grassroots mobilization in the broader context of the decentralization movement in Indonesia, but it is a unique variation on the sort of university–community and NGO–community partnerships that expanded participatory planning in other parts of the developing world over the past two decades. To understand the significance of the Sumedang case, it is necessary to see it against the backdrop of the larger decentralization movement in Indonesia that precipitated the changing paradigm in local planning.

Indonesian context

The case of Indonesia conforms closely to the model of changing development economics outlined by Mohan and Stokke (2000). The New Order regime from the mid 1960s through to the 1980s represented a case of a highly centralized governmental system that closely regulated both the economy and the supporting public institutions. President Suharto embraced privatization as a way to move towards market liberalism, and his government's direct authority over localities throughout Indonesia expanded the scope of privatization in addressing development needs.

Although the New Order government authored a "decentralization" statute (Law 5/1974) calling for a shift in decision-making to lower levels, the two decades following passage of the 1974 law saw the reverse process, that is, a consolidation of power in the central government ministries in Jakarta at the expense of local governments. This power was executed through the operations offices of central government ministries at the local level. Local legislatures (at the city, district and provincial levels) merely rubber stamped decisions made by local administrators who were appointed by, and therefore accountable to, central government. Reinforcing the control of central government was a system of public administration whereby all local government officials were employees of a central government agency, namely the Ministry of Home Affairs. Mayors, district heads as well as their senior staff relied upon detailed directives and plans from Jakarta, and were not accountable locally and made no effort to engage local stakeholders in planning.

In 1995, the New Order government took a tentative and belated step to operationalize the decentralization process outlined in the 1974 law. It launched a two-year district autonomy pilot project that transferred select functions from central and provincial levels to local government. It involved one district in each of the twenty provinces (not including Jakarta) and did not involve any of Indonesia's urban areas (Beier and Ferrazzi 1997). One fundamental limitation of the district autonomy pilot project was the limited scope of the transfer of responsibility. Another was that it did not include complementary transfers of central government funds to support new local functions in local government finance. All districts and cities (including the twenty-six districts in the pilot program) continued to rely on grants and loans emanating from, and administered by, the central government to meet virtually all local needs (Devas 1989). The purse strings held by the government in Jakarta made Indonesia one of the least decentralized countries in the world well into the 1990s, despite the rhetoric of the New Order government supporting greater decentralization and local participation in decision-making.

The economic and political crisis that hit Indonesia in 1997 (Forrester and May 1999) derailed privatization, led to the unanticipated demise of Suharto's New Order regime, and accelerated the process of decentralization in central–local government relations (*Jakarta Post* 3/10/01; Leigland, 1993; McAndrews 1986; Ranis and Stewart, 1994; Walker, 1991). Two laws enacted in 1999 under the short-lived presidency of B.J. Habibie (and prior to Indonesia's first democratic national elections in 1999) framed an imminent radical transformation of central–local relations. Law 22/1999 replaced the hierarchical governance system linking local governments to the central government with a system that granted local governments substantial autonomy. Mayors and district heads were no longer appointed by provincial government. This change made local government administrators accountable to the local population in a fundamentally new way (Alm and Bahl 1999). According to Ryas Rasyid, who briefly headed a ministry created specifically to oversee implementation of Law 22, the new paradigm in inter-governmental relations necessitated a fundamental shift from central to local dominance, with districts and municipalities receiving greatly expanded functions (US Embassy in Jakarta, July 21, 2000, Press Release).

Law 22 devolved power to local authorities by specifying a limited set of functions of central government (international policies, defense and security, the judiciary, monetary and fiscal policy, religion, national planning, natural resources utilization and the state economic institutional systems) and leaving all of the rest of the governmental responsibilities to localities. This included responsibility for health, education, urban services, agriculture, the environment and coastal management, all of which previously were the domain of central government ministries in Jakarta. The new law also removed another form of local government account-ability to provincial officials by stipulating that all decisions from the local legislatures and local administrators be reported to the Ministry of Home Affairs, thereby bypassing the provincial level. Although Law 22/1999 failed to specify what role the central government would exercise in reviewing local decisions, the assumption among local officials was that they now possessed full discretion so long as their decisions were consistent with national laws.

In addition, local government personnel were no longer employees of central government. Beginning in January 2001, in a process that generated considerable controversy, central government employees in ministry offices in Jakarta and in the localities throughout Indonesia were transferred to their local counterparts. Law 22 ended the practice of central government ministries influencing local affairs through deconcentrated regional offices. At the same time, the demise of the virtually one-party system of electing local legislators and the introduction of a multiple-party political system strengthened the resolve of locals to press for full decentralization. The companion act, Law 25, created the fiscal infrastructure for decentralization through the establishment of a new revenue-sharing grant from central government, *dana alokosi umum* (general revenue fund), and, by specifying that localities would be able to retain a substantial share of the proceeds from natural resource extractions within their jurisdiction, provided funds that previously went directly to Jakarta.

Deepening democratic process: university and community network in Jatinangor, Sumedang District

Although several participatory development programs emerged at the begin-ning of the 1990s, planning practices at the local level continued to be guided by Regulation 9, issued in 1982 by the Department of Home Affairs through *Pedoman Penyusunan Perencanaan dan Pengendalian Pembangunan Daerah* (Guidelines for Planning and Controlling Regional Development), commonly referred to as P5D. Under the planning process set forth in P5D, villages (*desa*) and sub-district government (*kecamatan*) propose a list of programs on the basis of their needs and priorities. On the basis of this list and sectoral priorities of all local government agencies, the local government formulated a development plan that would be submitted to the provincial government. Based upon all of the local government and sectoral agency proposals, the provincial government produced its own request to be submitted to the central government. The central government decided which components of the proposal to support as part of the national development program.

Although the government considers this regulation as a form of bottom-up planning in regional development, local priorities were inevitably lost in the process of developing the national program. In terms of participation by the local stakeholders, there was a wide gap between what the regulation prescribed and what happened on the ground. At the local level, P5D was dominated by the local government agencies and local parliament members and afforded limited room for non-governmental interests, especially marginal groups, to influence the outcome. The bottom-up planning process manipulated citizen participation to strengthen central government targets prescribed by sectoral objectives set forth in the Jakarta ministries. Even with decentralization, local participation mattered little, and this led to cynicism and apathy in the face of unresponsive higher-level decision-makers (Ferrazi 2001: 256). Furthermore, this process is still used by certain influential people as a way to get access to the public fund for their own interests through their connections to the local government officers. P5D was regarded as inconsistent with a real spirit of good governance demanding public participation and transparency in the planning process and budget policy.

In addition, community participation under the P5D process covered only the program suggestion stages from the village level, sub-district level and finally to the local government level. It did not cover budget decisions. Budget authority remained in the hands of local government officers and the local parliament members. Citizens lacked any access to the decision-making process to determine the priority of programs and their budget. Moreover, the P5D concept does not provide a clear mechanism to choose participants. In reality, the decision as to who would be invited to the planning workshop where priorities would be set was made exclusively by the government officers at each level.

Recognizing the limitations of the conventional local planning processes to fulfill the expectations of democratic decentralization and to address the variety of social, economic and environmental issues, a community-based participatory planning process was initiated by several non-governmental groups to model an alternative approach. The Jatinangor Forum was initiated in early 2000 by the planning faculty from the Institute of Technology, Bandung, in concert with a loosely aligned group of local activists. Jatinangor is a sub-district within the larger Sumedang regency, located in the West Java province adjacent to the highly urbanized and industrialized Bandung city and district, and traditionally grounded in agricultural activities. Jatinangor is distinguished by its designation by the national government as the place where two Bandung (city)-based public universities and two local government-affiliated educational institutions built new campus facilities on land previously used for agriculture. The effect of the campus building program in the 1990s was the rapid growth of the community, without any plan and without the infrastructure investment necessary to accommodate the growth.

Initially funded by a grant from the US Agency for International Development in collaboration with planning faculty from the University of Illinois, Urbana-Champaign, the pilot project later acquired critical financial backing from the Ford Foundation under its Civil Society and Governance initiative. The objectives of the Jatinangor pilot project were to establish a stakeholders' (or citizens') forum, to develop the planning and management agenda and to formulate collective action plans to address the issues in Jatinangor through a participatory planning process. The Jatinangor Forum was initiated following an organizational meeting of local stakeholders held on the Institute of Technology Bandung (ITB)'s Bandung (city) campus in August 2000. Subsequently, workshops involving all local stakeholders under the aegis of the Jatinangor Forum explored local needs, to assess the limitation of the conventional planning processes (P5D), and to produce an alternative local development planning process. Between the August 2000 gathering and June 2001, the Jatinagor Forum sponsored eight community-wide workshops that together drew into the participatory process hundreds of participants, mostly from the local community. The Forum established a permanent office, with staff, and the leadership group, which included representatives from all of the local stakeholder groups, met weekly for the first two years to craft its own indigenous brand of advocacy/participatory planning. Students and staff not only from ITB but also from the four local universities in Jatinangor provided a steady supply of labor to carry out action research projects and to respond to requests from local citizens for assistance. For many of the students involved in the activities of the Forum, they were learning firsthand the meaning of participatory planning while also contributing to the unique approach that was being formulated in the district (Silver and Sofhani 2001). What was unique about the Jatinangor approach to participatory planning, in the context of Indonesia's normal processes, was that it consistently engaged simultaneously all groups in the community, including the universities, local governments (both the Sumedang district government as well as that of the adjacent Bandung district), the local legislative assemblies, and every non-government institution down to block level. The activities of the Forum extended beyond the local capacity building workshops and involved community research, advocacy planning with local government, establishment of new institutions, creation of a network to link Jatinangor institutions for mobilization when necessary, and a monitoring process to ensure that the action plans were being implemented by the appropriate agencies. The Jatinangor initiative contributed to a deepening of democratic processes in Indonesia by, using Fung's term (2004), promoting the notion of empowered participation in the planning process. Specifically, five major characteristics of its participatory planning notion are explained below.

Scaling up of participatory planning from project to planning and policy

Stimulated by the notion that participation can be effective if it is followed by institutional change, the Jatinangor advocacy effort scaled up its participatory approach from projects to policies. During the1990s, Indonesian government projects, especially the poverty alleviation programs, adopted the participatory approach to manage the projects. However, as mentioned above, the regular (annual) development planning (P5D) maintained the apparatus of the New Order government's centralized development approach. To implement fundamental change in the participatory approach, the Forum pushed to reform the conventional planning process (P5D) through legislation reform in Sumedang, which was now legally possible because of decentralization.

By instituting participatory planning through a new local regulation rather than just through tacit support from the leadership, Forum members believed that the participatory approach was more likely to have a sustainable influence in the public decision-making process.

Gaventa has argued (2004: 18) that, "although the legal frameworks are not sufficient by themselves, they constitute an enabling factor to more empowered forms of participation." Furthermore Gaventa contends that "participatory approaches are more likely to have the greatest potential for influence if they can be strengthened by claims to participation as a legal right" (2004: 18).

In the case of the Jatinangor project, members of the Forum scaled up participatory planning from short-term government projects to the annual local development planning process. Similar to other municipalities in Indonesia, several government projects, especially poverty alleviation projects, have been performed on the basis of a participatory approach. Through continuous advocacy efforts, the Forum has been quite successful in expanding the approach covering planning process and budget policy. A decree (*Surat Edaran*) of the Sumedang District Head concerning the annual local development planning process passed in 2001 and shifted the public decision-making process from the government to the "governance" domain. The inclusiveness and deliberative democracy engendered by the decree altered the role of the local government agency to one of managing the planning process.

Nandang, one of the local leaders of the Jatinangor Forum, described the change first observed under the new decree:

Under the Misbah administration [which had enacted the decree], the implementation
. . . was better in terms of allocated time for every level of planning workshop [two days
for sub-district workshop and three days for district workshop]. The 2002 district
planning workshop lasted five days. Moreover, the number of participants increased
significantly [more than 100 people involved in the district workshop] coming from
different backgrounds.

These gains were shortlived, however. As Nandang noted, "the political change
in Sumedang District after the election of (a new) district head in 2004 made the
workshop less interesting. The number of participants declined."

The Sumedang District continued to rely on the District Head Decree to
guide its annual local development planning process in 2005 and 2006. In effect,
the decree binds only the executive agency, whereas the local legislative body,
DPRD, was not required to follow the recommendations of the planning process. As a result, members of DPRD still have a chance to change development
programs that have been agreed upon by stakeholders in the local planning
workshops and supported by the local executives. Disappointments were frequently
experienced among the workshop participants because some key proposals were
blocked by the members of DPRD. In other words, the deliberative democracy
that has been practiced at the workshop was undermined by the representative
democratic system at a later stage. In addition, the elimination of some of the
participant proposals has happened frequently, without a clear explanation why
this has occurred or even consultation with the participants. The final decision was
still in the hands of the small circle of the budget committees drawn from the
legislative and executive bodies.

Given the limited authority of the District Head Decree, the Forum pushed
for a local regulation on participatory planning and budgeting through continuous
discussion with the members of DPRD and the executive body. The intent of this
movement was to advance the values of inclusiveness and deliberative process within
the whole process of planning and budgeting, and to bind both the executive and
legislative bodies to support these values. However, the emergence of new political
leadership in Sumedang as a result of the 2004 general and district head election
hampered this movement. The limited understanding of participatory processes of
the new members of DPRD and the new district head delayed further reforms
through the legislative process.

In the middle of 2005, the Forum initiated its first workshop with the new
members of DPRD. This workshop was also attended by several experts from
non-governmental organizations and local universities who had experience in
formulating and advocating participatory planning. This workshop proved successful in generating a new awareness about participatory planning among members
of DPRD. Although the Jatinangor Forum did not officially sponsor the workshops

and meetings that followed this initial gathering, a Forum member became the key individual in stimulating continuous discussions involving members of DPRD, the executive and NGOs. By getting support and supervision from two local NGOs, the Inisiatif and the B-Trust, the discussions became a collective learning forum that infused their perspective on public planning into the approach of local decision-makers. After seven months of deliberations, a new local regulation about local planning and budgeting procedures passed in December 2006.

Members of the Forum were involved intensively in promoting the idea of a local regulation. According to Forum leader, Nandang:

> The Forum has mainly involved in *Musyawarah Perencanaan Pembangunan* [development planning workshop] at the sub-district and district level. Forum representatives provided constructive ideas on how to develop the workshop mechanism. Although the Forum did not participate officially in composing the local regulation, the Forum had a significant role in disseminating the notion of participatory planning and budgeting that eventually stimulated some members of DPRD to sponsor the initial 2005 workshop. This first workshop stimulated follow-up workshops that finally produced the local regulation.

Integrating planning and budgeting process

Proponents of participatory planning argue that development planning will be effective if it is an integral process with the budget policy (Gaventa 2004: 19). The planning process should be a rational action in which information on resource capacity is available before planners initiate a plan. Under the P5D planning process, there is no integration between planning process and budget policy. At the same time, however, critics of participatory planning in Jatinangor noted that the outcomes of the local planning workshops lacked information about the allocated budget for the proposed programs. Citizens made program recommendations without considering the financial capacity of the government to implement them. The budget process was separate and unconnected to planning, determined at a later stage by selected members of the budget committee, a group drawn exclusively from the executive and legislative bodies. Not only was the budget-making process inaccessible to the planning workshop participants, but in general it lacked transparency outside the governmental apparatus. Evidence of the disconnect between planning and budgeting was the fact that most of the proposed programs formulated during the Sumedang workshops were eliminated at the later step owing to budget limitations. For those actively engaged in planning the community's future, the lack of integration between planning and budgeting was a major disappointment. Forum members felt that they wasted their time in formulating programs when the final decision was in the hands of the limited circle of actors on the budget committee, most of whom, never participated in the planning workshop.

Drawing from the example of the Porto Alegre, Brazil, experience (Baiocchi 2003) provided by the Forum's academic partners, the Forum pushed for a change in the regulation of the local development planning process in Sumedang to integrate planning and budgeting. As in the Porto Alegre case, the Sumedang government would need to provide a preliminary budget for every village (*desa*) and sub-district (*kekamatan*) before the initial village planning workshop started. Based on the anticipated revenues available, every workshop at the village, sub-district and district levels would construct a work program. Informing participants about the budget parameters at the beginning of the planning workshops would enable the participants to produce an informed and reasonable program and avoid production of a project shopping list that could not be accommodated. In addition, it would educate the citizen and local government participants to produce a plan and to establish priorities on the basis of available resources.

Encouraging inclusion and strengthening deliberative process

The advocacy efforts of the Jatinangor Forum and its Bandung-based counterparts, Inisiatif and B-Trust, expanded the meaning of participation from a government activity to the governance domain, involving the three main agents of governance, namely the state, civil society and private interests. This expanded meaning of participation was demonstrated in the language of one of the articles of the local regulation of Sumedang District. It stated that the workshop participants should represent all local parties, including local government officers, local community organization leaders, NGO activists, professional organizations, religious leaders, university representatives and those involved in research centers. The spirit of inclusion of diverse communities to engage in the decision-making process was essential to the new planning system in Sumedang, made possible through the new regulations.

Besides embracing and affecting inclusiveness, the Sumedang regulations deepened democratic practices regarding the role of the community delegates in the local decision-making process. Although this was undertaken in the midst of a nationwide governmental reform movement in Indonesia, what was accomplished in Sumedang vastly outdistanced changes taking place in other localities. Elsewhere, the chief power in the process of public decision-making remained in the hands of the local government and its business allies. The role of the community residents in the planning processes continued to be largely one of receiving information or making some suggestions, but not directly as a part of public decision-making. By contrast, the Sumedang local regulation advanced participation beyond giving information and conducting a consultation process. It involved a degree of shared responsibility for decision-making in producing public plans that was unprecedented in Indonesia, as well as other developing nations dominated by centralized and bureaucratic systems.

Deepening democratic processes have also been promoted by the Forum Jatinangor through its institutionalized *forum warga* (citizen forum). The growing number of forums in many sub-districts in Sumedang since 2000, facilitated by several NGOs, including Forum Jatinangor, indicates the shift of democratic practices from—using Young's terms (2000)—the aggregative model to the deliberative one. This process is not a substitute for representative democracy in the Indonesian political system. Rather, it deepens democratic process by introducing the values of inclusion, political equality, reasonableness and publicity in the public decision-making process (Young 2000: 23).

In addition to the citizen forums, the deliberative process has also taken place in the public decision-making processes organized by the local government, such as the annual local development planning forum and budget committee. During the New Order regime, these annual rituals of decentralization and bottom-up planning had been controlled fully by the government officers and the members of the local legislative body (DPRD). The community did not have any access to this process because they were represented by the members of DPRD. The proponents of the regime at that time assumed that representative members—elected every five years through general election—could articulate the community needs and interests. However, criticisms from many parties, especially from NGOs working on the good governances issues, have brought about change in public decision-making mechanisms towards a deliberative democracy.

In the case of the Jatinangor Forum, the deliberative process has been modeled in the community workshops organized since 2000 and the annual local development planning forum. Through this deliberative process, several community proposals have been accommodated and supported by the local government. The workshops have become an effective medium for learning among the stakeholders. The process during the workshops has caused the participants to learn from each other about public participation in the planning process. The stages in the planning process were carried out in a participatory way where each stakeholder contributed their ideas and shared their own valuable experiences. From the stage of the formulation of issue, vision and mission of regional development, objectives and targets, up to the formulation of collective action plans, all were carried out in a deliberative process leading to social learning.

Promoting the devolution of fiscal from local government to the village institutions

In the state of Madhya Pradesh, India, the legal framework passed in 2001 transfers all powers of local development to the village assemblies, covering budgeting, levying taxes, village security and education, to name the most important components (Heller 2001; Isaac and Heller 2003). This legal framework is part of a broader strategy to strengthen participatory planning. To be effective on the ground, participatory planning practices should be accompanied by the legal framework providing the authority to the village institutions to manage certain affairs and budget.

In the case of Sumedang, Forum Jatinangor initiated regulation of fiscal decentralization from the district to the village level. Forum Jatinangor organized the village leaders and the members of the village consultative body (*Badan Permusyawaratan Desa* (BPD)) to push this regulation through the district legislature (DPRD). With support from the district head (*bupati*), a local regulation on fiscal relations between district and village levels was enacted in 2001. It was the first local regulation in Indonesia on fiscal decentralization from a district government regarding village institutions. Since 2001, each village institution (*desa*) in Sumedang receives annually a block grant from the district government that can be used at the village discretion to meet local needs.

Outcomes of the empowerment process: community and government

Lack of knowledge about public issues and policy, and limited skills of participatory planning have been a serious limitation for the community and local government officers prior to 1998 and the educational efforts of Forum Jatinangor. Restrictions on political discourse during Suharto's New Order regime hampered the growth of political knowledge and consciousness in the local community. The tradition of top-down planning in Indonesian public planning reinforced the view that decisions were made in Jakarta and impeded the opportunity for the community to cultivate participatory skills.

Forum Jatinangor introduced a new type of participatory planning beyond just achieving efficiency and effectiveness for predetermined projects. The essence of its participatory planning objectives was an empowerment process to strengthen community capacity and to increase government's responsive through citizen involvement in the planning process. Fung and Wright argue (2001: 32) that, "by exercising capacities of arguments, planning, and evaluation, through practice individuals might become better deliberators." In other words, community engagement in the planning process is a function of learning by doing. The type of participatory planning exercised in Jatinangor is consistent with the neo-Marxist notion of promoting participation as an end instead of as a means (Miraftab 2003; Parfitt 2004; Mohan and Stokke 2000).

In the case of the Jatinangor, the empowerment process was advanced by strengthening the capacity of local facilitators and community organizations through Forum Jatinangor. Training in organization and entrepreneurship for youth organizations sponsored by Forum Jatinangor, generated many innovative programs. Establishment of a community radio station, providing regular local bulletins, and launching several business activities to provide youth employment opportunities were all intended to increase the community's capacity by learning through doing. In addition, continuous public discussions and workshops attended by community leaders, government officers, university lecturers, NGOs and DPRD not only improved local knowledge of participatory planning and budgeting processes but also strengthened skills of communication, networking, conflict resolution and negotiation. Furthermore, advocacy efforts conducted by community leaders and the members of Forum strengthened their bargaining position in the decision-making process and widened their access to the decision-makers and resources throughout the district.

The Jatinagor Forum also facilitated establishment of new organizational communities that empowered locals to conduct collective actions in new ways. Youth organizations, *komunitas masyarakat peduli lingkungan* (community of environmentalists), a village leader association, a village representative association and a center for local community development and research are examples of community organizations established as a result of the dynamic interaction of the Forum and the broader democratization movement. Although some of these groups faced serious problems sustaining their activities, the learning process—generated through the interaction—generally increased the community's capacity to conduct both advocacy planning and internal management. The block grant policy from the district government to village institutions and the Sumedang District Head decree on participatory-based local development planning are the two main examples of the outcomes of their advocacy efforts. *Pusat Pengkajian dan Pengembangan Masyarakat Lokal* (P3ML) received a grant from the district government to conduct training in village government empowerment involving village institution leaders in the twelve sub-districts of Sumedang. P3ML also received financial assistance from the district government to participate in Jatinangor's spatial planning revision. Furthermore, P3ML got another project from the district government to train youth activists of Sumedang in participatory budgeting. The idea of participatory budgeting was transmitted by P3ML members to other nearby localities, such as Tasikmalaya and Subang District (West Java), Slawi District (Central Java), and other cities who learned about the Jatinangor model through seminars and workshops. This diffusion of ideas generated new awareness in citizens throughout Indonesia that they could be more involved in the budget planning process and could monitor planning and budget implementation.

Lessons learned

The success of Jatinangor in empowering a previously unorganized array of local stakeholders to address community needs offered not only a model to other

Indonesian localities but a way to understand change. The following six lessons can be gleaned from the Jatinangor experience:

1   Planning reform at local level is a result of change involving the macro context and the presence of a network of progressive local actors who translate national reform into local context. The collapse of the New Order regime in 1998, the subsequent decentralization policy emanating from a national social movement, and the support of international agencies created a greater opportunity for driving local planning reform. However, without the presence of the network of progressive local actors, the local planning reform probably would not have been advanced.

2   Local actors initiated the reform by establishing a broader network involving community leaders, local government officers and the district legislative body. The network became a learning environment that facilitated the diffusion of innovation process, collective learning and trust among actors that gradually transforms their understanding of planning practice at the local level. The need to reform the local planning practice and procedure emerged as a result of reflection on the limitation of the conventional state-driven planning.

3   Collective learning was accomplished through formal and informal training, and not simply but through a critique of the state-driven planning model. It was a result of creating an interactive learning environment that worked to transform the attitude, knowledge and skill not just of citizens but of key members of the bureaucracy. It produced the new planning practice and procedure not by opposing government but by engaging it. By creating a learning environment within the bureaucracy, the Jatinangor community had a wider opportunity to interact, share ideas and carry out experiments that gradually transformed a new understanding of planning into empowered participatory planning.

4   The broader network among the community groups, local executive and legislative bodies, the university community and various NGOs enabled the opinion leaders to spread the notion effectively to the entire bureaucracy. The opinion leaders, which in the case of Jatinangor included the higher-ranking government officials, helped to decide that the new planning procedures got institutional support. By involving the higher-ranking officials rather than merely the rank and file planners, there was a better chance that the new planning model would achieve broader acceptance. In the process of formulating and implementing a participatory planning and budgeting process, the involvement of key representatives of the leadership helped overcome operational problems within the existing planning system.

5   Local planning reform requires an extension of the role, methods and outcomes of the planner beyond plan-making. The role of planner needs to be broader than that of a technical advisor as prescribed by the modernist

planning paradigm. Reform requires an active role of the planner as a community advocate in the political process that encompasses both technical and political matters. The methods employed by planners involve more than the application of analytical and causal frameworks to complex phenomena. Reform necessitates a communicative rationality with greater emphasis on qualitative and interpretive inquiry. The products of a planner should be broader than a spatial or sectoral plan that emphasizes output, but also products that improve the quality of the public decision-making process. In the case of Jatinangor, that involved making new planners out of the citizens engaged in taking on the role of governing their community.

6   The success of the implementation of the new planning practices heavily depends on whether those new practices change the configuration of power and the capacity of all stakeholders, including previously marginalized groups, to participate meaningfully in the public decision-making process.

From pilot to permanency

Owing to the 1997 economic crisis and the fall of the New Order authoritarian regime in 1998, the political system, the apparatus of governance at all levels, and the processes of planning Indonesia's development efforts were transformed fundamentally. The typically extended process of introducing and implementing change, especially after more than thirty years of authoritarian rule under the New Order regime, makes the development of a new kind of political culture in Indonesia so remarkable.

The idea of civic engagement and participation in governance had been present in a rhetorical sense as a part of the bureaucratic machinery to justify predetermined government projects. In the post-1998 crisis and reform era, with its adoption from the neoliberalism paradigm in Indonesia's development policies promoted by the international funding agencies in the 1990s, the notion of participation has been implemented in government projects in order to get more support from non-state resources and increase the efficiency of the projects. However, this type of participatory planning was not followed by the change of power relations in the decision-making process indicated by the limited power of civil society organizations in the planning process. Following the fall of the Suharto regime in 1998, the need for deepening democratic processes has emerged, demanding the reformation of the public planning process. Several initiatives have been established between NGO, university and the local government to introduce an empowered participatory planning model through legislation processes and community development programs.

Five years of supervision, technical and financial support and hundreds of volunteer hours from students and the faculty at the ITB sustained the Jatinangor Forum. It now faces the challenge of consolidating its gains, especially when support is no longer available from external agents. Since 2004, ITB has been implementing an exit strategy by gradually decreasing its support of the Jatinangor Forum. Two of ITB's team still regularly provided supervision to the forum until 2005, but the financial support was reduced significantly. The main challenge for Forum Jatinangor is how to mobilize local institutions in Jatinangor—its universities and community groups—without the moral suasion of an initiative embraced by a prestigious public organization such as ITB, as well as the Ford Foundations. Furthermore, the Forum faces a challenge to maintain the open and inclusive nature of its organization and to avoid being a new group of local elites that creates a new type of polarization between that community and its leaders.

References

Alm, J. and Bahl, R. (1999) *Decentralization in Indonesia: Prospects and Problems*, paper prepared for the US Agency for International Development, Jakarta, Indonesia.

Antlov, H. (2003) "Not enough politics! Power, participation and the new democratic polity in Indonesia," in E. Aspinal and G. Fealy (eds) *Local Power and Politics in Indonesia, Decentralization and Democratization*, Pasir Panjang, Singapore: Institute of Southeast Asian Studies.

Baiocchi, G. (2003) "Participation, activism, and politics: The Porto Alegre experiment," in A. Fung and E.O. Wright (eds) *Deepening Democracy: Institutional Innovations in Empowered Participatory Governance*, New York: Verso.

Beier, C. and Ferrazzi, G. (1997) "The district autonomy pilot program: A new approach to decentralization in Indonesia," unpublished paper.

Devas, N. (1989) *Financing Local Government in Indonesa*, Athens, OH: Ohio University Center for International Studies.

Ferrazzi, G. (2001) "Regional planning reform in Indonesia," *Third World Planning Review* 23 (3): 249–72.

Forrester, G. and May, R.J. (eds) (1999) *The Fall of Soeharto*, Singapore: Select Books.

Fung, A. (2004) *Empowered Participation*, Princeton, NJ: Princeton University Press.

Fung, A. and Wright, E.O. (2001) "Deepening democracy: Innovations in empowered participatory governance," *Politics & Society* 29 (1): 5–41.

Gaventa, J. (2004) "Strengthening participatory approach to local governance: Learning the lessons from abroad," *National Civic Review* (winter): 16–27.

Heller, P. (2001) "Moving the state: The politics of democratic decentralization in Kerala, South Africa, and Porto Alegre," *Politics & Society* 29 (1): 131–63.

Isaac, T.M.T. and Heller, P. (2003) "Democracy and development: Decentralized planning in Kerala," in A. Fung and E.O. Wright (eds) *Deepening Democracy; Institutional Innovations in Empowered Participatory Governance*, New York: Verso.

Jakarta Post (2001) "Rupiah hits 10,000 on political concerns," January 3.

Leigland, J. (1993) "Decentralizing the development budget process in Indonesia: Progress and prospects," *Public Budgeting and Finance* 13: 85–101.

McAndrews, C. (1986) *Central Government and Local Development in Indonesia*, New York: Oxford University Press.

Mohan, G. and Stokke, K. (2000) "A participatory development and empowerment: The dangers of localism," *Third World Quarterly* 21 (2): 247–68.

Miraftab, F. (2003) "The perils of participatory discourse: Housing policy in post apartheid South Africa," *Journal of Planning Education and Research* 22 (3): 226–39.

Parfitt, T. (2004) "The ambiguity of participation: A qualified defense of participatory development," *Third World Quarterly* 25 (3): 537–56.

Pycroft, C. (1994) "Local government in the new South Africa," *Public Administration and Development* 16: 233–45.

Ranis, G. and Stewart, F. (1994) "Decentralization in Indonesia," *Bulletin of Indonesian Economic Studies* 30: 41–72.

Silver, C. and Sofhani, T.F. (2001) "Community-based planning and the decentralization rxperiment in Indonesia," unpublished paper presented at the World Planning Schools Congress, Tongji University, Shanghai, China, July 11.

US Embassy Jakarta website. Available online at www.usembassyjakarta.org, accessed July 21, 2000.

Walker, M. (1991) "Decentralized planning for sustainable development: The case of Indonesia," *Review of Urban and Regional Development Studies* 3: 94–102.

Wunsch, J.S. (1998) "Decentralization, local governance and the democratic transition in southern Africa: A comparative study," *African Studies Quarterly* 2(1).

Young, I. (2000) *Inclusion and Democracy*, Oxford: Oxford University Press.

Chapter 11

En(Gendering) effective decentralization

The experience of women in *Panchayati Raj* in India

Kajri Misra and Neema Kudva

The "deepening" of democracy is an important rationale offered for decentralization. This and other desired outcomes—efficient and effective service delivery, poverty remediation and sustainable development—are premised on including local citizens in decision-making. Democratization and decentralization are thus complexly interwoven. In practical terms, this focuses attention on the inclusion of marginalized groups, their involvement being seen as necessary to prevent perverse outcomes of localization, including increased corruption, persistence of discriminatory practices and capture of resources and decision-making processes by local elites (Bardhan 1996; Blair 1998; Manor 1999). The degree of inclusion of marginalized groups thus serves as an indicator of successful decentralization, particularly in the global South, where multiple and complex dependence relationships in localities severely limit informed citizen participation. One method that pushes inclusion is the imposition of quotas and reservations for marginalized groups. Here we analyze its efficacy by examining India's large-scale experiment with gender quotas in local government, imposed alongside decentralization reforms in the mid 1990s.

Women's under-representation in governance structures is pervasive across countries and cultures, diverse governance systems and arrangements.[1] Gender overlays all other identities that vivify societies such as class, caste, income, ethnicity or race. It makes women's inclusion particularly challenging, as multiple identifiers must be taken into account. As difficult is the issue of how interests are shaped by specific identities, the normative understanding being that there are gendered interests and needs, which leads "women" as a category to be more concerned with household and larger societal needs, even as it positions women as a unique repository of local knowledge and experience. Arguments for promoting gender equality through formal political channels rest on these normative propositions.

The impacts of strategies that seek to include women thus have wide-ranging consequences for gender equality, democratization and effective decentralization. This raises several questions, three of which we will examine through an analysis of India's experiment with gender quotas in decentralized governance: first, to what extent and in what ways have gender quotas enabled greater inclusion of women? Second, have the emergent patterns of inclusion and participation altered development and/or policy outcomes in any manner? And, third, what do the patterns indicate about how the two processes—decentralization and democratization—are linked, theoretically and practically?

The 73rd Constitutional Amendment of 1992–3 reinstated *Panchayati Raj* (PR) and mandated a gender quota in a three-tiered local government system. In the first elections in 1995, almost 800,000 women were elected to *Panchayats;* two more elections have been held since. We draw on a substantial literature mapping this decade-long experiment to answer our first two questions. Analyzing the impacts of gender quotas through the lenses of decentralization and feminist political theory allows us to get to the third question. In the process, it reveals gaps in empirical studies of the quota experiment that shape and limit our understanding of its efficacy in decentralized governance and the feminist project for gender equality.

The chapter is organized in four sections. We start by discussing feminist and decentralization arguments for women's inclusion. Next, we describe PR reforms and gender quota provisions in India, following which we summarize emergent patterns of women's participation in PR across India. In the fourth section, we analyze the quota experiment through the lenses of decentralization and feminist political theory to indicate the terms of future attention. In conclusion, we summarize our discussion and point to some theoretical and policy implications.

Decentralizing governance, engendering democracy: merging paths?

Feminist democratic theorists, notably Anne Phillips (1991; 1995; 1998), have problematized the issue of women's inclusion somewhat differently from the broader theorizing on the inclusion of ethnic and cultural groups (Kymlicka 1995; Young 1989). Although low economic positions and educational levels, social and cultural biases, and historical circumstances are seen as constraining the inclusion of both women and marginalized groups, the underlying *causes* of such patterns are theorized differently. Women's absence from governance is understood to be limited by their socialization against engaging in the public sphere, care-giving responsibilities, their under-representation in public work, and active exclusion by male selectorates (Phillips 1991). Underlying these reasons is the public–private divide that narrows the scope of politics in all versions of democracy currently practiced. Moreover, there is a "double separation" of the private–household, the public–social and the public–political (Arendt 1958; Pateman 1983) that hides the subversion of political equality by embedding inequalities in the private realms of marriage and household and the public domain of community. This analysis has widened the domains in which democracy is salient (workplace, home), identified the heterogeneity of power, and shown that domination is endemic. The range of admissible public policy concerns has accordingly broadened to include "personal" practices in the home and workplace, childcare, domestic violence, household division of labor and unpaid work—all of which burden women more, undercut their confidence and skills for public involvement, and hamper their development as citizens.

There is distinct overlap in the arguments for inclusion by feminists and decentralizers. Apart from the parity and justice ideal that underlies all inclusion, two other propositions are significant and persist despite their essentialist formulation. First, that women would bring overlooked matters of societal importance into policy-making; and, second, that their presence will change the quality of public life. The key assumption is that, despite their heterogeneity, women's different material experiences gives them *different interests*, perceptions on issues and attitudes to politics *from men*. Women's experiences of care and nurture lead them to define issues in relational terms, which alters market–society assumptions of an interest-group framework centering on individual gain, self-interest and instrumental advantage (Gilligan 1982; Hartsock, 1983). Their increased presence would, therefore, improve both the content and quality of politics.

Feminist theorists and decentralizers also overlap in their focus on structural and institutional change, agreeing that greater political equality is possible through reconstituting institutional arrangements, even pending fundamental social transformation (UNRISD 2005). Phillips (1995, 1998), in particular, has specifically made a case for quotas in elected seats and in party lists. This and also Young's (1989) suggestions for institutional mechanisms safeguarding marginalized and oppressed groups,[2] support for self-organization in civic and social space that would provide "political apprenticeships," (Cornwall and Goetz 2005) and connections between formal and informal political arenas are all seen as crucial to the project of gender parity (Niranjana 2002; Miraftab 2006).

These clear overlaps in arguments for the inclusion of women in the formal political realm open up possibilities for deepened democratization and effective decentralization.[3] We will examine how these are realized through the case of the Indian experiment with gender quotas in PR.

Panchayati Raj reforms

In 1992–3, the 73rd and 74th Constitutional Amendment Acts statutorily mandated the incorporation and the "right to life"[4] of multi-tier, elected local government in rural and urban areas across India. The 73rd Amendment Act specifies the constitution of *Panchayats* at the village (*Grama*), sub-district (*Taluka, Mandal* or Block) and district (*Zilla*) levels, with persons chosen by direct election from territorial constituencies. In addition, *Taluka* and *Zilla Panchayats* also include chairpersons from lower levels, as well as members from state and national legislatures whose constituencies wholly or partially include the *Panchayat* area. One-third of all seats at all three levels are reserved for women and allocated by rotation to different constituencies.[5] The *Gram Panchayat* periodically convenes

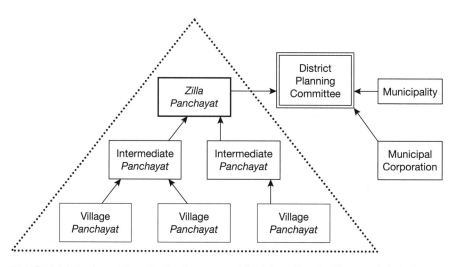

11.1 Skeletal structure of three-tier local government (in states with > 2 million population). Our discussion focuses on the structure within the dotted triangle.

an assembly of all voters in the village, the *Grama Sabha*. Figure 11.1 explains the local government structure.

Panchayats function as units of local self-government and are endowed with powers, responsibilities and resources for "the preparation of plans for economic development and social justice" and "the implementation of schemes . . . as may be entrusted to them" by superior levels of government (GOI 1992: 243G*). The 74th Amendment, which prescribes the local government structure for urban areas, also mandates the constitution of a District Planning Committee (DPC) in every district, to "consolidate the plans prepared by the *Panchayats* and the Municipalities in the district and to prepare a draft development plan for the district as a whole" (GOI 1992: 243ZD*).

Although these Acts provide a skeletal uniformity to local government across India, a number of provisions were left to the discretion of the respective state legislatures, to be specified in their conforming Acts.[6] Of these, the disparities in devolution of regulatory powers and financial functions to different tiers, the rules regarding composition of standing committees, nomination of *ex officio* members and election of chairpersons produced significant differences. In addition, legal, administrative and organizational reforms necessary to synchronize PR institutions and other administrative bodies were also left to state governments. This has resulted in significant variations in PR structure and functioning across states (Mathew 2000).

Implementation has been both reluctant and slow. Although service delivery and beneficiary selection functions have seen considerable devolution, planning functions have not. One notable exception is the State of Kerala, which initiated a state-supported, bilateral agency-funded local planning process that attracted wide attention (Isaac and Franke 2000). Although inadequate decentralization has clearly limited the scope for local decision-making, the sheer increase in the numbers of women has impacted local governance. We discuss these impacts and variations across place and time in the next section.

Patterns of women's participation in *Panchayats*

Women's involvement has three dimensions: presence, action and decision-making.[7] Although there are no country-wide surveys examining women's participation, a large number of smaller studies provide a surprisingly cogent and consistent picture of the general patterns. These include some work that is pan-Indian (Jain 1996; Jayal 2006; Narayana 2005; Pal 2004) or multi-statal in its scope (Buch 2000a, 2000b; Duflo and Chattopadhyay 2004; Kaushik 1998) and several case studies of selected *Panchayats* or elected women representatives in a district or state.[8] We also draw on our observations from work in six states over the past decade.

The characteristics of elected women are consistent across states: almost two-thirds are illiterate or minimally literate, Uttaranchal, Orissa, Tamil Nadu and Kerala being exceptions. In Kerala, more women have college education than their male peers (Radha and RoyChoudhury 2002). About 70 percent of elected women are under forty-five years. A little over half the women are either landless, or cultivators on small or marginal holdings. Close to a third are near or below the poverty line, and the largest proportion is from the lower or backward castes, except in Haryana and Karnataka. There is also variation between districts within states. In higher levels of local government, occupation and caste shift upwards, and more women have political connections and experience. The extent of political experience varies across regions and states, depending on the history of local government reform (as in Karnataka) and local political awareness or mobilization (as in areas where women's empowerment groups such as *Mahila Samakhya* are active).

Presence is not limited to that defined by the gender quota, with states such as Karnataka reporting higher numbers of elected women representatives. Several elected women were persuaded to run by males in their family and function as surrogate representatives (Leiten 1996; Pai 1998). Male relatives frequently campaign for women, even displaying their own names in publicity materials; though some women made their own decisions to contest despite family opposition and social controls (Mayaram 2002). Almost one-third of those in the Uttaranchal area did so (Kaushik 1998), as did many in *Mahila Samakhya* areas of influence in Andhra Pradesh and Karnataka (Anandhi 2002; Narayanan 2002). Proxy candidates are decreasing slowly with time, elected women are recognized as holding office, and more women are making the decision to contest elections (Buch 2000a; 2000b; Niranjana 2002). Attendance at meetings is good across states—almost two-thirds of women attend regularly, with numbers increasing. Reports of women coming to meetings unchaperoned is higher in the southern states of Kerala and Tamil Nadu. However, women's time commitment is variable, with two-thirds of women in Uttar Pradesh reporting that they spend little or no time at all on *Panchayat* work (Buch 2000a).

Active participation, such as speaking up at meetings, responding to constituents' petitions or raising issues for consideration, is linked to education, caste, prevailing cultural norms and prior experience in organizing. Participation is higher among women in Kerala and Tamil Nadu (where educational levels are higher) but, paradoxically, despite higher educational levels and, often, higher caste status, women in Orissa tend to remain silent. Similarly, more women speak out in Karnataka, which has a longer history of gender quotas (Kudva 2003). However, there are several reports of indirect strategies women adopt to get information as well as to convey opinions and ideas, from making use of household spaces to speak with husbands and younger male relatives, to loudly discussing *Panchayat* affairs with other women in the earshot of men (Strulik n.d.).[9]

Decision-making is most evident in attending to constituents' needs, in the selection of beneficiaries for welfare programs directed at individuals and households below the poverty line, and in directing infrastructure investment to areas impacting women's practical needs—with domestic water supply attracting the greatest attention almost everywhere, and roads, schools and other community facilities featuring prominently. A group of women chairpersons in West Bengal saw the creation of drinking water facilities, roads and community assets as their greatest achievement (Duflo and Chattopadhyay 2004). Monitoring progress of development projects is fairly common. Women representatives are also reportedly involved in helping women constituents settle household disputes over dowry, alcoholism, violence and abuse and even land.

What constrains active participation of elected women representatives? All studies demonstrate that stringent caste norms and patriarchal practices, low levels of education and awareness, and lack of prior political experience are significant obstacles. This complicates and compromises ideal notions of representation, agency and interests. Caste constrains both upper- and lower-caste women, through practices of *purdah* (seclusion) in the former and untouchability in the latter. *Purdah*, however, is not uniform across castes or regions and appears somewhat susceptible to change: 7 percent of elected women representatives reported giving up the practice (Buch 2000a). Caste-based exclusionary practices, on the other hand, are pervasive across states, more entrenched and less mutable. In places where customary practices have eroded with modernization, the participation of women is more extensive and active. Interestingly, upper-caste women are identified as being more closely linked to caste and community interests than lower-caste women (Clots-Figuera 2005).

Caste and gender intersect in the behavior of higher-caste male representatives towards others, with lower-caste women suffering the worst humiliations and abuses. This is reflected in the physical organization of *Panchayat* space: seating is segregated by sex and caste (Jayal 2006). In a Haryana *Grama Panchayat*, a scheduled caste chairman sat on the floor while upper-caste members occupied chairs (Tekchandani *et al.* 1997). The practice is endemic, as Misra noted recently in Madhya Pradesh, where upper-caste male villagers constrained lower-caste men to nominate their wives to fill quota requirements in *Panchayats* and standing committees.[10]

Active participation is also hindered by women's time constraints. For poor women, the onerous dual burden of domestic and livelihood work inhibits attendance and active involvement. Strong societal constraints on women's movement in public spaces or outside the village are also significant obstacles to participation. *Panchayat* meetings are often held in public spaces that customarily exclude women, in upper-caste localities that lower-caste members normally do not enter, or in hamlets and places within the *Panchayat* area that are considered outside the "village" boundary.[11] Withholding or controlling information on meeting times and agendas is another technique to exclude women and other minority elected representatives.

The majority of elected women cite illiteracy as a barrier that severely curtails, even precludes, their effective participation. Official communication uses legal and formal administrative vocabulary; and budgets, financial statements and account-keeping are in formats incomprehensible even to reasonably educated men *and* women. Kaushik's (1998) study reports another standard barrier: the exclusion of women from *Panchayat* committees such as finance and development administration, where many consequential decisions are made. Many elected women were not aware of committees; the few that were got relegated to health, women and child-care. By 2004–5, however, most states had mandated gender quotas within committees, though this is often bypassed by the election of proxy members.

In sum, there is a consensus on the efficacy of quotas in increasing women's presence in the formal structures of local government. Notwithstanding instances of inspired leadership and courageous action by individual women profiled in various case studies, the extent of active and decisive participation is both limited and highly variable. However, barring a severe backlash from those who would lose power, most observers anticipate positive change over time, even as they temper their optimism by recognizing the deeply entrenched nature of the barriers to women's participation.

Decentralization and women's inclusion—mutually hindered?

Decentralization reforms that strengthen local governments and simultaneously engineer the inclusion of women have extended democratization. The increased involvement of women appears to result in better targeting of welfare recipients and some improvements in infrastructure provision. Prima facie as democratic inclusion deepens, one can expect better local governance. However, seen through the eyes of decentralization and feminist literatures, there are gaps and disjunctures in the quota experiment that could impede change.

The first such gap lies in the explanation of differences in levels of participation. The quota literature turns to history, self-efficacy and individual attributes[12] or to the hurdles posed by institutionalized socio-cultural practices of caste and patriarchy. Accordingly, most authors expect positive change as more women gain political experience, and entrenched socio-cultural norms and practices erode or mutate. They suggest paying attention to women's literacy and awareness of institutional rules, procedures and programs. In practice, these suggestions have focused state and NGO attention on developing training programs and representative support networks in the decade since reforms were implemented (Behar and Aiyer 2003).

We find analyses that lead to such strategies partial. They result in an overemphasis on individual representatives, with very few authors seriously attending to differences in the formal organizational arrangements across states and their implications for variability in women's participation. Although the deeply gendered and casteist nature of organizational practice is noted, there is little serious analysis of it. Clearly, variations in "official" rules, procedures and practices can be more or less supportive of women's involvement and, given the amenability of these to engineered change (as compared with larger socio-cultural institutional patterns), could yield greater immediate gains. Evidence is already available from the increased presence of women on *Panchayat* committees after gender quotas were imposed, or the rule requiring office space and furniture to be provided to all women chairpersons in Haryana. Despite this, and recognition of the importance of organizational design for women's inclusion in other contexts (Cornwall and Goetz 2005), there is little attention being paid to identifying more such possibilities.

The second gap emerges in the ways in which the impact of inter-state variations in devolution is understood. Although these variations have troubled decentralization analysts and quota observers, in reality inadequate devolution affects both men and women representatives, thus losing relevance in the analysis of gender differences in patterns of involvement. Also, although extensive devolution looks desirable, greater local autonomy could well lead to the protection of local practices that inhibit women's participation, particularly in a situation of limited political mobilization and gender awareness.

The disconnect between decentralizers and the feminist sensibilities of several quota observers has also shaped the analysis of impacts. India's gender quota provisions at the sub-national level were not instituted as a result of advocacy by a strong women's movement; instead, it was initiated and piloted through the legislative process by largely male-dominated political parties (ISI 1997).[13] Once instituted, however, its efficacy and improvement have preoccupied feminists in diverse locations and disciplines, who have authored a large proportion of the quota literature. Feminist activists, academics and researchers, in turn, are influenced by debates of change and exclusion internal to feminism. These frame the issues raised in the quota literature in particular ways.

As Nancy Fraser (1997: 3) has pointed out, the cultural turn in second-wave feminism led, over time, to the "decoupling of the cultural politics of recognition from the social politics of distribution" and to an analysis and a politics that aimed to valorize difference rather than promote equality. The shift to words rather than things meant that bodies, individual attributes and cultural and consumption practices, not material needs or the political economy of our social reality, came to occupy the foreground in feminist discourse (Barrett 1999). This humanities-centered cultural turn has been, and will continue to be, enormously useful in uncovering the insidious ways in which hegemonic gender constructions and ideas are produced and maintained, but it is less useful in analyzing women's economic and political lives or in thinking through collective strategies for gender equality. Though the quota literature mostly remains at a distance from such theoretical discussions in feminist literature, it is influenced by the corporal–cultural turn and, consequently, privileges socio-cultural explanations of individual actors over political–institutional ones.

Equally important are the directions missed by the feminist focus on the double separation produced by the public–private divide, which focuses attention on power hierarchies in households and communities. While making public "private" concerns, it takes away analytical attention from more conventional "public" arenas of formal politics and ignores issues of institutional design and organizational practice.

We argue for a gendered scrutiny of formal rules, regulations and procedures in the conviction that the democratic pay-offs would be substantial. Gender quota provisions clearly demonstrate the efficacy of legislative mandates and procedural change. Paying attention to gendered and casteist organizational practices within institutions will reveal specific, micro-level, practical modifications to extend efficacy. Even more importantly, this can begin to undercut fairly entrenched customary practices owing to the overlap of formal and customary institutional domains, an important instrumentality in this process being the creation of opportunities for women themselves to counter discriminatory and oppressive socio-cultural norms and practices. A telling example is the slow discarding of *purdah* (Buch 2000a), as well as gradual changes noted in the practice of segregated seating and of women not speaking in the presence of men (Jayal 2006). In other words, some women are claiming spaces and initiatives to change customary norms that circumscribe their participation. Changing gendered organizational practices supports their efforts.

Another issue deserving more attention is "place." Although the historical, socio-cultural and developmental basis of difference across states is often noted, a deeper analysis of the mediation of *Panchayats* by the nuances of local context is noticeably absent. Institutional design and organizational practices vary by state,[14] and socio-cultural norms vary—sometimes widely—within States and sometimes even districts. This calls for a differentiated analysis that can identify local facilitative practices to support women representatives. Small variations across localities can be nested within broader, formal, state-wide rules for institutional design. Instances of such practices are already available in changes initiated by activists and NGOs who are involved in supporting women and lower-caste representatives: dates, times and locations of meetings are often tailored to fit local calendars, routines and norms.[15]

Our last concern is with the enthusiastic support for "networked governance" that links *Panchayats* to a range of civil society groups, from traditional village and caste *Panchayats* to community-based groups and NGOs. Although this is a useful proposition in its best manifestations, it needs to be carefully scrutinized on several counts. First, it is widely accepted that lumping together groups under the label of a benign civil society is problematic. This does not distinguish between groups involved in depoliticizing project development work, those embracing exclusionary practices, or others involved in decidedly uncivil activities. Second, in seeking greater engagement with traditional *Panchayats*, which tend to be exclusively male and reify caste distinctions, there is potential danger of elite collusion and further entrenchment of oppressive caste and patriarchal norms (AnanthPur 2004). Blaug's (2002) analysis of the interface between "incumbent democracy," characteristic of democratizing states, and norms of "participatory democracy" desired by many groups demanding inclusion, could, however, provide a useful differentiating principle. Regardless, the links between (incumbent) democratic *Panchayats* and (participatory) democratic community-based groups demand greater scrutiny.

In conclusion

Decentralization reforms with one-third seat-quota provisions for women have extended democratization and yielded some governance gains through improved welfare targeting and infrastructure provision. The impacts, however, vary greatly across India. We have suggested that the disconnects between the literatures on decentralization and gender quotas have produced gaps that have obfuscated the analysis of how we can support the further inclusion of women for gender parity and effective governance.

Our survey of the experience of women in *Panchayati Raj* indicates that there is evidence to support the imposition of quotas and, by implication, the utility of legal and institutional reform in creating opportunities for women to transform formal politics and the public domain. However, the efficacy of such strategies rests on public policy that takes into account the importance of institutional design and organizational practices mediated by place. As importantly, it rests on the robust nature of the linkages between *Panchayats* and a range of participatory, democratic civil society organizations.

Notes

* G and ZD stand for the pertinent sections of Article 243 of the Constitution of India.

1 Women's representation in national-level assemblies, for example, has gone up from a dismal 9 percent in 1995 to about 16 percent in 2004, with sixteen countries as different as Rwanda, Sweden and Argentina having used quotas to put a critical mass of 30 percent or more women into national legislatures (UNRISD, 2005).
2 These include rules that guarantee presence, obligate inclusion of views in decision-making and provide veto power over policies that directly affect them.
3 For a thorough analysis, see Kudva and Misra (forthcoming).
4 Personal communication, Mr Sivaramakrishnan, ex-Secretary, Ministry of Urban Development, Government of India. This means PR institutions are legally safeguarded against arbitrary dismissal, dissolution or supercession by state governments.
5 In addition to quotas assigned to other designated disadvantaged groups, including scheduled tribes, *adivasis*, and scheduled castes, *dalits*, in proportion to their population.
6 India's Constitution specifies local government as a "concurrent subject" that can be legislated on by both the central and the state government and is subject to national-level legislation only on the request of a minimum of three states.
7 We expand on Radha and RoyChoudhury's (2002) characterization (passive, active and decisive), but see presence itself being an act of contestation, while action and decision-making distinguish receiving authority from choosing to act on it through assertion of voice and power.
8 Space precludes our including a full list of all studies consulted.
9 Also Misra fieldnotes 2004–5.
10 Misra fieldnotes 2004–5.
11 Misra fieldnotes 2004–5.
12 Attributes such as age, education, prior political experience, capacity to counter prevailing norms, and leadership ability are seen as specific to individual woman.
13 We do not suggest that the inclusion of quota provisions was not informed by feminist discourses, but that PR reforms—of which the quota provisions were a part—are primarily informed and driven by decentralization discourses, where the dominant actors have been economists, development theorists, international donor agencies as well as national and subnational political elites and administrators.
14 Except in districts with large tribal populations.
15 We recognize the problems associated with increased localism but nevertheless contend that attention must be paid to framing organizational practices differently at various levels.

References

Anandhi, S. (2002) "Interlocking patriarchies and women in governance—A case study of Panchayati Raj Institutions in Tamil Nadu," in K. Kapadia (ed.) *The Violence of*

Development—The Politics of Identity, Gender and Social Inequalities In India, New Delhi: Kali for Women.

AnanthPur, K. (2004) "Interfaces in local governance—A study in Karnataka," Working Paper No. 187, Chennai: Madras Institute of Development Studies.

Arendt, H. (1958) *The Human Condition*, Chicago, IL: University of Chicago Press.

Bardhan, P. (1996) "Decentralized development," *Indian Economic Review* XXXI (2): 139–56.

Barrett, M. (1999) *Imagination in Theory: Culture, Writing, Words, and Things*, New York: University Press.

Behar, A. and Aiyer, Y. (2003) "Networks of Panchayat women: Civil society space for political action," *Economic and Political Weekly* (November 22).

Blair, H. (1998) *Spreading Power to the Periphery—An Assessment of Democratic Local Governance*, USAID Program and Operations Assessment Report No. 21.

Blaug, R. (2002) "Engineering democracy," *Political Studies* 50: 102–16.

Buch, N. (2000a) "Women's experience in new Panchayats—The emerging leadership of rural women," Occasional Paper No. 35, New Delhi: Center for Women's Development Studies.

Buch, N. (2000b) "Panchayats and women," in G. Mathew (ed.) *Status of Panchayati Raj in the States and Union Territories of India*, New Delhi: Institute of Social Sciences.

Clots-Figuera, I. (2005) "Women in politics: Evidence from the Indian states," PEPP 14, Political Economy and Public Policy Series, The Suntory Center, London School of Economics.

Cornwall, A. and Goetz, A.M. (2005) "Democratizing democracy: Feminist perspectives," *Democratization* 12 (5): 783–800.

Duflo, E. and Chattopadhyay, R. (2004) "Impact of reservation in Panchayati Raj—Evidence from a nationwide randomised experiment," *Economic and Political Weekly*, February 28: 979–86.

Fraser, N. (1997) *Justice Interruptus: Critical Reflections on the Postsocialist Condition*, New York: Routledge.

Gilligan, C. (1982) *In a Different Voice: Psychological Theory and Women's Development*, Cambridge: Harvard University Press.

GOI (1992) The Constitution (Seventy-third Amendment) Act, 1992. Available online at http://indiacode.nic.in/coiweb/amend/amend73.htm, accessed July 2006.

Hartsock, N.C.M. (1983) *Money, Sex and Power: Towards a Feminist Historical Materialism*, Bostob, MA: Northeastern University Press.

ISI (1997) *How and Why Women Entered Panchayat's Election Process*, New Delhi: Indian Social Institute.

Isaac, T.M.T. and Franke, R. (2000) *Local Democracy and Development: People's Campaign for Decentralized Planning in Kerala*, New Dehli: Leftword.

Jain, D. (1996) *Panchayat Raj: Women Changing Governance*, Gender in Development Monograph Series Number 5, New York: UNDP.

Jayal, N.G. (2006) "Engendering local democracy: The impact of quotas for women in India's Panchayats," *Democratization* 13 (1), February: 15–35.

Kaushik, S. (1998) *Participation of Women in Panchayati Raj in India: A Stock Taking*. A study of six states sponsored by the National Commission for Women, New Delhi.

Kudva, N. (2003) "Engineering elections—The experiences of women in Panchayati Raj in Karnataka, India," *International Journal of Politics, Culture and Society* 16 (3), Spring.

Kudva, N. and Misra, K. (forthcoming) "Gender quotas, the politics of presence and the feminist project: What does the Indian experience tell us?," *Signs: Journal of Women in Culture and Society* 34(1).

Kymlicka, W. (1995) *Multicultural Citizenship: A Liberal Theory of Minority Rights*, Oxford, New York: Clarendon Press.

Leiten, G.K. (1996) "Panchayats in western Uttar Pradesh: 'Namesake Members,'" *Economic and Political Weekly* XXXI (39): 2700–5.

Manor, J. (1999) *The Political Economy of Democratic Decentralization*, Washington, DC: World Bank.

Mathew, G. (2000) "Panchayati Raj—An overview," in G. Mathew (ed.) *Status of Panchayati Raj in the States and Union Territories of India*, New Delhi: Institute of Social Sciences.

Mayaram, S. (2002) "New modes of violence—The backlash against women in the Panchayat system," in K. Kapadia (ed.) *The Violence of Development—The Politics of Identity, Gender and Social Inequalities in India*, New Delhi: Kali for Women.

Miraftab, F. (2006) "Feminist praxis, citizenship and informal politics," *International Journal of Feminist Politics* 8 (2): 194–218.

Narayana, D. (2005) "Local governance without capacity building—Ten years of Panchayati Raj," *Economic and Political Weekly*, June 25: 2822–32.

Narayanan, R. (2002) "Grassroots, gender and governance—Panchayati Raj experiences from Mahila Samakhya Karnataka," in K. Kapadia (ed.) *The Violence of Fevelopment—The Politics of Identity, Gender and Social Inequalities in India*, New Delhi: Kali for Women.

Niranjana, S. (2002) "Exploring gender inflections within Panchayati Raj institutions— Women's politicization in Andhra Pradesh," in K. Kapadia (ed.) *The Violence of Development—The Politics of Identity, Gender and Social Inequalities in India*, New Delhi: Kali for Women.

Pai, S. (1998) "Pradhanis in new Panchayats, field notes from Meerut district," *Economic and Political Weekly* XXXIII (18): 1009–10.

Pal, M. (2004) "Panchayati Raj and rural governance—Experiences of a decade," *Economic and Political Weekly*, January 10: 137–43.

Pateman, C. (1983) "Feminism and democracy," in G. Duncan (ed.) *Democratic Theory and Practice*, Cambridge: Cambridge University Press.

Phillips, A. (1991) *Engendering Democracy*, Cambridge: Polity Press.

Phillips, A. (1995) *The Politics of Presence*, Oxford: Clarendon Press.

Phillips, A. (1998) *Feminism and Politics*, New York: Oxford University Press.

Radha, S. and RoyChoudhury, B. (2002) "Women in local bodies," Discussion Paper No. 40, Kerala Research Programme on Local Level Development, Thiruvananthapuram, Center for Development Studies.

Strulik, S. (n.d.) "Women-Panchayat-electives at the interface of state and village politics: Gendered constructions of the political space," paper presented at the 18th European Conference on Modern South Asian Studies at Lund University, Sweden.

Tekchandani, B. Jyoti, K. and Sharma, P. (1997) *They Call Me Member Saab: Women in Haryana Panchayati Raj*. New Delhi: MARG.

UNRISD. (2005) "Gender equality: Striving for justice in an unequal world." Available online at www.unrisd.org/unrisd/website/document.nsf/(httpPublications)/1FF4AC64C 1894EAAC1256FA3005E7201?OpenDocument, accessed May 2006.

Young, I.M. (1989) "Polity and group difference: A critique of the idea of universal citizenship," *Ethics* 9: 250–74. Reprinted in A. Phillips (ed.) (1999) *Feminism and Politics*, Oxford: Oxford University Press.

Chapter 12

Decentralization and social capital in urban Thailand

Amrita Daniere and Lois M. Takahashi

Introduction

Decentralization and social capital have become the twin pillars on which good governance is defined. Good governance and planning are associated with efficient, effective and responsive government institutions. Decentralization is seen as necessary to improved local governance as it presumably disperses the power and authority that uphold bloated bureaucracies, patronage and corruption. This, in turn, implies that social capital, which many believe is crucial to more effective local capacity, is also critically important to better governance.

This chapter explores the decentralization efforts in Thailand and its potential linkages to social capital, with a focus on urban environmental planning and governance. We analyze survey data that we collected in low-income communities in the Bangkok metropolitan area in 1995 and 2000 to explore two dimensions of the potential interactions between decentralization and social capital: complementarity and embeddedness (Evans 1996).

Decentralization and social capital: conceptualizing the linkages

If, as many argue, good planning and governance rely on local institutions and expanded participation by the citizenry, then the composition, characteristics and policy capacity of local institutions become vital (Dupar and Badenoch 2002). It should come as no surprise that good governance and decentralization are associated with sufficient and effective social capital, and vice versa. Like many before us, we define social capital as a resource available to individuals that emanates from group interaction through trust, reciprocity and cooperation (Bourdieu 1986; Coleman 1988). Putnam (1993) notes that civic-minded communities, those rich in positive social capital, expect better government and are able to achieve good governance largely through their own actions. Ostrom (1990), among others, argues that trust and shared values among members of a group or community are fundamental attributes of sustainable community-based natural resources management (Bebbington and Carroll 2002; Wai 1996).

Since the mid 1990s, scholars have explored the interaction of social capital and governance. The state can provide resources to enhance social capital by providing environments that are conducive to social capital formation (Gertler 1997), and social capital may act as a guide for good governance through civic engagement (Putnam 1993). Evans (1996) identifies two synergistic possibilities for governance and social capital: complementarity and embeddedness. Complementarity means the state and the community having clear and separate tasks and skills in governing; this division of labor is made more effective and efficient by the well-working day-to-day interactions of government officials and community members. Evans cites Tendler's (1997) case study in northeastern Brazil to show that actions that make sense for the state because of economies of scale, such as media publicity, can bolster a societal "call" to public service, thereby enhancing a sense of civic engagement. Evans defines embeddedness as those networks that breach the division between public/state/government and private/society/community. Evans turns again to Tendler (1997), who finds that health service agents provided health services but also helped with household tasks, such as childcare. There was a high level of "enmeshment" (Evans 1996: 185), or multifaceted social ties, in Tendler's Brazilian case, between government agents and community members.

Both the ideas of embeddedness and complementarity also have, it can be argued, a connection to decentralization. Complementarity can be enhanced as part of a decentralization process that clarifies the relative responsibilities of the local government and of the communities it hopes to serve. Similarly, embeddedness, which suggests that governance can be enhanced through practices that:

1   breach traditional notions of the public sector; and
2   focus on generating networks between the state and society (perhaps though collaborative planning efforts) that can be facilitated under conditions of decentralization.

Local authorities, given additional resources and decision-making capacity, would be well placed to identify opportunities to create enmeshment.

Social capital and its relationship to governance have also drawn scathing critiques. Molyneux (2002), for example, argues that there are multiple problems, not the least of which is the unproblematized role of gender in (unpaid) voluntarism, especially women's role in community development, and the at times exclusionary nature of social networks, especially in contexts driven by patron–client relationships. We believe, however, that, given careful attention to these critiques, the social capital lens offers important lessons for designing and implementing decentralization that is more sensitive to community norms and values than top-down policy design.

Decentralization in Thailand

Like many countries, Thailand has initiated decentralization, but primarily deconcentration (Dupar and Badenoch 2002: 11). The overall result is that, although the Thai government has taken a number of legal steps to initiate and formalize decentralization, in fact, much remains to be done in terms of the actual transfer of power and resources to locally elected officials and representatives, NGOs and communities.

Historically, Thailand has three levels of government: the central, the provincial and the local. The central government, located in Bangkok and organized into a number of ministries, makes almost all government decisions and controls the vast majority of resources. The provincial administration is divided into two separate strands. In each of the provinces, district offices and district branch offices, representative of each central ministry, are responsible for policy design and implementation. The provincial administrations have the responsibility for providing basic services such as irrigation, healthcare, education and police. Since 1997, provincial governors have been elected by provincial council members who are elected by citizens. Traditionally, the districts are divided into areas comprising several villages (*tambon*), which are often led by traditional leaders or headmen. The Provincial Governor interacts with villagers through the *tambon* headmen, who must be authorized by the one of the high-ranking officials in charge of the province.

The local administration in Thailand is composed of Provincial Administrative Organizations (PAOs), Municipalities, Sub-district (*tambon*) Administrative Organizations (TAOs) and the Bangkok Metropolitan Area (BMA) and Pattaya City. These latter cities have special standing in terms of their local governance structures. The BMA, in particular, owing to its size and financial importance, generally functions as an autonomous local state. The residents directly elect the governor of the BMA and its council members. As is true for all the other provincial and district administrative organizations, however, the Minister of Interior can dismiss the governor and councilors of the BMA with Cabinet approval.

In similar fashion, *tambon* councils and their members are elected from the respective villages. In 1994, the Thai government passed the *Tambon* Administrative Act, which made local development planning and implementation (including local infrastructure, education, health, welfare and natural resources management) the responsibility of the newly created TAOs. In addition, when Thailand rewrote its constitution in 1997, in response to a series of political crises in the early 1990s, it called for decentralization.

The new constitution entitles local people and organizations to formulate their government organizations to consist of locally elected council and executive bodies. In addition, the Decentralization Act of 1999 established that local governments are entitled to an increased share of total revenues and expenditures and that, furthermore, inter-governmental transfers are supposed to be more transparent and predictable.[1]

These central government policy changes seem to indicate significant shifts downward in decision-making and authority. However, at least since 2002, most decentralization efforts occurring in Thailand fall under the label of "deconcentration"—shifting responsibility and decision-making to lower/local government entities in a strong vertical relationship with central government. For example, all local governments, including the TAOs, the PAOs and the various municipalities, must seek and obtain approval for all their budget appropriations from a governor or a district chief officer (Shiroyama 2003). The power to raise local taxes still resides with the central government. In addition, the historical devolution of power has taken place in typical Thai fashion, so that multiple agencies at different levels have *de jure* authority for the same functions and services (Kuwajima 2003: 198).

In a similar way, the impetus to open up traditionally closed decision-making processes to public participation and democratic elections is difficult to reconcile with the traditional mandates of line agencies. Dupar and Badenoch (2002) suggest that introducing transparency and participation (i.e. the decentralizing of decision-making) is particularly problematic in the areas of water and forests. In Thailand, most residents believe that water is a right and that it should be provided for free. The Royal Irrigation Department would, thus, prefer to have the power to implement pricing and management changes without worrying about resident dissatisfaction. Decentralization has made implementing policy in this area much more difficult and controversial (International Rivers Network 2000).

In terms of politics, Thailand's recently deposed Prime Minister, Thaksin, was widely seen as someone who "emphasizes tackling inefficiency and sectionalism of the public sector" (Kuwajima 2003: 208). He hoped to eliminate duplication across government departments and urged the bureaucracy to begin to act more as a facilitator as opposed to a ruler. Thaksin implemented a number of measures designed to increase the role of local politicians, such as increasing the number of grants awarded to villages for economic development. However, given that Thaksin's leadership approach relied predominantly on his individual influence, his lack of interest in actual political decentralization led to a lack of progress in transfer of power or fund-generating authority. For example, the multi-stakeholder committee formed in 1999 to implement decentralization, the National Decentralization Committee, ceased its activities in 2002.

There are, however, some signs of progress in terms of actual decentralization. The central government, as of 2006, has been obligated to increase the volume and number of grants received by local administrative units because of the guidelines established in the 1999 Decentralization Act. As a consequence, a variety of structures and services, such as "small-scale civic construction work, garbage collection, provision of school meals and other services [are] now being undertaken by local government organizations" (Kuwajima 2003: 207–8).

Social capital in Bangkok's low-income communities

In the context of Thai decentralization, the role of social capital is important, but unclear. To some extent, the BMA is also in the midst of a national effort to decentralize funding, decision-making and implementation of urban infrastructure projects. One large and important element of these decentralization efforts is community participation in planning. However, there is still a severe lack of understanding of the dynamics inherent in facilitating community-based planning in slums and low-income neighborhoods. Shatkin (2004), for example, examines the case of Chonburi, Thailand, to assess how urban political governance has changed with increased fiscal and economic pressures created by globalization. He finds that there are windows of opportunity for local decision-making and collaborative planning, especially through public–private financing. This has led to the increasing influence of businessmen-cum-politicians who can exert economic and political dominance at the local level (also Evans 1996). These individuals, who breach the boundaries between the civil society and the state, act as intermediaries between central governments and local citizenry by mobilizing local institutions and solidifying a political base for central development policy.

Dupar and Badenoch (2002) argue that creating social capital, particularly in terms of mobilizing communities and raising awareness of environmental issues, will need the proactive leadership of local agencies and government institutions. In the northern province of Mae Chaem, for example, TAO officials were not motivated by environmental concerns and decided to focus instead on elections and economic development policy. A local NGO, however, recognized the importance of environmental management and planning and eventually directed the local environmental agenda. The NGO served as a conduit between the various ethnic groups in the region and was able to coordinate a regional planning network dedicated to the protection of natural resources, effective watershed protection and assigning fire control responsibilities. The NGO and the people's network have received funding from the Ministry of Science, Technology and Environment and several donor organizations to support their efforts. The NGO is now working to help increase TAO capacity to engage in collaborative natural resource management and planning (Dupar and Badenoch 2002: 31).

These examples make clear the potential productive relationship between social capital and decentralization for enhancing good governance. We turn now to an analysis of survey data from Bangkok that focus on social capital to further clarify these interactions. We focus on two cross-sectional surveys in low-income communities in the BMA in 1995 and 2000. Although this is not a panel or longitudinal data set, the two samples generally have comparable characteristics. The socio-economic characteristics of the households surveyed in both efforts are summarized in Tables 12.1 and 12.2.

Social capital in 1995

We use the state–society synergy elements of complementarity and embeddedness (Evans 1996) to assess the interactions between social capital and decentralization.

Table 12.1 Summary characteristics of 1995 sample

Variable	Proportion
Geographic location	Inner: N = 232 (43%)
	Middle: N = 238 (44%)
	Outer: N = 70 (13%)
Gender	Male 21%; female 79%
Household heads in sample	32%
Education	Average = 5.8 years
Age	Average = 38 years
Household size	Average = 5 persons
Household earnings per month	Average = 10,562 baht (US$420)

Source: Daniere and Takahashi 1997.

Table 12.2 Summary characteristics of 2000 sample

Variable	Community				
	1 (N = 200)	*2* (N = 30)	*3* (N = 50)	*4* (N = 90)	*5* (N = 130)
Community					
Size of community	2,800	160	185	538	600
Location	Urban	Urban	Suburb	Urban	Suburb
Respondent					
Average age (years)	42.7	40.6	42.8	41.2	41.8
% born in community	32.0	3.0	42.8	9.0	29.0
% lived in community longer than 5 years	92.0	72.0	88.0	79.0	72.0
Average number of adults in household	3.1	3.4	3.7	3.2	3.1
Average number of children in household	1.8	1.0	1.8	1.6	1.5
Total average expenses per month					
in baht[b]	11,561	11,890	14,048	10,464	8,482
in US$	289	297	351	261	212
Gini coefficient[a]	0.24	0.18	0.24	0.26	0.25

Source: Daniere *et al.* 2002.

a The Gini coefficient is a measure of inequality that varies between 0 (when all have the same expenditure, or incomes) and 1 (when one person has everything). The closer a Gini coefficient is to 1, the more unequal is the distribution. For most developing countries, Gini coefficients for expenditures or incomes range between 0.3 and 0.6.
b 40 baht=$1.

Complementarity is characterized as state and society having clear and distinct roles (Evans 1996)—here we focus on the perceived responsibilities and capabilities of the state and society in addressing environmental management issues. Interestingly, when respondents were asked who had responsibility for dealing with infrastructure problems (e.g., water and sanitation), the largest proportion said that individuals (i.e. the citizenry) were primarily responsible (over one-third of the respondents), with government officials (BMA and District Offices) indicated by less than one-fifth of the respondents (Table 12.3).

Very large proportions of respondents, however, believed that community members and local government agencies, perhaps through community-based planning efforts, could both be very effective in improving infrastructure conditions at the local level. There is consequently a slight mismatch between who might be seen as capable of dealing with what were in 1995 significant infrastructure problems, and those who are seen as primarily responsible. There are two dimensions to this mismatch between capability and responsibility. The 1995 survey indicated that no group or agency was seen by a large majority of respondents as primarily responsible for managing urban environmental problems. Perhaps related to this, there was in the 1995 survey very limited community-based planning or other types of involvement in urban environmental management activities. Less than one-third of the respondents in the 1995 survey reported that they had participated in a community-based planning project in the previous year, though for those who did report that they had participated, about two-thirds were involved in efforts to clean the community rather than in planning projects. Consequently, it was unclear which institution or groups were seen to be responsible by these respondents for urban environmental quality, and, in addition, there was very limited community-based planning effort to improve urban environmental conditions.

Those respondents who did participate in community projects and, therefore, presumably saw themselves in part responsible for urban environmental quality, had specific characteristics. Those respondents who reported that they participated in community projects during the previous year tended to have lived longer in the neighborhood (Daniere and Takahashi 1999a). Also related to community participation were overall household earnings (respondents who reported that income or earnings were a major problem were more than twice as likely to have reported that they participated in a community project in the prior year).

Embeddedness consists of breaching the usual boundaries between public and private spheres (e.g., public infrastructure programs and private household tasks/community cleaning (Evans 1996)). We explore the ways that participation in community-based planning efforts was related to trust in and belief in the capability of government to deal with infrastructure problems (Table 12.4).

When respondents reported that they had participated in community activities in the past three years, they also tended to report that individuals could play a role in improving local environmental conditions. In contrast, these respondents tended

Table 12.3 1995 survey results: complementarity

Questions about responsibility, capability and participation (N = 540)	Response	
		%
In your opinion, who has responsibility for solving water quality and sanitation problems in Bangkok?	Individuals/everyone	36.2
	The BMA	20.8
	Governor of the BMA	15.4
	District Office	8.8
	Garbage collectors	6.6
	National government	6.2
	Community committee	5.3
Do you believe that people:	%	
• in this community can improve water and sanitation conditions in the community itself?	81.7	yes
• in this community can improve water and sanitation conditions in Bangkok, at large?	66.7	yes
• who work for the BMA can improve water and sanitation in your community and in Bangkok?	70.6	yes
Aware of NGO in community	51	yes
Participated in a community project during the past year (most common types: community cleaning: 67%; joining a savings group: 14%; fund raising: 12%)	30	yes

Source: Daniere and Takahashi 1999a; 1999b.

to report that they did not believe that the BMA (municipal-level government agencies) could solve water and sanitation problems. This indicates that there is less embeddedness between government officials and community members for respondents who engaged in community activities. Although a lack of faith in local state institutions might lead to greater engagement in community-based planning, this also leads to a lack of embeddedness (or dense networks between government officials and community members (Evans 1996)).

In Thailand, embeddedness might more likely exist for those who believe in, and benefit from, patron–client relationships. Patron–client relationships are a common form of social capital that is prevalent in many Thai households and family groups. The divisions between the private/community sphere and government institutional sphere are breached when patron–client relationships are present, though these relationships tend to be vertical rather than horizontal. Although the government–community divide may be breached with patron–client relationships, the benefits of such relationships to decentralization are likely to remain within the vertical social relationship, rather than spread horizontally through so-called bridging relationships across communities. Patron–client relationships were measured in the 1995 survey using a Likert scale, where respondents were

Table 12.4 1995 Survey results: embeddedness

Characteristic or behavior	Attitude	Percent exhibiting attitude	X^2	P
Is aware of community organizations	BMA can solve problems	57	6.7 (df = 1)	0.010
Is aware of community organizations	Individuals can solve community problems	57	4.5 (df = 1)	0.035
Has not participated in community group/activity in past 3 years	BMA can solve problems	31	8.4 (df = 2)	0.015
Has participated in community group/activity in past 3 years	Individuals can solve community problems	30	9.6 (df = 2)	0.008

Source: Daniere and Takahashi 1999b.

asked how much they believed that "If my patron asks me to do something unpleasant, I should not do it." Respondents who reported a lack of belief in patron–client social norms (i.e. those who agreed with this statement) were more than twice as likely to participate in community projects.

Social capital in 2000

In our 2000 survey, we again investigated the level of engagement of residents with community groups and projects to understand the drivers of participation and the ways that government action could facilitate social capital for improving urban environmental conditions. We found low levels of community group membership across the five communities, but high levels of participation in community-based planning projects across almost all of the communities (with the exception of Community 5; Table 12.5). The largest proportion of respondents who reported belonging to a community group was 20 percent in Community 4 (but respondents in Community 2 reported the highest proportion of participation in community-based planning projects: 80 percent). The lowest proportion of respondents reporting participating in community-based planning projects lived in the most geographically isolated community, Community 5. There was quite a low level of confidence reported by respondents in almost all of the communities that community groups could provide assistance. Less than 10 percent of the respondents in Communities 1, 3, 4 and 5 indicated that community groups could provide assistance; over half of respondents in Community 2, however, reported that they believed they could get assistance from community groups (however, only 13 percent of respondents in this community reported that they belonged to a community group). Consequently, it appeared that community

Table 12.5 2000 survey results: complementarity

Variable	Community				
	1 (N = 200)	2 (N = 30)	3 (N = 50)	4 (N = 90)	5 (N = 130)
Gini coefficient	0.24	0.18	0.24	0.26	0.26
% belonging to community groups	17.5	13.3	8.0	20.0	3.1
% participating in community projects	57.5	80.0	56.0	63.3	24.6
% believing they could get assistance from community groups	1.0	56.6	10.0	3.3	0.0
% believing they could get assistance from neighbors	41.5	36.7	34.0	43.3	27.7
% reporting that government helped the community solve its garbage problem	62.5	96.7	82.0	63.3	37.7

Source: Daniere *et al.* 2002.

groups provided little in terms of confidence about being able to deal effectively with the direct needs of these respondents. Community-based planning projects seem to be taking place outside the governing ability of recognized community groups, perhaps in a more ad hoc fashion. Respondents appeared to have much more confidence that their neighbors would assist them rather than community groups. For example, sizable proportions of respondents indicated that they could ask their neighbors for help and that their neighbors would provide assistance; the proportion was highest in Communities 4 and 1, and lowest in Community 5.

When asked specifically about whether government was effective in addressing solid waste (garbage), large majorities of respondents across almost all the five communities (with the exception of the geographically isolated Community 5) reported that government agencies had helped the community "solve its garbage problem" (Table 12.5). Consequently, the 2000 survey showed that respondents believed that government agencies could be effective in dealing with at least one urban environmental issue through a process best described as collaborative planning.

In measuring embeddedness, the most direct measures of potential breaching of the public/governmental and private/community divide were of trust of community respondents in NGOs and government officials. NGOs, in Thailand, are ubiquitous (Bradshaw and Schafer 2000), and many engage in collaborative planning with members of the community and different government agencies. As such, few, if any, respondents were unfamiliar with a number of both local and international NGOs operating in and around their communities. However,

the 2000 survey provides a complex portrait in terms of community residents trusting NGOs in a general sense (Table 12.6). When asked about whether or not they
trusted NGOs, very low proportions of respondents across the five communities
indicated that they could trust most or all NGOs.[2] The largest proportions were
in Communities 4 (24 percent), 1 (18 percent), and 3 (16 percent). Many
reported that some NGOs could be trusted, but not most nor all NGOs. Over
one-third of respondents in Communities 2, 3 and 4 reported that they could trust
some NGOs, with smaller proportions reporting the same in Communities 1 and
5. But there were also very low proportions of respondents across the five
communities that indicated that they did not trust any NGOs, with Communities
1 (22 percent of respondents) and 5 (the most geographically isolated community, 12 percent of respondents) indicating the most distrust in NGOs. This
suggests that experience with NGOs was not directly related to trust in NGOs, as
Community 1 respondents likely had the most experience with NGOs among the
five communities surveyed (given their location next to the port and their

Table 12.6 2000 survey results: embeddedness

Variable	*Community*				
	1 (N = 200)	*2* (N = 30)	*3* (N = 50)	*4* (N = 90)	*5* (N = 130)
Gini coefficient	0.24	0.18	0.24	0.26	0.26
NGOs					
% can't trust any NGOs	22.0	6.7	8.0	8.9	12.3
% can trust some NGOs	20.0	33.3	38.0	38.9	11.5
% can trust most NGOs	10.0	3.3	12.0	14.4	0.8
% can trust all NGOs	8.0	0.0	4.0	8.9	1.5
% don't know if NGOs can be trusted	32.5	56.7	34.0	26.7	64.6
Government officials					
% can't trust any government officials	39.0	3.3	6.0	15.6	20.0
% can trust some government officials	26.0	33.3	36.0	46.7	28.5
% can trust most government officials	1.5	3.3	22.0	13.3	4.6
% can trust all government officials	1.0	0.0	4.0	5.6	3.1
% don't know if government officials can be trusted	25.0	60.0	26.0	17.8	36.9

Source: Daniere *et al.* 2002.

development history), and Community 5 respondents had the least experience. From one-third to two-thirds of the respondents reported that they did not know if NGOs could be trusted, indicating a potentially large window of opportunity for NGOs to build trust among community members, perhaps through careful implementation of collaborative planning initiatives.

There was a bit more certainty in the respondents in these five communities about whether or not government officials in general could be trusted or not. Community 1 respondents indicated the highest distrust of government officials, with about 39 percent reporting that no government officials could be trusted; the most geographically isolated respondents in Community 5 had the second highest proportion of distrust in any government officials at 20 percent. Sizable proportions of respondents across all five communities, however, indicated that they believed that some or even most government officials could be trusted, with Communities 3 and 4 having more than half of the respondents indicating that they thought some or most government officials could be trusted. Many respondents, especially in Community 2, reported that they did not know if government officials could be trusted. Similar to the trust measures associated with NGOs, these results suggest that there is a fragmented sense of trust associated with government officials, and that, consequently, there is a large opportunity for building trust between the government agencies and officials who will be increasingly called upon to interact with the citizenry.

Policy implications/future research

Thai decentralization is proceeding, but in a cautious manner. The central government still wields much governing power, and the recent coup[3] does not really bode well for decentralization as it is likely to be resisted by various interests for different reasons. In this turbulent political environment, the potential advantages stemming from decentralization will likely depend in large part on local government capacity and social capital.

We argued that the linkages between decentralization and social capital should be conceptualized through a state–society synergy lens. Such synergy can be characterized in terms of two important components, complementarity and embeddedness (Evans 1996). We used survey data from 1995 and 2000 in Bangkok to highlight the complexities inherent in any potential synergy between Thai decentralization and social capital. Measures of social capital differed somewhat between the surveys, perhaps because of the slightly different methodologies used to select respondents as well as a refinement in the survey instrument over time. In addition, the survey conducted in 2000 was specifically designed to evaluate social capital within communities, whereas the survey implemented in 1995 aimed at uncovering the relationship between community-based planning efforts and environmental quality of life. In addition, the prevalence of NGOs and community-based initiatives through government and donor auspices increased markedly between 1995 and 2000, which may, in effect, have heightened cynicism on the part of respondents of the 2000 survey.

Especially in the 2000 survey, we saw a substantial proportion of respondents across communities express deep distrust of government officials and NGOs. However, this sizable level of distrust was expressed at the same time as respondents indicated that government had successfully engaged in collaborative planning on specific problems and that community-based planning also held out some potential to resolve environmental problems. Respondents indicated, for example, that governments had been seen as being effective in addressing community problems with garbage in both our 1995 and 2000 surveys. In addition, in both the 1995 and 2000 surveys, although there were few respondents who belonged to community-based planning groups, or believed that community groups could provide assistance in times of need, we found that very large proportions of respondents across most of the communities reported that they had participated in community-based planning projects in the previous year.

The explanation for this seeming contradiction between stated satisfaction with government services and lack of trust in government officials and NGOs may lie in respondents' fractured perception of government and community organizations/NGOs. That is, one potential reason for higher levels of reported trust in some or most government officials and NGOs in our 2000 survey is the differentiation that might be made between levels of government and, associated with this, the responsiveness of government to public needs. However, the large proportion of respondents, especially in the 2000 survey, that indicated that they did not know whether NGOs or government officials could be trusted points to a significant window of opportunity to create and enhance embeddedness. That is, to leverage existing social capital (and there does appear to be trusting and reciprocal relationships at the community level), breaching typical government–community roles, through greater reliance on collaborative planning techniques, may be necessary to enhance trust and build potential synergy between social capital and decentralization. Thai decentralization and social capital appear, from our 1995 and 2000 survey data, to be confined primarily to the complementarity dimension of the state–society synergy framework, without the substantial possibilities for good governance offered by the breaching of typical government–community relations (see e.g., Tendler, 1997). As such, whatever social capital exists and can be sustained in resource-poor communities in Thailand remains largely disconnected from formal administrative governance.

We saw such deep divides between government action and community efforts in the 1995 survey data, where respondents who had participated in group or community activities also tended to report that they did not believe that the BMA could address water and sanitation challenges. Community participation came at the cost of faith or trust in the Thai state's ability to address environmental issues, or, put in another way, when there was a loss of faith in state institutions, community participation became more prevalent.

There is a clear need to examine more fully the cultural and political–economic reasons for the disjuncture between community participation and Thai state action. Without a detailed understanding of the mechanisms underlying state–society relations, especially the role of social capital in governance, policy levers for building and leveraging social capital are likely to be ineffective. In general, future research on this issue needs to focus on the details of community-based planning and participation in governance (Agarwal and Ribot 1999).

The Thai central state's typical bureaucratic routines, including duplication of responsibilities, lack of emphasis on training of staff/upgrading capacity and resistance to devolving financial and decision-making authority, will make any meaningful decentralization difficult at best. In this complex and challenging political–administrative context, there are avenues for expanding complementarity and embeddedness so that social capital becomes an integral component of a productive decentralization effort.

First, as our 1995 and 2000 surveys showed, there is still much room for building trust between community members (who are expanding and using social capital and community-based planning efforts to cope with local problems) and NGOs and government officials. There is an opportunity for not only emphasizing the complementarity in decentralization (e.g., distinct government and community roles in environmental management, such as garbage collection by government agencies and community clean-up by local residents) but also expanding embeddedness through collaborative planning initiatives, where government officials can provide for private/household/community needs (e.g., working with communities to design and implement solid waste collection or improve the cleanliness of slum pathways and lanes). Although patron–client relationships (a problematic form of social capital that is quite prevalent in Thailand) would appear to be a short-term strategy for expanding embeddedness, this approach comes at the cost of reinforcing rather than dismantling parochial community-centered networks and, consequently, should be leveraged with caution.

Second, decentralized Thai government agencies can work with relatively minimal financial resources to create environments that are conducive to the expansion of intra- and inter-community networks. Within communities, Thai government agencies can diffuse knowledge and information about environmental improvements within villages and small communities to build resident capacity for helping one another. At a larger spatial scale, Thai government agencies can help support leadership development of officials/representatives who want to work across villages, *tambons* and urban communities. Building a political leadership base that is sensitive to cross-community issues may help to leverage bridging social capital (i.e. vertical patron–client relationships) across communities (i.e. horizontal networks of leaders).

Although the portrait of Thai decentralization and Thai social capital does not appear to be one of radical change or substantial democratization, there are opportunities for building social capital and pushing decentralization in a direction that reallocates power and resources more evenly across the nation. As such, future research should focus on the role of social capital and how it can be harnessed in areas outside the capital city of Bangkok (i.e. in smaller municipalities and TAOs). Although we focused much of this discussion on the BMA's urban dwellers, the potential impact of social capital on decentralization will also largely depend on the smaller and perhaps more flexible local institutions outside the BMA. Future researchers should ascertain the nature, form and functionality of social capital in these smaller jurisdictions and the possible lessons for decentralization and community-based planning.

Acknowledgements

The authors express their gratitude and appreciation to Dr Anchana NaRanong at the National Institute for Development Administration in Bangkok, Thailand, without whom this research could not have been conducted. We also thank Molly Davidson-Welling, Nadia Abu-Zahra and Jill Wigle of the Department of Geography at the University of Toronto for their substantial contributions. We are grateful to the University of California Pacific Rim Research Program and the Social Science and Humanities Research Council of Canada for funding this research. We remain responsible for all errors and omissions.

Notes

1   The Decentralization Act established that local revenues are supposed to reach 35 percent of all government revenues by 2006 (up from less than 10 percent in the 1990s).
2   The wording of the questionnaire, including the notion of trust, was extensively pretested for comprehension during the pilot phase of the survey. There was little or no confusion regarding the use and meaning of the word trust expressed by either respondents or field assistants.
3   In September 2006, the Thai military engineered a coup d'état while Prime Minister Thaksin was out of the country. At the present time, a caretaker government, led by the army, is ruling the country with the apparent tacit approval of the Thai constitutional monarch, King Bhumipol (*The Economist*, 2006).

References

Agarwal, A. and Ribot, J.C. (1999) "Accountability in decentralization: A framework with south Asian and west African cases," *Journal of Developing Areas* 33 (4): 473–502.
Bebbington, A.J. and Carroll, T.F. (2002) "Induced social capital and federations of the rural poor in the Andes," in C. Grootaert and T. van Bastelaer (eds) *The Role of Social Capital in Development: An Empirical Assessment*, Cambridge: Cambridge University Press: 234–78.

Bourdieu, P. (1986) "The forms of capital," in J.G. Richardson (ed.) *Handbook of Theory and Research in the Sociology of Education*, New York: Greenwald Press.

Bradshaw, Y.W. and Schafer, M. (2000) "Urbanization and development: The emergence of international nongovernmental organizations amid declining states," *Sociological Perspectives* 43: 97–116.

Coleman, J. (1988) "Social capital in the creation of human capital," *American Journal of Sociology* 94: 95–120.

Daniere, A.G. and Takahashi, L.M. (1997) "Environmental policy in Thailand: Values, attitudes, and behavior among the slum dwellers of Bangkok," *Environment and Planning C* 15: 305–27.

Daniere, A.G. and Takahashi, L.M. (1999a) "Environmental behavior in Bangkok, Thailand: A portrait of attitudes, values and behavior," *Economic Development and Cultural Change* 47(3): 525–57.

Daniere, A.G. and Takahashi, L.M. (1999b) "Public policy and human dignity in Thailand: Environmental policies and human values in Bangkok," *Policy Sciences* 32: 247–68.

Daniere, A., Takahashi, L. and NaRanong, A. (2002) "Social capital, networks and community environments in Bangkok, Thailand," *Growth and Change* 33: 453–83.

Dupar, M. and Badenoch, N. (2002) *Environment, Livelihoods, and Local Institutions: Decentralization in Mainland Southeast Asia*, Washington, DC: World Resources Institute.

The Economist (2006) "Special report: Old soldiers, old habits—Thailand's military coup," September 23, 380 (8496): 27–9.

Evans, P. (1996) "Government action, social capital and development: Reviewing the evidence on synergy," *World Development* 24 (6): 178–209.

Gertler, M.S. (1997) "The invention of regional culture," in R. Lee and J. Wills (eds) *Geographies of Economies*, London: Edward Arnold, pp. 47–58.

International Rivers Network website, "Agricultural sector program loan Thailand." Available online at www.irn.org/programs/mekong/adb.php?id=adbbp9.htm.

Kuwajima, K. (2003) "Health sector management and governance in Thailand," in Y. Shimomura (ed.) *The Role of Governance in Asia*, Singapore: Institute of Southeast Asian Studies, pp. 190–252.

Molyneux, M. (2002) "Gender and the silences of social capital: Lessons from Latin America," *Development and Change* 33 (2): 167–88.

Ostrom, E. (1990) *Governing the Commons: The Evolution of Institutions for Collective Action*, New York: Cambridge University Press.

Putnam, R. (1993) *Making Democracy Work: Civil Traditions in Modern Italy*, Princeton, NJ: Princeton University Press.

Shatkin, G. (2004) "Globalization and local leadership: Growth, power and politics in Thailand's eastern seaboard," *International Journal of Urban and Regional Research* 28 (1): 11–26.

Shiroyama, H. (2003) "Regional governance in Asia: Comparative analysis of experiments of decentralization and deconcentration in Indonesia, Thailand and Korea," in Y. Shimomura (ed.) *The Role of Governance in Asia*, Singapore: Institute of Southeast Asian Studies, pp. 6–26.

Tendler, J. (1997) *Good Government in the Tropics*, Baltimore, MD: Johns Hopkins University Press.

Wai, F.L. (1996) "Institutional design of public agencies and coproduction: A study of irrigation associations in Taiwan," *World Development* 24 (6): 1039–54.

Chapter 13
Decentralization and the struggle for participation in local politics and planning
Lessons from Naga City, the Philippines

Gavin Shatkin

The paradox of decentralization is simple and apparent—addressing inequities in power and resources cannot be achieved simply by reallocating governmental resources and responsibilities from one scale to another. International aid organizations focus on city and metropolitan government as the ideal scale to which power over urban development should be allocated. It is at this scale, they argue, that "essential public services are delivered . . . and where policy meets the people" through popular participation (World Bank 2000). Yet, particularly in the context of severe power and resource disparities that exist in most cities in developing countries, civil society organizations working with the urban poor are profoundly disadvantaged in urban politics. For corporations, large landowners, developers, and other elite political and economic actors whose social networks and economic interests naturally span the scale of cities and metropolitan regions, the means and motives exist to assert influence at this level. With the inter-urban economic competition that comes with globalization, these elite actors have become increasingly organized and resolute in pursuing their shared interests in the commodification of urban land, a position that frequently places them in conflict with the community and public uses required by the less powerful. Hence, for organizations of civil society representing community interests, entering the lion's den of urban politics can prove a daunting experience, even where they enjoy some strength in numbers.

It is all the more intriguing, then, when such organizations do break through, governments bring people into decision-making, and community needs become a central focus of attention. Particularly in Asia, where globalization-led growth has fostered intense pressures for urban redevelopment, non-governmental and community-based organizations (NGOs and CBOs) representing low-income groups have generally influenced urban policy and planning only at the margins. This chapter examines one notable exception, that of Naga City, the Philippines, based on an exploratory field research trip taken in July 2005.[1] Although this is a preliminary investigation, the research suggests that Naga City is in many respects the exception that proves the rule—reform only came about when a mayor who gained office through his membership in an elite family shifted his power base by connecting directly to low-income communities. Yet it also suggests that his success in doing so points to opportunities in the Philippines' shifting political economy that have important implications for the strategies of organizations and political parties that ally themselves with less powerful groups. Specifically, it suggests that, although civil society empowerment is not a foregone conclusion under decentralization, it can be encouraged through a focus on promoting the development of a new brand of progressive city leaders and building community capacity to participate in local politics. In the post-authoritarian settings that characterize many countries, at least a basic infrastructure of civic organizations often exists, but these organizations often lack capacity or opportunity to engage effectively in political participation. With the emergence of city leadership that is effective and inclusive, the potential may emerge for a virtuous cycle to form, as progressive city leaders encourage the strengthening of civic organizations representing the poor and disenfranchised, and these groups in turn encourage and contribute to progressive policy and planning and form a political base for progressive leaders.

Decentralization, civil society and urban governance: the Philippine experience

There is increasing interest in the role of progressive city regimes in enhancing civil society participation in urban politics in developing countries. Research has naturally focused on Latin America, where nine of the twelve largest cities were governed by left or center-left mayors for at least part of the 1980s and 1990s, and many experienced significant experiments with broad-based participation in governance (Fox 1995; Chavez and Goldfrank 2004). The most closely watched case has been Porto Alegre's model of participatory budgeting, in which a Worker's Party administration created a process that resulted in the participation of tens of thousands of city residents in formulating the city budget, resulting in significant changes in spending. Research has pointed to the administration's critical role in emphasizing the need for participation by all segments of society in the rhetoric surrounding the budgeting process, and in providing an equity-focused political platform that legitimized participation by the poor (Abers 2000; Baiocchi 2001).

In most of Southeast Asia, however, left political parties are weak, and city governments that focus on an agenda of broad-based participation and social equity are exceedingly rare. Despite the fact that most large cities in the region have a history of civic activism and large contingents of NGOs and CBOs, reform for democratization and decentralization has not translated into a strong voice for these organizations. Rather, reform has generally resulted in the emergence of what one analyst has termed "elite democracy," in which "formal institutions of representative democracy and civil and political rights have been established, but limits to effective citizen participation remain in place" (Rocamora 2004: 9).

The Philippines' experience is of particular interest because reform came earlier and went far deeper than elsewhere in the region. In the years after the "People's Power" street demonstrations that overthrew the Marcos regime in

1986,[2] a hodgepodge of interest groups, including business associations, former members of the revolutionary underground, NGOs and CBOs, and others, have all sought to influence the direction of the post-authoritarian Philippine state. All generally favor decentralized governance, but there has been less agreement on the role of civil society and anti-poverty strategies. The reforms that ensued have had a dramatic impact on the urban planning system. Municipal and neighbourhood-level officials are now elected, and enjoy considerable new powers in land use and infrastructure planning, education, public health and a variety of other areas (Brillantes 2003). The landmark Local Government Code (LGC) of 1991 mandates that representatives of NGOs and CBOs make up at least 25 percent of city and *barangay* (neighborhood/village) councils that approve or disapprove major projects. More controversial has been legislation for urban and rural land reform. Of particular interest to this chapter is the Urban Development and Housing Act (UDHA), passed in 1992 following intensive civil society mobilization. It provides legal protections against eviction for informal settlers, mandates resettlement for those displaced involuntarily by redevelopment projects, and requires local governments to register informal settlers and identify land for social housing (PHILLSA 1997).

In practice, however, urban planning decision-making in most cities and municipalities remains quite closed. Mayors often control NGO and CBO participation in LDCs by such means as exclusionary rules that prevent the registration of oppositional organizations (Clarke 1998). The Philippines' tradition of dynastic mayoral rule by elite families is still in evidence—mayors effectively exceed the legal maximum of three consecutive terms by having other members of their family serve a term until they are eligible to run again. Planning and policy are often driven largely by patronage and rent-seeking. Philippine courts regularly uphold evictions of informal settlements that are in clear violation of UDHA, and local government non-compliance with aspects of the law goes largely unchallenged.

There are several reasons for the continued limitations to the role of NGOs and CBOs in urban politics. The first is the political power of elite local families, which scholars of Philippine politics attribute to the distinct colonial history of the country. To summarize this argument, the American colonial regime that was in place during the first half of the twentieth century enacted political reforms for electoral democracy that subverted the power of national government to local political strongmen in an effort to gain the support of rural elites. This resulted in a reengineering of the Philippine state as a mechanism to provide a steady flow of resources to these local elites (Hutchcroft 1998; Sidel 1999). What emerged out of this system was a social stratum composed of powerful families, often large landowners, who view political office almost as a birthright. Sidel (1999) has used the term "bossism" to describe the resulting model of patronage politics and the monopolization of force by local political families.

Second, the aspirations of Southeast Asian nations to follow the path of the "Tiger" economies of Taiwan, South Korea, Singapore and Hong Kong have shaped government and elite discourses about city governance by providing a powerful tool to legitimize growth-oriented urban policy and planning (Kelly 2000). The concept of a "developmental state," characterized by a strong authoritarian state that uses its influence to assert the power of the bureaucracy and the rule of law towards developmental ends in opposition to both oligarchic groups and the left, has emerged as an ideal type for many Filipinos (Rocamora 1994: 175). Hence, even when reformist mayors do emerge they tend to fashion themselves in the mold of leaders such as Singapore's Lee Kwan Yew in pushing urban redevelopment projects that appeal to a middle-class and business constituency, and law and order policies that have broader appeal among many sectors.

Finally, left political parties that might provide some political support to organizations working with the urban poor are notably ineffective and ill-represented at all levels of government. This is largely owing to the divisions that have emerged in the post-Marcos period between those within the left who prefer to continue the Maoist insurgency that has been ongoing since the early 1970s, and those who believe that the new context of democracy and decentralization requires a shift to aboveground community organization and participation in politics (Rocamora 1994). Many NGOs and CBOs that identify with the left also continue to eschew ties to political parties out of concerns over the possibility of cooptation.

Although the obstacles to civil society participation in municipal politics are significant, Philippine politics is also changing. Until recently, the overwhelmingly agrarian nature of the Philippine economy meant that, in contrast to Latin America, the bureaucratic and managerial middle class and industrial working class did not represent a significant political force. Urbanization and industrialization have, however, led to a debate within NGOs and political parties as to whether the hold of landowners and other local elite politicians might be weakening, and what this might mean for organizations of civil society (Lacaba 1995). Second, legislation for decentralization has regularized the flow of state resources to local governments and increased them significantly, thus reducing the amount of pork-barrel spending and arguably rendering national officials somewhat more independent of elite influence (Rocamora 2004). At the same time, recent generations within elite families have tended to be more educated than their predecessors and have greater exposure to new political ideals. Finally, the media has recently emerged as an alternative basis for political mobilization, and popular media figures (including movie actors, news reporters and basketball stars) have gained elective office both at the local and national level in recent years. Although they tend to take populist positions and to follow in the footsteps of elite families in using political power for personal gain, some have used political office to push a reform agenda.

Finally, although it has had its drawbacks, the initiation of a party list system for some seats in the House of Representatives has created a channel for parties based on sectoral interests to gain some representation in national government, as groups claiming to represent the urban and rural poor, labor, women and other interests have been able to garner the required number of votes. One of these, AKBAYAN, has had success in developing an electoral platform based on the input of affiliated associations that concern themselves with a range of sectoral interests, and has begun to shift its focus to pursuing this platform in local politics. I will return to a discussion of AKBAYAN's efforts in this regard later in the chapter.

The direction of urban policy change is as yet undetermined. Mayors in many cities have proven quite adept at mobilizing the forces of the media and the rhetoric of globalization to pursue an agenda of growth that appeals to the middle class and business interests while paying marginal attention to the needs of low-income groups. Although the expectation among advocates that decentralization would create a pervasive atmosphere of civil society empowerment has certainly not materialized, however, some opportunity has emerged. The Naga City case offers insight into the possibilities and limitations of the current political framework, and the strategies that civil society organizations and political parties might employ in taking advantage of what opportunities do exist.

The Naga City case

In Naga City, the disparate elements of the left—former underground activists, NGOs and people's organizations (POs), and reformists in city hall—were able to overcome political resistance and seize the opportunities presented by national legislation to create new institutions for political participation and new programs for poverty alleviation. The model that emerged from this coalition was notably eclectic in its approach, borrowing elements from models of community organization developed within civil society, left activists, and international case studies in governance. Many of the "innovations" in Naga represent little more than the city's relative success in implementing existing national laws and programs concerning shelter and participation by civil society. The analysis that follows will focus on two key factors that made the Naga City experience possible—the role of leadership from the mayor's office, and the existence of a strong NGO network that focused on community organization for political participation.

Naga City has a population of about 150,000 and is located 450 kilometers southeast of Metro Manila in the Bicol region, one of the poorest regions of the Philippines (Naga City 2006). It is the capital of the province of Camarines Sur and functions as a local trading center for this predominantly agricultural region. It also contains several universities, hospitals, and regional television and radio stations.

During the Marcos dictatorship, NGOs based in the liberation theology model made inroads in organizing a network of CBOs in urban poor communities throughout Camarines Sur. In the mid 1980s, the Naga City Urban Poor Federation (NCUPF) was established by the COPE Foundation, a national community organizing entity that employs the radical model of Saul Alinsky (Angeles and Clavecillas n.d.). By 1986, the NCUPF was actively agitating for greater attention to the situation of informal settlements, which represented about 25 percent of the population, and was also involved in protest rallies organized by leftist political organizations.

As the Philippines transitioned to the post-Marcos era, however, Naga City and Bicol were like many other localities in that local politics remained largely controlled by a small number of elite families. The key figure was the provincial governor, Luis Villafuerte, who came from a family with a long history of political power and who himself had risen to regional and national power under the patronage of President Marcos (Kawanaka 2002). The transformative moment occurred when Villafuerte sponsored his nephew, Jesse Robredo, for the mayorship in an effort to consolidate his influence in Naga City politics. The son of a modestly wealthy family of Chinese heritage, Robredo was 29 when elected, held a bachelor's degree in engineering and a masters of business administration, and had previously worked in a managerial position for the San Miguel Corporation, one of the Philippines' most prominent companies. Robredo went on to hold office from 1988 to 1998, left office owing to term limit requirements, then returned to power in 2001.

Unbeknownst to Villafuerte, Robredo was seized with the ideals of the anti-Marcos movement during his time as a student in Metro Manila during the mid 1980s. After winning his first election by a narrow margin, Robredo quickly earned the ire of his uncle by exhibiting considerable independence in his administration of the city, broadening his political base by reaching out to the NGOs and POs representing urban poor settlements. He has won overwhelming victories in subsequent elections and has successfully sponsored a number of local professionals and people with backgrounds in the underground left and civil society for positions in city council. Hence, he has proven successful at recruiting a core of responsive and competent politicians and administrators that draws on his key constituencies in the left and the middle class.

The first major innovations of the Robredo administration were in the area of urban poverty alleviation. COPE and its affiliated CBOs met with Robredo on his first day in office, and an Urban Poor Affairs Office was created in 1989. The city soon initiated the *Kaantabay sa Kauswagan*, or Partners in Development program (Prilles 2004). Based on a philosophy of "tripartism," the program utilizes the existing network of NGOs and CBOs in low-income communities to organize residents for self-help improvement initiatives, while local government mediates between communities and private landowners in efforts to legalize tenure. The program draws some inspiration from the national government's Community Mortgage Program (CMP), which provides a pool of credit for CBOs to purchase land. Under the CMP, CBOs must negotiate purchase of the land from the existing owner, reblock the community and rebuild housing and infrastructure, and organize collection of loan repayment from households. Yet *Kaantabay* also recognizes the major impediments to success of the CMP—resistance from landowners, the difficulty of negotiating an affordable price, and the difficulty of organizing residents to undertake such a major task (Berner 2000). The city government plays a much more activist and hands-on role in *Kaantabay* by: acting as advocates for communities, for example by pleading restraint by courts and the police in cases where an eviction is imminent; cajoling and pressuring landowners to accept below-market prices; and working closely with NGOs to coordinate community organization and redevelopment (Prilles 2004). Program staff seek creative ways to finance schemes, employing such measures as land sharing, land swapping, land banking, as well as the CMP. Thus the program has relied on buy-in from, and coordination among, a number of city agencies, and more generally on an emphasis on competence and non-corruptibility throughout city hall. It is credited with legalizing tenure for more than half of the city's informal settlers and reducing the population of informal settlements dramatically, while many other cities have seen an increase.

Based on the concept as embodied in *Kaantabay sa Kauswagan*, the Robredo administration has sought to institutionalize "tripartism" by increasing formal channels for civil society participation in politics through the enactment of what has come to be known as the Empowerment Ordinance in 1995. This ordinance was inspired by the concept of "People's Councils," originally proposed by President Corazon Aquino and seized upon by some left activists in their effort to formulate a program of engagement with electoral politics (Santos 1998). The concept behind People's Councils is to bring POs and NGOs together in a forum to develop consensus around a political agenda, and provide them with a forum to voice this agenda in local politics. Authored by a city council member, a lawyer who was once part of the underground left, the Empowerment Ordinance creates the Naga City People's Council (NCPC), made up of accredited POs and NGOs in the city (Santos 1998). It mandates a minimum of 20 percent representation by representatives of the NCPC on the city council and on a variety of executive committees dealing with such issues as land use, urban poor affairs, public safety, transportation and others. The NCPC representatives are entitled to:

> observe, vote and participate in [program and project planning], propose legislation and participate and vote at the committee level of the [City Council], and/or act as the people's representatives in the exercise of their constitutional rights to information or matters of public concern and of access to official records and documents.
>
> (Santos 1998: 48)

A modest portion of the city budget is also set aside for use by the NCPC to organize various interest groups to participate in the council.

The Empowerment Ordinance attempts to create a parallel structure of NGOs and CBOs that is self-organizing and self-perpetuating, and that acts as a counterweight to government, holding politicians accountable and ensuring a voice for civil society in policy-making. It notably avoids the direct involvement of government in organizing participation, allowing organizations themselves to strike a bargain as to the relative influence of different sectors and interests. Hence, the Empowerment Ordinance model places considerable faith in the capacity of these groups to mobilize and organize independently, and to represent citizen interests effectively. In practice, their ability to do so has been a source of considerable debate and controversy. The NCPC has debated the degree of representation of sectoral interests in its membership, and some city officials complain that NCPC representatives are often passive and unable to provide meaningful feedback on government initiatives. This has led some to suggest that local government should play a stronger role in providing technical assistance and training to the NCPC and regulating its activities.

How and why has Naga City been able to resist the undercurrent of patronage politics? And what factors have allowed Mayor Robredo to pursue an agenda of popular participation that is also (modestly) redistributive? People involved with the Naga City experience frequently point to the tradition of civic awareness and political activism in the city as a deciding factor. Yet it resembles other cities in terms of the historical strength of elite families and the marginalization of urban poor issues. It is noteworthy that Robredo himself essentially slipped through the cracks of the bossist system—elected as a client of a local political boss, he turned his back upon his patron once in office and opened the doors of city hall. He did so partially out of conviction and partially in recognition that broadening his political base by responding to the demands of civil society could be good politics. As expressed by one Robredo associate with deep roots in the local NGO network:

> We don't have to go into this thing of really caring for the poor. We only have to think of the election and we will always come to the conclusion that we must help the poor [because] we have more poor than rich. . . . But most politicians tend to protect the interests of the moneyed sector because they are the ones that contribute to the fund come election time. . . . One thing we have realized is that, once the urban poor come to the conclusion that you are really sincere in helping them, no amount of vote buying will make them change their mind.

Of course, good intentions are insufficient—effectively addressing the concerns of low-income groups requires strong movement against corruption in city hall, a workable political program and a competent bureaucracy that can realize program goals. The question that arises is how a reformist regime can overcome the initial obstacles to gaining office and thereby earn the time to achieve these objectives. The Robredo associate argues that:

> The crucial period is election time, the first time you enter into politics. If you spend, more [during the campaign] than what you will receive as your salary you have to think of how you can recover that and then get more for the next election . . . So, once in office, you start recovering three times as much [through corruption] to pay for your elections. So our young politicians start out with ideas, but then . . . they start thinking, maybe I will compromise now and, when I am in power, I can change.

Without a base of political, financial and media support, avoiding this pitfall is difficult.

The experience of Naga City therefore raises three issues. The first is the difficulty that politicians who do not have the access to influence that Mayor Robredo had face in winning those critical first elections without being drawn into "politics as usual." The second is that, particularly in the period before they have been able to solidify a political base, progressive administrations face significant obstacles to carrying out their programmatic agenda in the continued strength of the opposition in elite families and business. It is notable that Mayor Robredo was able to build a broad-based coalition that included elements of the middle class and business because his business background appealed to these groups. He has also combined his anti-poverty agenda with support of the national government's agenda of globalization-oriented economic growth. The fact that Naga City's economy remains fairly stagnant has probably allowed him to avoid the potential contradictions in this stance—in a rapidly developing city conflicts between elite interests and informal settlements over access to land would likely force a mayor to be more explicit in making choices between community and commodity interests in land. The third issue is the difficulty of sustaining reform beyond the term of a reform regime. It is notable that, in the interim between Robredo's two periods in power, Mayor Sulpicio Roco, who had been sponsored for election by Robredo, made significant efforts to curtail civil society influence.

Yet the Naga City experience also highlights the potential for change that is inherent in the emergence of new constituencies in urban politics and the growing role of civil society. The case study points to two factors that enhance these possibilities for change, each of which has implications for organizations that are interested in fostering progressive local governance.

The first critical factor is the emergence of local politicians who are competent and creative and who are able to formulate a political platform that appeals to civil society organizations as well as some elements of the middle class, business and the media. There are several ways that this outcome might be encouraged: by facilitating networking and information-sharing among local leaders; by providing a programmatic base that they can draw on in developing a campaign platform; by mentoring them in such areas as public relations; and, perhaps, by providing resources (either financial or human) for their campaigns. A political party is obviously the ideal entity to perform many of these functions. One political party, AKBAYAN, has recently begun to focus on such activities with modest success. AKBAYAN currently counts 124 local officials, including nineteen mayors of small to medium sized municipalities, as members (AKBAYAN 2006).[3]

The second factor is the existence of an infrastructure of civil society organizations that has a strong base of support in communities and that is critical in its relations with local government yet willing to engage officials if the forum is amenable to meaningful influence. Such a base of collective action exists in many parts of the Philippines, having organized as part of the opposition to the Marcos dictatorship and/or to provide self-help solutions to meet shelter, infrastructure and other needs in the face of government neglect. This base can prove critical and perhaps essential to the efforts of progressive politicians to get elected and successfully pursue a planning and policy agenda. Although a large number of NGOs in the Philippines engage in community organizing, most focus on program or project level organizing. Few focus specifically on participation in local governance, and fewer still do so on a nationwide scale. One significant recent initiative in this regard has been the work of the Barangay–Bayan Governance Consortium (BBGC), a consortium of NGOs, community groups and local officials that has focused on exploiting the potential for civil society participation in *barangay* (village/community) governance embodied in the LGC (Villarin 2004). Its activities have included: providing training to NGOs, CBOs and other actors on *barangay* governance; developing models of participatory planning that communities can employ to identify community needs and make demands on local officials; and organizing women for political participation (Villarin 2004). The BBGC is currently working in about 2,500 of the Philippines' 42,000 *barangay*.

Conclusion

In their paper on the contested meaning of "participatory development," Mohan and Stokke (2000) differentiate between what they call a "revised neoliberal" and a "post-Marxist" interpretation of the term. The former is rooted in a belief that "empowerment of the powerless could be achieved . . . without any significant negative effects on the power of the powerful," whereas the latter posits that such a change can only come about with "'bottom-up' social mobilization . . . as a challenge to hegemonic interests within the state and market" (Mohan and Stokke 2000: 249). These interpretations imply very different political agendas with regards to when and how people should participate, and how power and resources should be allocated amongst interests. Which of these models of participatory development prevails in practice is determined by a contest of ideas in the realm of politics, and decentralization shifts the focus of this contest to the city and neighborhood scales.

The preceding analysis has demonstrated that the relative weakness of organizations and political parties in the Philippines that employ a "post-Marxist" framework for participation has led to the emergence of "elite democracy" as the prevailing form of politics in most cities. The ferment of ideas that emerged in the post-Marcos era, and the efforts of hundreds of organizations, have opened up new possibilities for citizen engagement, but this potential remains unrealized in most localities. A significant task of advocates of less powerful groups is now to understand the factors that lead to change in city politics and develop strategies on the basis of this understanding.

Through a case study of Naga City, this paper has tentatively identified two such factors. The first is the emergence of political leaders who actively pursue a redistributive and participatory agenda through both programs and institutional reforms. The second is the development of an established infrastructure of NGOs and CBOs that focuses on broad-based community participation and that sees a role for itself in pushing city government towards a participatory model of decision-making. Additional research and debate will be required to verify this finding and suggest other possible avenues of change. What is apparent is the need to recognize that decentralization does not inevitably lead to civil society empowerment and redistributive policy and planning. Rather, it renders city politics an important and potentially fruitful new forum for pursuing these objectives.

Notes

1   This case study is based primarily on a review of government and NGO documents and previous academic studies pertaining to Naga City, interviews with twelve city officials and representatives of NGOs and CBOs in the city, and correspondence over a period of several months with several individuals involved in Naga City politics. The interviews took an average of an hour.

2   President Ferdinand Marcos ruled the Philippines from 1965 to 1986, including a period from 1972 to 1981 under martial law. He was overthrown in 1986, following allegations of fraud in elections held that year, and was replaced by his main opponent in that contest, Corazon Aquino.

3   Mayor Robredo was briefly affiliated with AKBAYAN, but is currently affiliated with the Liberal Party.

References

Abers, R. (2000) *Inventing Local Democracy: Grassroots Politics in Brazil*, Boulder, CO: Lynne Rienner.

Akbayan. (2006) "The Akbayan! Story." Available online at www.akbayan.org/about.com, accessed August 9.

Angeles, J. and Clavecillas, F. (n.d.) "Community organizing and tripartism: The Bicol experience," unpublished manuscript.

Baiocchi, G. (2001) "Participation, activism and politics: The Porto Alegre experiment and deliberative democratic theory," *Politics & Society* 29 (1): 43–72.

Berner, E. (2000) "Poverty alleviation and eviction of the poorest: Towards urban land reform in the Philippines," *International Journal of Urban and Regional Research* 24 (3): 554–66.

Brillantes, A. (2003) *Innovations and Excellence: Understanding Local Government in the Philippines*, Quezon City: CLRG.

Chavez, D. and Goldfrank, B. (eds) (2004) *The Left in the City: Participatory Local Governments in Latin America*, London: Latin American Bureau.

Clarke, G. (1998) *The Politics of NGOs in Southeast Asia: Participation and Protest in the Philippines*, London: Routledge.

Fox, J. (1995) "The crucible of local politics," *NACLA Report on the Americas* 29: 15–19.

Hutchcroft, P. (1998) *Booty Capitalism: The Politics of Banking in the Philippines*, Ithaca, NY: Cornell University Press.

Kawanaka, T. (2002) *Power in a Philippine City*, Chiba: Institute of Developing Economies, Japan External Trade Organization.

Kelly, P. (2000) *Landscapes of Globalization: Human Geographies of Economic Change in the Philippines*, London: Routledge.

Lacaba, J. (ed.) (1995) *Boss: 5 Cases of Local Politics in the Philippines*, Manila: Institute for Popular Democracy.

Mohan, G. and Stokke, K. (2000) "Participatory development and empowerment: The dangers of localism," *Third World Quarterly* 21 (2): 247–68.

Naga City. (2006) "City profile." Available online at www.naga.gov.ph/cityprofile/eco.html, accessed August 14.

PHILSSA (Partnership of Philippine Support Service Agencies) (1997) *The Urban Development and Housing Act of 1992: Republic Act 7279*, Quezon City: PHILSSA.

Prilles, W. (2004) "The Kaantabay sa Kauswagan program: A close look at a 'secure tenure' poverty reduction program in Naga City, Philippines," unpublished Master's dissertation, University of Cambridge, Department of Land Economy.

Rocamora, J. (2004) "Legal and policy frameworks for participation in Thailand, Indonesia and the Philippines," in H. Antlov, A. Fabros, N. Iszatt, B. Orlandini and J. Rocamora (eds) *Citizen Participation in Local Governance: Experiences from Thailand, Indonesia and the Philippines*, Quezon City: Institute for Democracy.

Rocamora, J. (1994) *Breaking Through: The Struggle Within the Communist Party of the Philippines*, Pasig City: Anvil.

Santos, S. (ed.) (1998) *The Theory and Practice of People's Councils: Focus on the Naga City Model*, Quezon City: Institute of Politics and Governance.

Sidel, J. (1999) *Capital, Coercion, and Crime: Bossism in the Philippines*, Stanford, CA: Stanford University Press.

Villarin, T. (2004) "Finding meaning in local governance through popular participation in the Barangay-Bayan," in M. Estrella and N. Iszatt (eds) *Beyond Good Governance: Participatory Democracy in the Philippines*, Quezon City: Institute for Popular Democracy.

World Bank (2000) *Cities in Transition: World Bank Urban and Local Government Strategy*, Washington, DC: World Bank.

Chapter 14

Making sense of decentralized planning in the global south

Christopher Silver, Victoria A. Beard and Faranak Miraftab

Introduction

The reach of the decentralization movement, especially since the early 1990s, has substantially changed governance structures in the global south. The pervasiveness of decentralization is clear, as seen in the case studies and demonstrated by Table 14.1. What cannot be read from the chart, however, are the motives that have driven this movement, nor its implications. Those questions remain matters of considerable controversy. One of our aims as we examined decentralized planning in the global south has been to assess its potential for the distribution of resources to disadvantaged groups, and for empowering them to influence planning processes and their outcomes. From that vantage point, we have sought to clarify whether the decentralization movement has in fact improved local governance as its proponents had envisioned that it would. The case studies in this volume illuminate the motives that prompted decentralization, document the institutional and legal changes made to support decentralization, and explain the ways in which various political actors shaped the decentralization process and its outcomes. The case studies demonstrate that no simple answer can be given to the question of decentralization's outcome, especially when the experiences of decentralization are examined across the diverse social and political landscapes that comprise the global south. Nonetheless, it is possible to draw some conclusions from the collective observations here that enhance our understanding of decentralization and its implications for planning.

Drawing on the case studies in this volume, we can outline three broad lessons for appropriate and effective decentralized planning:

1   to take into account the socio-historical legacies that influence the institutional and political culture where decentralized planning is practiced;
2   to decouple the aims of efficiency and of equity when assessing decentralized planning; and
3   to recognize the critical role of social movements, civil society groups and local leaders in achieving democratic planning and decision-making.

The chapter reviews each of these points and identifies future research priorities.

Table 14.1 Select decentralization laws and statutes

Country	Year	Statute/law
Argentina	1977	Buenos Aires (province) transferred planning to municipal governments, Urban Code 8912; Law 9347
Bolivia	1994	Law of Popular Participation Law of Administrative Decentralization
	1996	Election Law
	2005	Law calling for direct election of departmental prefects
	2006	National referendum supporting departmental autonomy
	2006	Constitutional Assembly (still in progress and currently deadlocked) with greater autonomy for indigenous regions and departments
Chile	1974–80	Chile divided into 13 regions, 52 provinces and 325 municipalities (DL 573/74); Municipal Law (DL 1289/76) defined local functions and DFL 1/80 provided for local administration of health and education
	1988	Constitutional Municipal Law (18,695)
	1992	Law 19,130 set democratic election of local authorities
	1993	Regional Government and Administration Law (19,175)
	2005	Law 20,035 granted new powers to regional governments
India	1992–3	73rd and 74th Constitutional Amendment Acts devolving governance powers to local governments with seat quotas for women
	1996	83rd Constitutional Amendment Act (*Panchayats* Extension to Scheduled Areas Act)
	1993–5	Various State *Panchayat* and Municipal Acts
Indonesia	1974	Basic Principles of Government at the Regional Level
	1999	Law 22 on Regional Governance Law 25 on Fiscal Balance between the Central and Regional Government
	2004	Law 32, Regional Autonomy Law 33, Regional Fiscal Balance
Kenya	late 1990s	Local Authority Transfer Fund Local Government Reform Program
Philippines	1987	Constitution drafted that calls for decentralization
	1991	Local Government Code, mandating decentralization
	1992	The Urban Development and Housing Act
South Africa	1996	Constitution of the Republic of South Africa
	2000	Local Government Municipal Services Act 32
Thailand	1994	*Tambon* Administrative Act
	1997	Constitution called for decentralization.
	1999	Decentralization Act
Uganda	1993	Local Government Statute
	1995	Uganda Constitution
	1997	Local Government Act/Local Government Finance Commission
Vietnam	1986	National Policy of Renovation (*Doi Moi*)
	1992	Constitution stipulated that the People's Council is the "local organ of the state"
	1994	Law on Organization
	1996	Ordinance on Concrete Tasks
	1995, 2001	Public Administrative Reform Program

Accounting for socio-historical legacies

One basic insight drawn from the case studies is that decentralization varies markedly across the global south, even though many instances of it have adhered faithfully to the model of inter-governmental finance that is endorsed in the West and promoted by the international donor community. That model assumes that the devolution of administrative and planning responsibilities from central to local governments is the key to greater market participation and to efficient delivery of services that traditionally were provided by inefficient, centralized state structures. The financial framework thus propounded ways to strengthen local revenues so as to reduce the significant dependence on inter-governmental transfers; to bring the cost of, and the revenue from, services into closer geographical proximity; and, for inter-governmental transfers, to use block grants rather than earmarked transfers whenever possible and thus to enhance local discretion. The assumption is that, if local governments are given more flexibility in allocating funds, they will do a better job of matching resources with needs than central government agencies did. The fiscal decentralization package also includes tax reforms; new sources of local revenue; more effective revenue collection (presumably due to greater local involvement); and raising the rates charged for basic public services so that residents bear more of the costs. Finally, the fiscal decentralization model calls for a system of inter-governmental transfers using distribution formulas that would be more transparent, removing opportunities to exact rents in return for favorable treatment, and that would enable localities to anticipate revenue flows better and thus plan effectively for future needs (see Smoke, Chapter 6). Even in the case of Thailand, where central control of revenue distribution remains strong, a 1999 decentralization law states not only that local governments should get a larger share of revenues to handle their greater responsibilities, but that the transfer of funds should be more predictable in order to facilitate the expanded local functions (see Daniere and Takahashi, Chapter 12).

Although often the same model of fiscal and administrative decentralization was being implemented, the timing and the forms of the legislative changes were strongly influenced by diverse national and local political cultures. In Bolivia, for example, decentralization displayed the full sweep of the "new development paradigm" focused on "community development, deregulation, privatization, minimal government, popular participation and flexible forms of foreign aid" (Werlin 1992: 223)—but the outcome took a very local twist. It was thought that achieving such a high level of local engagement was likely to blunt the power of national labor unions (which had initially opposed decentralization) and to increase political stability in a nation known for forceful regime change. Decentralization indeed "channeled the attention of political groups to the local arena to prevent greater democratic participation at a national level." However, to an unexpected degree it also generated a local movement for social reform that challenged local leaders in unprecedented ways (Kohl and Farthing, Chapter 5, p.23). Local Bolivians appropriated "political decentralization for their ends," Kohl and Farthing point out, "rather than those envisioned by national elites and international financial institutions" (ibid., 23–4).

The opposite set of consequences followed in Thailand, where the rhetoric of decentralization should be viewed in the context of local governance that has remained firmly under the control of the national and regional governments. Rather than authority and resources shifting to the local level, in urban Thailand decisions still emanate from the central government, and taxing powers also remain there. Moreover, "in typical Thai fashion," Takahashi and Daniere point out, "multiple agencies at different levels have *de jure* authority for the same functions and services" (p. 4), and thus local leaders are marginalized. In 2006, the central government increased the size and number of grants to local government under the authority of the 1999 decentralization law, which has made possible a variety of small-scale projects led by local government agencies. Although for Thailand that clearly constitutes a step towards greater local engagement, the shift is a minor one compared with what occurred in Indonesia after its landmark decentralization legislation in 1999, which followed the Asian economic crisis and President Suharto's resignation.

Indonesia and also Uganda, Kenya, India, Chile, Vietnam and the Philippines lie somewhere between the extremes of Thailand and Bolivia in terms of the changes made to establish new institutional decentralization within the framework expected by the international donor community. The roads taken towards decentralization in these nations varied greatly, but typically reduced central government's oversight of local administration and development. For example, in Indonesia, local governments had historically relied on the central government for anywhere between 60 and 80 percent of their budgets. Decentralization made it mandatory for the central government to transfer at least 25 percent of the national domestic revenues, as well as a set proportion of revenues from natural resources, but as discretionary funds and according to an explicit formula not susceptible to administrative whims. That creation of a public allocation fund (*dana alokasi umum*) ushered in new relations between central and local institutions. Similarly, Uganda's decentralization created the Local Government Finance Commission, an independent body prescribed by the constitution and accompanying legislation to ensure sufficient resource allocations to local, elected administrations. In recent years, however, the inability of local officials to exercise their authority effectively in delivering services has reduced their administrative autonomy. In another variant of decentralization, Vietnam's institutional changes cannot be separated from market liberalization. Spencer shows how *Doi Moi* created new, complex institutional relationships in which the state and local leaders interact with community-level entrepreneurs in distributing water.

Too frequently, because research on decentralization in the global south focuses on short-term changes, the context examined often includes only the period just before decentralization policies were adopted, or in some cases the country's post-independence history as well. That limited perspective ignores the long-term political dynamics influencing contemporary processes and the outcomes of decentralization. More systematic, comparative research is needed to trace the relationships between countries' historical legacies and their institutional decentralization. For example, research should consider how the institutional structure of states varies with the modes of colonial governance under which modern states were created. How did the experience of centralization vary across British, French, Dutch, Spanish and United States colonies? Other important considerations are how each state has traditionally treated market forces, citizen participation and social movements. How do these historical legacies influence each state's institutional and political culture and, hence, the ways in which the stated objectives of decentralization have been formulated and implemented? In summary, an historically nuanced analysis of state decentralization is essential if the opportunities and limitations of decentralized planning are to be assessed accurately.

Decoupling efficiency and equity

Another insight offered by the case studies in this volume concerns decentralization's implications for efficiency and equity. Proponents argue that decentralization more clearly delineates local government functions vis-à-vis central government agencies. One expectation is greater local control over hiring within the public administrative system. Where central government previously intruded in local affairs, operating efficiency is expected to improve because the duplication of service delivery agencies has been eliminated. Another key expectation of proponents is stakeholder participation in local governance, either in planning or through the direct election of local administrators and legislators (almost unheard of throughout the global south before decentralization). Through such participation, community residents would presumably influence local government to be more permeable and accountable, improving the likelihood of achieving equity.

Several case studies in this volume suggest that the initial motivation for decentralization was fundamentally political, whether in places with traditions of national as well as local instability or in places struggling to break free from despotism (see Beard *et al.* in Chapter 9 and Shatkin in Chapter 13). Strengthening popular participation in local governance through formal institutional channels or through the advocacy of community-based organizations was intended only to produce greater efficiency that would be accompanied by greater social and political stability. But, as Bond noted about South Africa's privatization of water supplies, many of the functional shortcomings seen in centralized, despotic governance did not vanish with decentralization, but simply shifted to administration at the local level. Bond's notion of "decentralized despotism" describes the extreme form of a common phenomenon: the processes of decentralization rested on an assumption of local competency that local performance could not match.

Where inter-governmental systems of fund transfers fail to support the new responsibilities for local governments, they may turn to "entrepreneurial governance" to fill the fiscal gap. Miraftab demonstrates how, in the case of South Africa, such a policy shift has elevated profit-making above the social objectives of decentralization. The poignancy of the Cape Town case lies in the contrast to the broader mandate in South African society to model the "unmaking of apartheid's social and spatial inequalities." That stark irony differs from the many other cases of decentralization in the developing world that were tied more explicitly to economic factors. The paradox in Cape Town is a microcosm of the "paradox of South Africa's post-apartheid state," which has sought to engage simultaneously in "political liberation and economic liberalization," two endeavors likely to embody cross-purposes. The Cape Town case, as well as several others, undercuts the assumption that local decision-making inherently fosters equality. Mirfatab's case study concludes that "local participation can indeed generate greater injustice from the inequality" already present in local communities.

The South African case underscores the value of systematically examining the conjuncture and also the disjuncture between two outcomes of decentralization that are often conflated: efficiency and equity. We need to identify those institutional forms of decentralization that not only improve the efficiency of service delivery, but also improve the equity of resource distribution. As evident in the Argentinian and South African cases, the cost of improving efficiency can be greater inequity. Research on the equity implications of decentralization is called for. Comparative research also might examine the institutional mechanisms used to protect participatory processes, which often influence equity, from elite capture. Such research could examine how decentralization affects disadvantaged and marginalized groups, and how participatory planning strategies may help to resolve conflicts between groups with competing interests interacting in a context of asymmetrical power relationships. When implementing change under the rubric of decentralization, planners should break apart the concept of citizen participation to examine critically the respective roles of local leaders and development facilitators. They should also warily examine the specific forms of participation (e.g., rules for exit, horizontal monitoring between actors, and the role of public education and the media).

The role of social movements, civil society groups and local leaders

Along with raising the question of efficiency versus equity, the cases in this volume clearly document how the organizational strength of social movements, civil society organizations and disadvantaged groups has the potential to contribute to more equitable and democratic decentralization. The Urban Poverty Program (UPP) launched by the World Bank in Indonesia, which is discussed in the case study by Beard, Pradhan, Rao, Cartmill and Rivayani, challenges the simplistic notion that the orthodoxy of neoliberalism is monolithic. Devised in response to the fiscal crisis that arose in Indonesia in 1999, UPP was designed to bring resources directly to the community, as both a short-term strategy to relieve suffering and a long-term strategy to reduce the influence of central government in allocating resources. Channeling funds directly to community-based organizations was intended to reduce the likelihood of them being diverted. Of course, this strategy also opened the possibility for local elites to capture the funds and for traditional unequal power relations to be sustained (a form of "decentralized despotism"). The case study shows that the UPP was relatively successful in delivering resources to the poor, but that it was less successful in overcoming the anticipated problem of "elite control" over local decision-making and not notably successful in providing ways for women and members of disadvantaged groups to exercise leadership. Shatkin concludes, for the case of Naga City in the Philippines, that "decentralization does not inevitably lead to civil society empowerment and redistributive policy and planning." These authors' observations do not, however, rule out the alternative possibility that social movements, civil society groups and disadvantaged groups may take advantage of the new spaces for public action that decentralization creates. This is evident, for example, in Misra and Kudva's chapter, which explains how, despite "gaps and disjunctures" in the gender quota system, India's poor women of lower castes took advantage of a legislated gender quota system to create new spaces for women's participation, thus opening up possibilities for broader social transformation in the future.

As shown in the cases of El Bosque in Chile and Naga City, leadership matters when transforming institutional directions and mitigating flawed strategies. The leadership of Mayor Sadi Melo in El Bosque and Mayor Jesse Robredo in Naga City had beneficial consequences because they used their institutional role to ameliorate the potentially explosive conditions. In another instance, the case of Jatinangor, Indonesia, the district head fully supported the aims of the community-based organization that pushed for meaningful participation in local decision-making, even though the legislative authorization for that had not been tested.

In the cases examined in this volume, the key to countering "decentralized despotism" proved to be the degree of democratization of the local governance structure and the effectiveness of community-based organizations and interest groups to ensure accountability of local officials. Several authors suggest that the decentralization process, with all its flaws, created spaces of public action that some disadvantaged groups were able to use—for example, Bolivian indigenous groups (Chapter 5) and poor, low-caste Indian women (Chapter 11). These openings, which decentralization created, surpassed the possibilities available under highly centralized and frequently despotic states. Decentralization's redistributive outcome thus appears when disadvantaged populations can organize and make use of the new spaces mandated by decentralization laws to articulate their interests effectively. To the extent that such ability exists among populations disadvantaged by class, race, gender and caste, decentralization can have progressive and transformative outcomes. Clearly, strong social movements and civil society groups among disadvantaged populations are fundamental to pushing decentralization beyond the rhetoric of inclusion and democratic practices to achieve broader social transformation.

Conclusion

Decentralization has become a mantra for international development circles and especially for the powerful international development agencies. Its critics view it as just another product from the west being sold to developing states already heavily in debt. Decentralization policies are marketed as a tool-kit that can help developing nations achieve a range of improvements including, but not limited to, more efficient service delivery, more accurate beneficiary targeting, empowerment of disenfranchised populations and democratization of planning and development. The case studies in this volume reveal how far these visions diverge from actuality. Where decentralization policies are being implemented, planners and policymakers should consider critically the socio-historical context, political culture and economic environment, and the capacity of civil society groups and social movements. Equally important are the technical and legislative details of specific decentralization policies.

It should also be noted that most of the chapters in this volume have focused on how decentralization affects urban areas. Additional research should compare and contrast those outcomes with experiences of decentralization among local governments and planners working for rural constituents. Rural settings pose distinctive challenges for decentralized planning and decision-making. For example, a local government that depends on input from a large number of dispersed localities with relatively fewer inhabitants faces major constraints of time, resources and the effort necessary to reach agreements among settlements. Furthermore, in many countries the political–administrative system differs between rural and urban jurisdictions, which have different service needs and varying capacities for collective action. Research nuanced by the physical characteristics of locales is needed, to clarify how the impact of decentralized planning differs in urban and rural settings.

It is clear from the cases examined in this volume that decentralization is *not* a magic bullet guaranteeing efficient, equitable, democratic and environmentally sustainable outcomes. To the extent that the reach of decentralization continues to broaden and deepen in the global south (which seems likely from the case studies examined here), further institutional changes will ensue. Whether they lead to more effective and responsive local governments, to greater transparency and equity in the distribution of resources, and to more meaningful roles in the political process for a broader segment of society will only become clearer as the decentralization movement matures and as it is exposed to rigorous, comparative research. What is apparent is that decentralized planning creates new spaces where the state, the private sector, community-based groups and social movements may engage in public action. This question, however, remains highly contested: which of set of actors will ultimately have the most influence on planning and development outcomes?

References

Werlin, H. (1992) "Linking decentralization and centralization: A critique of the new development administration," *Public Administration and Development* 12: 223–35.

Index